"Christensen is an excellent guide to the complex moral issues that arise when we shift our attention to the global level, and he makes a number of valuable contributions to the various debates he assesses. Highly recommended."

– Chris Armstrong, University of Southampton, UK

"An excellent book to learn about global justice; lucid, concise, balanced, systematic, up-to-date and impressively wide-ranging. My students will be reading his book, and thanking the author for it."

– Paula Casal, Universitat Pompeu Fabra, Spain

"This excellent textbook addresses some of the most pressing issues of our time with intellectual clarity and moral concern. It is an essential introduction for students of global justice."

– Kevin K W Ip, Hong Kong Baptist University, Hong Kong

GLOBAL JUSTICE

JAMES CHRISTENSEN

© James Christensen, under exclusive licence to Macmillan Education Limited 2020

All rights reserved. No reproduction, copy or transmission of this publication may be made without written permission.

No portion of this publication may be reproduced, copied or transmitted save with written permission or in accordance with the provisions of the Copyright, Designs and Patents Act 1988, or under the terms of any licence permitting limited copying issued by the Copyright Licensing Agency, Saffron House, 6–10 Kirby Street, London EC1N 8TS.

Any person who does any unauthorized act in relation to this publication may be liable to criminal prosecution and civil claims for damages.

The author has asserted her right to be identified as the author of this work in accordance with the Copyright, Designs and Patents Act 1988.

First published 2020 by
RED GLOBE PRESS

Red Globe Press in the UK is an imprint of Macmillan Education Limited, registered in England, company number 01755588, of 4 Crinan Street, London, N1 9XW.

Red Globe Press® is a registered trademark in the United States, the United Kingdom, Europe and other countries.

ISBN 978-1-137-60678-5 hardback
ISBN 978-1-137-60677-8 paperback

This book is printed on paper suitable for recycling and made from fully managed and sustained forest sources. Logging, pulping and manufacturing processes are expected to conform to the environmental regulations of the country of origin.

A catalogue record for this book is available from the British Library.
A catalog record for this book is available from the Library of Congress.

For my mum,
Angela Christensen,
with love and gratitude.

ACKNOWLEDGEMENTS

While writing this book, I have benefitted from the input of several friends and colleagues. For their helpful feedback on earlier drafts of various chapters, I would like to thank Susanne Burri, Mollie Gerver, and Caleb Yong.

I would also like to thank three anonymous reviewers who read the manuscript for Red Globe Press. I am grateful not only for their helpful feedback but also for their efforts to defend my approach against potential editorial interventions. Having said that, I should immediately add that these potential interventions rarely materialized. My editor, Lloyd Langman, gave me the time and the space to write the kind of book that I wanted to write, along with some helpful advice.

As this book is aimed at students, among others, I would like to use this as an opportunity to thank those who taught me during my own student days. In particular, I would like to thank (in the order that they taught me) Paula Casal, Annabelle Lever, and Simon Caney. Without the encouragement and inspiration that these people provided, it is highly unlikely that I would have pursued a career in political theory.

The book's front cover was designed by Sandy Matta. I think that she has done an excellent job.

Finally, I would like to thank my parents, Angela and William Christensen.

CONTENTS

Acknowledgements   vii

1 **Introduction**   1
    1.1   A troubled world   1
    1.2   Human rights and global justice   3
    1.3   The nature of justice   6
    1.4   Arguing about justice   8
    1.5   Replying to the "realists"   11
    1.6   Everyday "realism"   16

2 **Rights**   19
    2.1   Understanding rights   20
    2.2   Understanding human rights   22
    2.3   Justifying human rights   26
    2.4   Cultural relativism   29
    2.5   A Western imposition?   33
    2.6   Toleration and respect   35
    2.7   Rawls on toleration   38
    2.8   Diversity   42

3 **Poverty**   45
    3.1   Peter Singer and the drowning child   46
    3.2   Alternatives to Singer's view   50
    3.3   Symptoms and institutions   54
    3.4   Is poverty caused by local or global factors?   55
    3.5   Is the global order really harming the poor?   61
    3.6   Conclusion   64

4 **Inequality**   65
    4.1   Cosmopolitanism   65
    4.2   The case for global equality   68
    4.3   The case against global equality: The Coercion argument I   71

4.4	The case against global equality: The Coercion argument II	77
4.5	The case against global equality: Cooperation	80
4.6	Conclusion	83

5 Nationalism — 85
- 5.1 Nations and nationality — 85
- 5.2 National self-determination — 88
- 5.3 National self-determination and international redistribution — 90
- 5.4 National self-determination and global egalitarianism — 92
- 5.5 Global egalitarianism and special duties to compatriots — 95
- 5.6 Global egalitarianism and national responsibility — 96
- 5.7 The limits of human motivation — 98
- 5.8 The value of natural resources — 102
- 5.9 Conclusion — 104

6 Immigration — 105
- 6.1 Immigration and radical global inequality — 106
- 6.2 Immigration and the domestic poor — 114
- 6.3 Freedom of movement — 117
- 6.4 Immigration and cultural preservation — 121
- 6.5 Moving beyond the status quo — 125

7 Trade — 127
- 7.1 The world poverty argument for free trade — 127
- 7.2 The sweatshop argument for trade restrictions — 129
- 7.3 The domestic labour argument for trade restrictions — 133
- 7.4 A nationalist perspective — 136
- 7.5 Special and differential treatment for developing countries — 137
- 7.6 Fair trade as reciprocity — 140
- 7.7 Fair trade as equality — 142
- 7.8 Conclusion — 145

8 Climate — 147
- 8.1 The nature of the problem — 148
- 8.2 The moral dimensions of our task: Avoiding the violation of human rights — 151
- 8.3 The moral dimensions of our task: Sharing the burden — 156
- 8.4 Why not make future generations pay? — 164
- 8.5 The problem of uncertainty — 169

9 War — **171**
- 9.1 *Jus ad bellum*: Regulating the resort to war — 173
- 9.2 *Jus in bello*: Regulating conduct within war — 180
- 9.3 The relationship between *jus ad bellum* and *jus in bello* — 183
- 9.4 The blameworthiness of unjust combatants — 187
- 9.5 Conclusion — 190

10 Intervention — **191**
- 10.1 State sovereignty and communal self-determination — 193
- 10.2 Humanitarian intervention and the principles of just war — 199
- 10.3 Massacres and poverty — 212

Bibliography — 215

Index — 225

1 INTRODUCTION

1.1 A troubled world

To those of us who grow up in affluent Western countries, the world can feel very small. During our childhoods, the boundaries of our home towns constitute, for the most part, the borders within which we live our lives. Our experiences are narrowly circumscribed, and we take them to be representative. To the extent that we think about other people, we imagine them living lives not dissimilar to our own. Often, the trips we take abroad reinforce rather than undermine these perceptions. Our parents take us on holidays to other rich societies or to tourist enclaves within poorer countries where we are cut off from the lives of the natives. We are perhaps vaguely aware of a wider, less familiar world, but our vision of it remains hazy and obscured.

Gradually, however, the fog starts to lift. Events from the outside begin to intrude upon our insulated bubble. At one point in the Philip Roth novel *American Pastoral*, the narrator describes a scene in which the main character ("the Swede"), his wife (Dawn), and their young daughter (Merry) are confronted with a shocking news broadcast concerning a street protest in South Vietnam. During the protest, a Buddhist monk had set himself on fire. We are told that the disturbing footage seems to appear in their home "[o]ut of nowhere", leaving "Merry and the Swede and Dawn, horrified together in their living room".[1]

Young Merry is especially upset by the experience and is unable to sleep alone for a week. Countless children undoubtedly endure similar experiences, their perception of the world recast by fragmentary images of distant tragedy: of mass graves in Srebrenica; emaciated peasants in Sahel; an apparently endless procession of stretchers wheeling lifeless protesters into an overwhelmed Bahraini hospital in the midst of the Arab Spring. When I began work on this book, newspapers were displaying harrowing images of dead refugee children washed up on our beaches like driftwood.

---

1 Philip Roth, *American Pastoral* (London: Vintage, 1997), p. 153ff.

These events trouble us. They bring sharply into focus the existence of a world beyond our own, a world populated by individuals living lives that we struggle to comprehend. They also reveal the indifference with which these people are so often regarded. Reflecting on his daughter's reaction to the monk's act of sacrificial protest, the Swede observes that "for her it had only to do with the extremes to which gentle people have to resort in a world where the great majority are without an ounce of conscience".[2] As we grow older and the fog obscuring the tragedies unfolding beyond our borders begins to lift, the worry that we are living our lives without an ounce of conscience only grows stronger.

Moreover, we learn that we are not mere bystanders. On the contrary, our lives are bound up with those of the poor and dispossessed in multiple ways. Our clothes are manufactured in Asian sweatshops, the oil that fuels our cars is purchased from African and Middle Eastern dictators, and our consumer lifestyles generate climatic changes that threaten Bangladeshi peasants with drought and famine.

These discoveries prompt us to reflect on our conduct. Is our behaviour justified? Should we be doing more to help the distant needy? What do we owe to disadvantaged individuals living in other countries? What can these people demand of us as a matter of right? Of course, not all advantaged individuals think to ask these questions. Some instead become so inured to their privilege that they begin to regard it as a natural and innocent feature of the world.

Some readers of this book will perhaps have had experiences very different from those described above. Some will have grown up in countries devastated by poverty and war or have been raised by parents who immigrated to richer nations in order to escape from such evils. For some readers, the fog that shrouds one's horizons during childhood may have obscured not the severe hardships that are endured by so many but rather the highly unequal distribution of those hardships; the fact that so many of the world's inhabitants are left relatively unscathed by the crushing burdens that devastate the lives of others.

Still, first-hand experience of deprivation does not resolve moral questions. Being saddled with any given burden does not, in itself, enable one to determine who is required to do what (if anything) in order to alleviate that burden. On the contrary, deprivation may actually *reduce* one's ability to answer such questions. Just as the fortunate can become habituated to their privilege, so the worse-off can become habituated to their disadvantage. In order to gain an adequately critical perspective on the troubled world in which we live, whatever our personal experience, we shall have to engage in moral theory. More specifically, we shall have to engage in philosophical reflection on the nature of *justice*.

---

2   Ibid., p. 155.

1.2 Human rights and global justice

In the international domain, concerns about justice are often framed using the language of human rights. Traditionally understood, human rights are entitlements that all human beings possess simply by virtue of their humanity. These entitlements, which find legal expression in a variety of national and international documents, include rights to life, to freedom of thought, to education and healthcare, and to much else besides. In international politics, the language of human rights carries considerable weight. Neglecting human rights is widely regarded as a serious offence.

Despite the prominent role it plays in international affairs, human rights discourse is unlikely to be able to capture every dimension of global justice. As we shall see, recognizing the full extent of justice requires us to venture beyond the domain of human rights, at least as that domain is commonly conceived. This book, then, is not simply a book about human rights. On the contrary, a large part of the debate around human rights will not be addressed. In recent years, the traditional understanding of the nature of human rights has been challenged. According to revisionist thinkers, human rights are best understood not as entitlements grounded in a common humanity but as standards that enable us to assess the legitimacy of states and the appropriateness of international intervention.[3] Important and interesting as these issues are, they shall here be set aside.

Nevertheless, many of the issues to be addressed in this book have a human rights dimension, and reflection on human rights provides a useful starting point to our enquiry. Chapter 2 provides an account of the nature of rights and sketches one approach to justifying their existence. Chapter 2 also addresses a common criticism of human rights, according to which the universalist perspective embodied in such rights is unduly insensitive to radical cultural diversity. Chapter 2 shows how this challenge can be met and thereby paves the way for the debates that occupy the rest of the book.

Among the most important human rights are those to subsistence. As Charles Jones writes, "To subsist is to survive… Subsistence rights are rights that protect and promote our interests in obtaining what is necessary to survive".[4] Elaborating, Jones notes that the goal of subsistence rights "is to ensure that each person has secure access to clean water, adequate food and shelter, and basic health care".[5] These rights are especially basic, for without them, we would struggle to enjoy any other rights.[6]

---

3 John Rawls, *The Law of Peoples* (Cambridge, MA: Harvard University Press, 1999); Charles Beitz, *The Idea of Human Rights* (Oxford: Oxford University Press, 2009); Joseph Raz, "Human Rights without Foundations", in Samantha Besson and John Tasioulas (eds.), *The Philosophy of International Law* (Oxford: Oxford University Press, 2010).

4 Charles Jones, "The Human Right to Subsistence", *Journal of Applied Philosophy*, vol. 30, no. 1, 2013, pp. 57–72, at p. 61.

5 Ibid.

6 Henry Shue, *Basic Rights: Subsistence, Affluence, and U.S. Foreign Policy* (Princeton, NJ: Princeton University Press, 1980).

If there is a human right to subsistence, the existence of extreme poverty represents a catastrophic failure to respect human rights. At present, hundreds of millions of human beings lack access to the various goods that the right to subsistence is supposed to protect. With regard to some goods, the number is in the billions. For example, according to the World Health Organization, two billion people are forced to rely on contaminated drinking water sources.[7]

Considerations such as these prompt us to ask what is owed, morally, to those living in extreme poverty. To what extent must better-off individuals sacrifice their own wellbeing in order to ensure that the world's poorest people can satisfy their vital interest in subsistence? If the more advantaged have obligations to the world's poor, what is the source of these obligations? Are they grounded in the mere fact that the better-off have the capacity to assist? Or are these obligations grounded, as some philosophers have claimed, in the fact that the better-off are actually *contributing* to world poverty? These questions are taken up in Chapter 3.

Rights to subsistence are extremely minimal. As we have seen, they are rights to survival, not to a decent existence. Even if extreme poverty were erased, millions of people would continue to lead lives marked by various deficiencies. Significantly, many people would lead lives that are considerably worse than those enjoyed by individuals residing in the world's most privileged countries. Global *inequality* would endure even if global poverty were eliminated.

Rectifying material inequality is often thought to be beyond the purview of human rights. Indeed, the human rights project is sometimes criticized for failing to take inequality seriously. According to this line of critique, human rights activists have set their sights too low. Social rights have been subordinated to civil and political rights, and the social rights that are recognized are conceived too narrowly, as protections of only the most fundamental human interests.[8]

As we shall see in Chapter 4, there are compelling reasons to think that global justice requires the elimination of material inequality. The disadvantages that many people suffer are traceable to the bad luck of being born in the "wrong" country, and many philosophers believe that justice cannot allow people's life prospects to be determined by luck. If human rights do not guarantee equality, human rights cannot be the whole of global justice.

This view is not shared by all. While there is consensus about the need to alleviate severe deprivation, some philosophers doubt that justice requires us to aim for the more ambitious goal of equality. Nationalist philosophies are especially sceptical of this claim. As we shall see in Chapter 5, nationalists

---

7 World Health Organization, "Drinking Water", 7 February 2018, available at https://www.who.int/news-room/fact-sheets/detail/drinking-water.

8 Samuel Moyn, *Not Enough: Human Rights in an Unequal World* (Cambridge, MA: Harvard University Press, 2018).

maintain that global inequality is a natural concomitant of national responsibility. As nations must be held responsible for their actions, global inequality must be tolerated. If the case for global equality is to be successfully made, this nationalist challenge must be answered.

Chapter 6 is about immigration. This issue interacts with the themes of earlier chapters in multiple ways. First, a right to immigrate is conspicuously absent from the major human rights documents. While some of these documents acknowledge a right to *internal* free movement (i.e., within states), they do not recognize a right to move freely *between* states. Many have found this asymmetry puzzling. After all, our interest in moving between states might be just as weighty as our interest in moving within a state. Second, if movement across borders were less restricted, many of those who suffer from poverty and inequality would be able to escape their plight by emigrating to a wealthier country. If we prevent them from doing so, we are arguably neglecting our duties of justice. Third, nationalists are concerned to preserve the cultural integrity of their nation, and many think that this requires restrictions on immigration. But can such restrictions be reconciled with the claims of needy outsiders?

Questions about immigration concern the regulation of state borders. This issue is further explored in Chapter 7, which is about international trade. International trade is governed by the World Trade Organization (WTO), the primary aim of which is to "open up" or "liberalize" trade by encouraging the removal of various obstacles such as import tariffs and quotas. This aim can seem laudable. Many economists tell us that free trade is important for economic growth and that growth in turn is important for economic development. If we care about the world's poor, perhaps we should support the WTO's mission of liberalizing trade.

On the other hand, there are reasons to be suspicious of free trade. Many of the goods imported from poor countries are produced in gruelling "sweatshop" conditions, and it is natural to worry that, by purchasing these goods, rich-world consumers are implicating themselves in the exploitation of very poor workers abroad. Moreover, cheap imports can appear to undermine domestic industries and destroy the jobs of our fellow citizens. Whether trade ought to be freed is therefore a difficult question to answer.

We just noted that economic growth can be important. But growth traditionally has been pursued in a manner that we now realize is causing profound and perhaps irreparable damage to our planet. Economic progress has been driven by the reckless burning of fossil fuels, a process that has caused carbon dioxide and various other greenhouse gases to accumulate in the atmosphere and prevent heat from escaping into space. The resulting climatic changes could be devastating. Most significantly, these changes pose severe threats to fundamental human rights such as the right to subsistence. These matters are taken up in Chapter 8.

Burning fossil fuels is one activity through which political communities impose harms on outsiders. In Chapter 9, we address one of the most harmful practices of all: war. War is often spectacularly unjust, but can it ever be justified? How can we distinguish between an unjust war and a just one? A right to wage war is not usually among the entitlements that we first think of when human rights are discussed, but it is plausible to think that there is such a right. After all, if we are morally entitled to certain goods, it would be odd to think that we are not also morally permitted to take the necessary steps to retain those goods when unjust individuals try to take them away. And perhaps these necessary steps will sometimes involve taking up arms. Needless to say, if we are permitted to wage war, we are permitted to do so only under extraordinary circumstances.

Among these extraordinary circumstances are perhaps those that often provoke calls for "humanitarian intervention". When a government is massacring its people and military action seems necessary to end the massacre, many people are inclined to think that war can be justified. But is intervention in such cases always permissible? What about in cases where governments are violating the rights of their citizens in less extreme ways? Can intervention be permissible in less dramatic circumstances? These important questions are addressed in Chapter 10.

1.3 The nature of justice

So far, I have relied on an intuitive grasp of the kind of thing that justice is, but we should now consider its nature in a bit more detail. It might be helpful to start by distinguishing between the *concept* of justice and a *conception* of justice.[9] The concept of justice refers to the proper or correct distribution of rights and duties, benefits and burdens. A conception of justice describes what such a distribution would look like. For example, we might endorse an *egalitarian* conception of justice, which says that the proper distribution of relevant goods is one that gives everyone a roughly equal share. Alternatively, we might prefer a more minimal conception of justice, which says that the proper distribution of relevant goods is one that ensures everyone can lead a minimally decent life.

Often, when people profess scepticism about justice, what they are sceptical about is not the concept of justice, but a particular conception. They recognize that rights, duties, benefits, and burdens can be distributed improperly, but they have doubts about a particular account of what a proper distribution entails. Indeed, their doubts arise precisely because they are attracted to a different, rival conception.

Many people have great faith in the various ethical convictions that their conceptions of justice comprise. They confidently proclaim that foreign aid should be cut, say, or that immigration should be reduced. But this confidence is rarely justified. Consider an analogy. While walking in the woods,

---

9　John Rawls, *A Theory of Justice*, Revised Edition (Cambridge, MA: Harvard University Press, 1999), pp. 5, 8–9.

Amy notices a shiny, metallic object, apparently lying on the ground. Believing the object to be a cigarette lighter, Amy reaches down to pick it up. On closer inspection, the object turns out not to be a cigarette lighter but one corner of a larger object that is jutting out of the earth. Her curiosity piqued, Amy begins digging with her hands but finds herself unable to extract the object. Undeterred, Amy runs home to fetch a shovel. After spending several minutes digging with the shovel, Amy realizes that the object is *much* larger than she originally believed and that extricating it from the ground will probably require mechanized equipment.

When we first encounter an issue of justice, what we typically see is an outer edge of a much larger problem. We may feel confident that we understand the nature of the issue – in the same way that Amy felt confident that the object in the ground was a cigarette lighter – but further exploration will reveal that our confidence is unfounded. Different people have different amounts of time and patience for philosophical investigation. Some are willing to dig about a bit with their hands (listen to a podcast), others to fetch a shovel (read an article or two); very few engage in the extended philosophical deliberation that would be the equivalent of commandeering powerful digging machinery.

One may lose interest in philosophical inquiry and choose to bow out of the debate. And doing so is one's prerogative. But if one does this, one cannot expect to be taken seriously if one nevertheless continues to make bold ethical proclamations. One cannot justify believing that foreign aid should be cut, or immigration reduced, if one is unwilling to put in the philosophical legwork necessary to evaluate the plausibility of such beliefs. Of course, not everyone enjoys the luxury of being able to devote large amounts of time to philosophical reflection. One aim of this book is to introduce readers to some of the results achieved by the heavy lifting of others.

As the above remarks suggest, a conception of justice can be more or less fully developed. A fully developed conception will specify several aspects of justice: its *content*, its *scope*, and its *grounds*. (A word of warning: the remainder of this section is somewhat technical. Readers who are new not only to global justice but to philosophy more generally may wish to skim these paragraphs and not worry too much about their finer details.) The *content* of a conception of justice specifies a state of affairs that should be brought into being. For example, a particular conception might recommend a state of affairs in which all relevant persons can live a minimally decent life. This recommendation often will be said to reflect the fact that all relevant persons have a *right* to a particular state of affairs. (The concept of a right will be explored in detail in the next chapter.)

The *scope* of a conception has multiple dimensions. First, it answers what we might call the *rights-bearer question*. In other words, it specifies by whom each right is possessed. Is a particular right possessed by all human beings or only by the members of a particular group or association? Second, the scope of a conception answers the *duty-bearer question*. That is, it specifies upon whom a particular right imposes duties. A right to a particular good (such as a minimally decent life) may be possessed by all human beings but this does not mean that the duty to provide this good to each individual also falls on all human beings. The duty *might* fall on all human beings or it might fall on some subset of the global population (e.g., one's fellow citizens). Third, the scope of a conception answers the *comparator question*. This third dimension of a conception's scope comes into view when we notice that certain goods make essential reference to the condition of others. Most notably, some theories maintain that all relevant persons should enjoy some kind of *equality*. But this raises the question: to whom must they be equal? For example, must they enjoy equality with all human beings or only with their compatriots? (Notice that our answer to the comparator question does not determine our answer to the duty-bearer question. Even if equality must be enjoyed only among compatriots, it does not follow that the duty to ensure this equality is possessed only by one's compatriots. Individuals or organizations in one country may have duties to promote equality within another.)

Finally, the *grounds* of a conception refer to the reasons that we have to endorse it. In order to win our allegiance, a conception of justice must provide a compelling defence of its content. In other words, it must be able to explain *why* certain persons should be thought to possess certain rights and duties, why they should be entitled to certain goods, and why they should be expected to bear certain burdens. Contrary to what the behaviour of our politicians and other public figures might sometimes seem to suggest, moral disputes are not resolved by raising one's voice, shaking one's head, or repeating appealing soundbites. Rather, we must endeavour to support our position with well-developed *arguments*.

1.4 Arguing about justice

People who have not been trained in moral thinking, along with students who are just beginning their training, sometimes express the worry that we will not be able to make progress in resolving justice-based disputes. But this worry often arises prematurely. In many cases, we can effectively adjudicate among rival ethical positions by scrutinizing the arguments that are made, or could be made, in their defence.

Now, when first exposed to philosophical reasoning, some people are slightly puzzled by the arguments that they encounter. When you move on to the more substantive chapters that comprise the majority of this book, you might feel a little lost at first, at least if this is your first foray into philosophical debate. It is therefore important to emphasize that although they depart markedly from the vapid sloganeering of much popular debate, the arguments employed by philosophers are not actually that different from many of those that we encounter in quite ordinary, everyday, scenarios. They are just a bit more sophisticated.

Allow me to illustrate. Suppose your friends are trying to persuade you to go on holiday with them. They say: "you should come with us. We're going to go bungee jumping. It will be fun!" When they say this, your friends are attempting to defend a particular claim or conclusion (that you should go on holiday with them), and they are doing so by offering an argument. Their argument has two steps, or "premises". The first premise is factual: they inform you that the holiday will involve bungee jumping. The second premise is evaluative: they assert that bungee jumping is fun. From these two premises they infer their conclusion. Stated much more formally than it ever would be in a normal conversation, your friends' argument has the following structure:

Premise 1: The holiday involves bungee jumping;

Premise 2: Bungee jumping is fun;

Therefore,

Conclusion: You should come on the holiday.

Now, you might challenge your friends' argument in a variety of ways. You might challenge it by criticizing the second (evaluative) premise. Your friends have asserted that bungee jumping is fun, but you might simply deny this; you might point out that you are scared of heights and that you cannot imagine anything worse.

Alternatively, you might challenge the argument not by criticizing either of its premises but rather by criticizing its overall structure. Suppose you say: "that does sound fun, but my mum is unwell, and I have to stay home to look after her". When you say this, you do not deny that bungee jumping is fun (you do not object to any of the premises that make up your friends' argument); rather, you question the significance of the fact that bungee jumping is fun. You say: from the fact that bungee jumping is fun, it *does not follow* that I ought to go on the holiday. The fact that bungee jumping is fun gives me *a* reason to go on the holiday (what philosophers call a "pro-tanto" reason), but it does not give me a conclusive, *all-things-considered* reason to do so. By pointing out that your mum is unwell, you demonstrate that, although you have *a* reason to go on the holiday, you also have a reason (a "countervailing" reason) *not* to go on the holiday and that reason may well outweigh the first one. To use the philosophical jargon, you show that your friends' argument is a *non sequitur*; that is, you reveal that their conclusion does not follow logically from their premises. (To say that a conclusion "does not follow" from a set of premises is to say that you can accept the premises without being logically committed to accepting the conclusion; rejecting the conclusion is logically consistent with accepting the premises.)

Your response can also be framed in a slightly different way. We might say that your reply reveals that your friends' argument is *incomplete*; the considerations you put forward reveal that, in order for the argument to yield its conclusion, it will need to be supplemented with at least one additional premise, something like: "you ought to take advantage of opportunities to do fun things". Adding this premise makes the overall structure of the argument a little more robust, in the sense that, if we were to accept it, we would be a little closer to arriving at the conclusion that you should go on the holiday. But it should be pretty clear that we should *not* accept this new premise, for such an unqualified claim is obviously implausible. We could accept a *similar* premise – something like, "you ought to take advantage of opportunities to do fun things *when you can do so without neglecting your duties to others*" – but this more modest premise will not enable us to arrive at the conclusion that you ought to go on the holiday. This is because going on the holiday would prevent you from looking after your mum, and it seems reasonable to suppose that looking after your mum is something that you have a duty to do. Thus, if you should take advantage of opportunities to do fun things only when you can do so without neglecting your duties to others, you should *not* go on the holiday.

Many familiar arguments that we hear when growing up are vulnerable to the kinds of philosophical strategies that I have just described. Parents often tell their young children that they should finish their dinner "because there are children in Africa who are starving to death". But this argument appears to be an obvious non sequitur. How could it follow from the fact that there are children starving in Africa that we ought to finish our dinner? After all, it is not like finishing our dinner would *benefit* Africa's starving children. Many of us will remember times in our childhood when we attempted to justify our behaviour to our parents by pointing out that we were simply acting in the way that we had been instructed to act by an older sibling or friend, and many of us will remember our parents responding to these attempts at justification by asking: "If your brother told you to jump off a cliff, would you jump?!" Our parents might not have realized it, but by asking this rhetorical question they were making two important contributions to our intellectual development: they were teaching us to challenge the dictates of those we regard as authority figures, and they were introducing us to a well-known type of philosophical argument known as the *reductio ad absurdum*. This argument works by revealing that a particular claim has absurd consequences that no one would be willing to accept. When we tell our parents that we, say, smoked a cigarette because our older brother told us to, we seem to be making the following argument:

Premise 1: My brother told me to smoke a cigarette;

Premise 2: I should do whatever my brother tells me to do;

Therefore,

Conclusion: I should smoke a cigarette.

When our parents ask us if we would follow our brother's instruction to jump off a cliff, they criticize our second premise; they point out that that premise commits us to absurd conclusions that we could not possibly accept and that it should therefore be abandoned. But if we abandon that premise, the argument we offered in defence of our cigarette-smoking collapses.

The point that I want to make here is that although philosophical argumentation might seem very unfamiliar at first, some of the arguments that philosophers use actually have the same form or structure as arguments that we regularly encounter in everyday life. In subsequent chapters, we shall see how the non sequitur and the reductio ad absurdum can be employed in a more political context and can help us to make progress in debates about justice. Needless to say, these two kinds of argument are far from the only kinds used by philosophers – we will encounter other kinds over the course of the book – but hopefully what I have said will help to make subsequent chapters more accessible than they might otherwise have been.

1.5 Replying to the "realists"

I have been talking about how we might make progress with moral debates. However, it is sometimes said that, in the context of world politics, invoking considerations of morality and justice is misguided. In later chapters, I will address "statist" and "nationalist" attempts to identify considerations that drastically constrain the demands of global justice. Here, I want to consider a more fundamental challenge. Often, students who enrol in classes on global justice also take classes on International Relations in which they are introduced to a school of thought known as "realism". Realism challenges the very possibility of global justice and of international morality more generally. According to realist doctrine, either moral considerations have no application in the international domain or those considerations license the single-minded pursuit of self-interest.

When Charles Beitz addressed realist arguments in his pioneering 1979 book *Political Theory and International Relations*, he wrote: "For many years, it has been impossible to make moral arguments about international relations to its American students without encountering the claim that moral judgments have no place in discussions of international affairs or foreign policy".[10] Thankfully, this is no longer the case. Since the publication of Beitz's text, serious academic inquiry into the nature of international morality has flourished. The literature on global justice has burgeoned, and classes exploring that literature have proliferated. (That this book was commissioned is a testament to that fact.) Moreover, students who enrol in these classes often do so because of an antecedent conviction that international affairs are currently marked by deep *in*justices and that various international practices require radical reform or even abolition. They purchase Fair Trade products, belong to human rights organizations such as Amnesty International, and take to the streets to protest their governments' involvement in unjust wars.

---

10 Charles R. Beitz, *Political Theory and International Relations* (Princeton, NJ: Princeton University Press, 1979), p. 15.

Indeed, it is safe to say that in recent decades there has been something of a sea change: the realist scepticism that once dominated academic discourse has been supplanted by an altogether more humanitarian outlook. For this reason, I do not want to say much about the realist tradition, but I do want to say something. (It should be noted that some of the "statist" arguments to be examined in Chapter 4 have a realist pedigree.) In what follows, I briefly elaborate on some of the main arguments that underpinned the erstwhile realist hegemony and I sketch some of the key considerations that have been instrumental in turning the tide.

Realism can be interpreted either morally or non-morally.[11] On the moral interpretation, states are morally permitted (or perhaps even morally required) to pursue the national interest and to disregard the wellbeing of other states and their citizens: in other words, focusing exclusively on the promotion of the national interest is compatible with the dictates of morality, even when doing so imposes large burdens on others. By contrast, according to the non-moral interpretation of realism, it is misguided to invoke moral concepts such as "permissions" and "requirements" in discussions about international affairs, for morality has no application in the international domain: the foreign policies of governments can be neither just nor unjust. The arguments that I discuss below demonstrate that we can circumvent both versions of the realist challenge.

Realism is an extraordinary view. In our everyday lives, most of us (including most realists) believe that morality constrains our freedom to pursue our ends: it compels us to recognize – and to accommodate – the rights and interests of others. But according to the realist view, no comparable constraints regulate the interactions of states. In the international domain in which states operate, "to have all, and do all, is lawful to all".[12] This startling phrase is taken from the work of Thomas Hobbes, the 17th-century philosopher who provided much of the inspiration for contemporary realist thought. According to Hobbes and his followers, international affairs take place in a "state of nature", a realm characterized by the absence of an overarching authority capable of guaranteeing the security of its denizens. While the interaction of individuals within states is regulated by governments, there is no world government with the capacity to regulate the interactions of states themselves. It is this feature of international relations – its "anarchic" character – that grounds realist claims about the freedom of states to pursue their own interests. Given the nature of international relations, realists maintain that states have little choice but to focus on their self-preservation. In a state of nature, it is unreasonable to expect states to comply with principles that require them to respect the rights of others since there can be no guarantee

---

11 Jeff McMahan, "Realism, Morality, and War", in Terry Nardin (ed.), *The Ethics of War and Peace: Religious and Secular Perspectives* (Princeton, NJ: Princeton University Press, 1996), p. 79.

12 Thomas Hobbes, *De Cive* [1642] (New York: Appleton-Century-Crofts, 1949), p. 28.

that their counterparts will do likewise, and any state that did comply would thereby render itself vulnerable to exploitation. As Hobbes puts it: in a state of nature, it is irrational for an agent to adhere to other-regarding precepts, "for that were to expose himself to prey, which no man is bound to".[13]

Ironically, a central objection to realism is that it is not at all realistic. According to this objection, the picture that realists paint of international relations is a poor representation of the world that we know. Although it is of course true that there is no world government, the Hobbesian account is overly simplistic. Hobbes compared the international domain to an "interpersonal" state of nature that he imagined individual men and women inhabiting prior to the establishment of a sovereign power. He identified principles that he believed would be appropriate for the latter scenario, and his followers have applied these to the former. But there are important differences between the two scenarios, differences which undermine the suggestion that a single set of principles could be appropriate for each.

To begin with, states are not as vulnerable as individuals are in the interpersonal state of nature. As Marshall Cohen notes, "nations are not overcome by sleep every day, they are not afflicted with diseases of mind and body, and they are not prostrated by old age".[14] When individuals in a state of nature expend time and energy assisting others, they deplete their stock of scarce natural resources and thereby jeopardize their own safety. But states lack many of the susceptibilities that render individuals so insecure.

Second, while Hobbes stipulated that individuals in his imagined interpersonal state of nature were of equal power, the distribution of power among states is hugely *un*equal. Thus, while burdening weak developing states with demanding other-regarding responsibilities may drastically undermine their viability (and therefore be unreasonable), stronger developed states can often bear such burdens at little cost.[15]

Third, unlike individuals in the interpersonal state of nature, states are not radically ignorant about the intentions of their counterparts. As Cohen observes: "Individuals in the Hobbesian state of nature are anonymous and ahistorical. But nations have names and reputations, geographies and histories, principles and purposes, and these allow others to judge their intentions with considerable confidence".[16] The knowledge that states have about their counterparts enables them to forge alliances and to engage in cooperative and altruistic endeavours without fear that others will take advantage of them. States have managed to overcome a number of the obstacles generated by

---

13   Thomas Hobbes, *Leviathan* [1651], in William Molesworth (ed.), *The English Works of Thomas Hobbes: Volume 3* (London: John Bohn, 1841), p. 118.

14   Marshall Cohen, "Moral Skepticism and International Relations", *Philosophy & Public Affairs*, vol. 13, no. 4, 1984, pp. 299–346, at p. 326.

15   Beitz, *Political Theory and International Relations*, pp. 41–42, 49; Cohen, "Moral Skepticism and International Relations", pp. 326–327; Simon Caney, *Justice Beyond Borders* (Oxford: Oxford University Press, 2005), p. 137.

16   Cohen, "Moral Skepticism and International Relations", p. 327.

uncertainty in international affairs by establishing international "regimes". Regimes enable states to overcome these obstacles by facilitating communication and the exchange of information. As Robert Keohane explains, regimes stimulate the development of "'[t]ransgovernmental' networks of acquaintance and friendship ... with the consequence that supposedly confidential internal documents of one government may be seen by officials of another" and "informal coalitions of likeminded officials develop to achieve common purposes".[17] Indeed, although there is no world government, there are various practices and institutions that make the international arena a more secure and cooperative domain than Hobbes's interpersonal state of nature.[18]

None of this is to deny the obvious fact that states often feel – and sometimes are – threatened by others. But it hardly follows from this fact that states are free to disregard the interests of outsiders. After all, there are plenty of acts that states can – and often do – perform that are not necessary for self-preservation.[19] A state's army bombing a school in a rival's territory, for example, cannot typically be construed as an act of self-defence. This point is acknowledged by the laws of war, which prohibit attacks that cannot be expected to confer a military advantage during a conflict. Similarly, as noted above, there are various other-regarding acts that developed states could perform without thereby jeopardizing their security.

Of course, developed states often *decline* to act altruistically, even when they can do so at little cost to themselves. Indeed, they often act with ruthless disregard for the welfare of others. As Cohen writes, "the history of international conduct is to an alarming degree the history of unconscionable insolence, greed, and brutality".[20] But this does not show that the requirements of justice are suspended in the international domain; it shows simply that states frequently *violate* those requirements. It would be different if states were *incapable* of accommodating others' interests. (According to a well-known philosophical maxim, "ought implies can": we cannot say that an agent ought to do something that she is incapable of doing.)[21] It would also be different if accommodating the interests of others were unduly burdensome. But realists have failed to provide evidence that either of these conditions holds.

---

17 Robert O. Keohane, "The Demand for International Regimes", in Keohane (ed.) *International Institutions and State Power: Essays in International Relations Theory* (Boulder, CO: Westview Press, 1989), p. 120.

18 Beitz, *Political Theory and International Relations*, pp. 36–40, 42–49; Aaron James, *Fairness in Practice: A Social Contract for a Global Economy* (New York: Oxford University Press, 2012), Ch. 3.

19 Cohen, "Moral Skepticism and International Relations", p. 322ff.

20 Ibid., p. 307.

21 James, *Fairness in Practice*, p. 84.

Sometimes, realists suggest that states are not merely permitted but morally *required* to set aside other-regarding concerns and focus exclusively on the national interest. According to this line of thought, states have a special duty to promote the wellbeing of their own citizens, a duty they neglect when they cater to the interests of outsiders. One obvious response to this argument is that individuals often want their government to pursue an ethical foreign policy that is sensitive to the interests of those in other countries. Thus, satisfying the preferences of their own citizens requires governments to act in an other-regarding fashion.[22] But there is also a deeper problem with the realist argument, one which arises even in the case of a hypothetical country where everyone is thoroughly selfish. The problem is that we do not generally think that our agents may do anything and everything to promote our interests.[23] For example, we do not think that a lawyer may destroy evidence in the course of defending her client. Although agents are often allowed a degree of partiality toward their principals, their partiality is always constrained by moral considerations. There is no reason to think that the relationship between states and their citizens should be any different. (The degree to which states are permitted to show partiality toward their citizens is an issue to which we shall have reason to return at multiple stages throughout this book.)

Two final points should be made about the realist challenge to global justice. First, although realists often present themselves as opposing the application of any form of other-regarding morality (or even morality per se) to the international domain, the specific complaints that they articulate often reveal that their real grievance is with *a particular conception* of (other-regarding) morality – that is, with a particular interpretation of what morality in fact demands.[24] Importantly, it will sometimes be possible to advocate global justice while also recognizing the legitimacy of realist grievances. After all, it does not follow from the claim that a particular conception of international morality is deficient that we must abandon the notion of other-regarding international morality altogether. Instead of doing that, we could advocate an *alternative* conception of international morality that is capable of accommodating legitimate realist concerns.

Second, realists often object to specific policies or courses of action that some individuals or groups have supported in the name of global justice. But, again, we might continue to advocate global justice while agreeing that the policies in question are misguided; we might argue that any conception

---

22 David Reidy, "Philosophy and Human Rights: Contemporary Perspectives", in Claudio Corradetti (ed.), *Philosophical Dimensions of Human Rights: Some Contemporary Views* (New York: Springer, 2012), p. 29.

23 Beitz, *Political Theory and International Relations*, pp. 23–24; McMahan, "Realism, Morality, and War", p. 81; Allen Buchanan, "The Internal Legitimacy of Humanitarian Intervention", *Journal of Political Philosophy*, vol. 7, no. 1, 1999, pp. 71–87, at p. 78.

24 McMahan, "Realism, Morality, and War", p. 83; Cohen "Moral Skepticism and International Relations", p. 300.

of global justice that endorses those policies is deficient. It should go without saying that a commitment to global justice does not entail a commitment to any and every policy that has ever been advocated in its name.

1.6 Everyday "realism"

The arguments addressed in the previous section are associated with a specific intellectual tradition. But it should be noted that theories of global justice might also attract "realist" criticism of a more general, less formal, kind. I shall conclude this introductory chapter by describing the kind of criticism that I have in mind and by explaining how I believe it should be answered.

Many of the political theorists who contribute to the global justice debate defend rather heterodox views, views which depart quite radically from the dominant strands of public opinion. Many citizens of affluent Western democracies are eager to preserve their privileges. They believe that their own interests, and those of their compatriots, should be prioritized by their governments, and they oppose even the minimal efforts that are currently made to alleviate the plight of distant strangers. In the face of these convictions, political theorists have argued for large transfers of wealth to the world's poor, for minimal controls on immigration, and for radical reform of the international trading system.

One might be tempted to dismiss these proposals on the grounds that they are unrealistic, perhaps even utopian. But it is important to ask what exactly is meant by such claims. It is true that, given the current political climate, many of the proposals in question are politically unfeasible. But this is simply a shorthand way of saying that many people are unwilling to support these proposals and that, for this very reason, they will not be advocated by politicians anxious to be (re)elected. But the reason that many people refuse to support the radical ideas endorsed by political theorists is that the former do not believe they are morally required to do so. When they insist that their government prioritize their own interests, they believe that they are exercising a moral permission. In fact, they often believe that their government is morally *obligated* to make their interests their top priority and that they are simply demanding that their government honour its moral obligations.

This is an important point, for it reveals that part of what is involved in making radical proposals feasible is *challenging* these beliefs and demonstrating that they are unfounded. Nobody wants to think of themselves as a "bad guy", as a defender of injustice. People support the policies they do because they believe those policies to be morally defensible. If we can demonstrate convincingly that those policies, or the principles which underpin them, are *not* morally defensible but are in fact deeply misguided, we will be better placed to mobilize against them.

Political theorists may seem to operate at some distance from political reality but this simply reflects the discipline's distinctive role. The role of political theory is not the sociological or anthropological one of documenting the moral views that people actually hold – what we might call *conventional* morality – but rather the philosophical one of developing a robust *critical* morality that can be used to evaluate and scrutinize conventional views. If political theorists embraced, as a form of methodological constraint, a refusal to stray too far from conventional morality – if they insisted on tethering themselves to the status quo – the whole enterprise would prove to be an unduly conservative endeavour. In order to make a valuable contribution to the movement for global justice, political theorists must "call them as they see them", even when – *especially* when – this means going against the grain of public opinion.

2 RIGHTS

A conception of justice identifies ends that we should endeavour to realize and proposes moral principles to guide the conduct of those it addresses. It accords "rights" and specifies the kinds of duties that those rights impose upon others. A conception of *global* justice aspires to identify the moral principles that should govern the global domain. It begins with the thought that if some entities (such as individual human beings) possess rights, those rights may generate duties that extend beyond the borders of nations and states. This book is devoted to exploring the ongoing debate over what the content of a plausible conception of global justice might look like.

In popular political discourse, the debate about global justice is typically framed in terms of "human rights". As Charles Beitz has written, "To whatever extent contemporary international political life can be said to have a 'sense of justice', its language is the language of human rights".[1] This is not to say that the debate about global justice is *reducible* to the debate about human rights. The former is often understood to be a broader discussion, which addresses certain issues (such as "distributive" justice, considered in detail in Chapters 4 and 5) not covered by the latter.[2] That is one reason why this book is called *Global Justice* and not *Human Rights*.

Nevertheless, human rights are an important part of global justice, which is why they are considered here, at the very beginning of our enquiry. I start by exploring the nature and justification of human rights. I ask what rights are and how we might make the case for their existence. I then address what we might call *the cultural critique of human rights*. According to this critique, the human rights movement should be opposed, for it seeks to foist a narrow, Western conception of morality upon a diverse range of cultural communities. I canvass a number of considerations which demonstrate that the cultural critique is unpersuasive.

---

1. Charles Beitz, "Human Rights as a Common Concern", *The American Political Science Review*, vol. 95, no. 2, 2001, pp. 269–282, at p. 269.
2. James Griffin, *On Human Rights* (New York: Oxford University Press, 2008), pp. 39–44; Charles Beitz, *The Idea of Human Rights* (New York: Oxford University Press, 2009), pp. 141–144.

2.1 Understanding rights

As Martha Nussbaum has written, human rights discourse expresses "the most common and influential form of the view that all human beings everywhere have certain fundamental entitlements".[3] As we shall see, there is disagreement about which entitlements count as genuine human rights, but it may be helpful to begin by mentioning some commonly cited examples. These entitlements can be grouped into a number of different categories, including *security rights* (such as the right to life and bodily integrity), *due process rights* (such as the right to a fair trial and the right against arbitrary detention), *basic freedoms* (such as the right to freedom of thought, expression, association, and religion), *rights to political participation* (such as the right to vote and hold office), *equality rights* (such as the right to equality before the law and the right to equal pay for equal work), and *economic and social rights* (such as the right to education, healthcare, and rest).[4]

For those of us living in liberal democracies, these entitlements will be reasonably familiar. But what exactly does it mean to say that a particular entitlement should be classed as *a right*? And what does it mean to say that a particular entitlement should be classed as a *human* right? In order to answer the first of these two questions, we should consider several distinctions. Once these distinctions are drawn, we shall be in a better position to answer the second question. Whereas the majority of this book is concerned primarily with *normative* questions relating to what we ought to do and why, this section and the next are primarily *conceptual* in nature. The conceptual issues addressed in these sections set the stage for the normative analysis to follow.

We can begin by familiarizing ourselves with an important and illuminating distinction that the jurist Wesley Hohfeld drew among "claims", "liberties", "powers", and "immunities". Hohfeld observed that the notion of a right was used to refer not to a single concept but to any one of these four "incidents".[5] Let us consider each in turn.

If I have a *claim* to something, then a second party has some kind of duty toward me. For example, my claim not to be punched imposes upon others a duty not to punch me. This duty is *negative* in character: it requires the duty-bearers to refrain from performing a particular kind of act. But the duties associated with a claim can also be *positive*: that is, they can require the duty-bearer(s) to provide something. For example, my claim to be paid is associated with my employer's duty to pay me. Notice that, irrespective of whether they are negative or positive, the duties associated with a claim are duties *owed to the right-holder*. They are not duties owed to god or society or

---

[3] Martha Nussbaum, *Creating Capabilities: The Human Development Approach* (Cambridge, MA: Harvard University Press, 2011), p. 102.

[4] James Nickel, *Making Sense of Human Rights*, Second Edition (Malden, MA: Blackwell Publishing, 2007), p. 11.

[5] Wesley Hohfeld, *Fundamental Legal Conceptions as Applied in Judicial Reasoning* (New Haven: Yale University Press, 1919).

any other entity. In other words, they are "directed duties", or, to use Allen Buchanan's terminology, they are "solely subject-grounded".[6]

While claims indicate the presence of a duty, *liberties* are associated with the *absence* of a duty. I am at liberty to perform a particular act when I have no duty not to perform that act. For example, I am at liberty to part my hair on the left side, because I have no duty not to do so.

The distinction between claims and liberties can be further illustrated by thinking about a trip to the cinema. Sometimes, when we buy our ticket, we are told that we have not been allocated a specific seat; rather, we can sit wherever we like. In such cases, we have a liberty. If I wish to sit in a particular seat – D1, say – I am permitted to do so. I have no duty not to sit there. But, similarly, no one else (who's bought a ticket) has a duty to refrain from sitting in that seat. If I arrive in the auditorium and find that D1 is already occupied by another cinemagoer, I cannot demand that she move. She is not violating my rights by sitting in D1; my rights do not impose on her a duty not to sit there.

By contrast, sometimes, when we buy our ticket, we are allocated a specific seat. If I book D1, this means that in addition to having a liberty to sit in that seat (no duty not to), I have a claim. If I arrive in the auditorium and find that another cinemagoer is sat in D1, I can reasonably ask him to move. In this case, my rights *do* impose on others a duty not to sit there.

Let us now consider the next two Hohfeldian incidents. A *power* is a capacity to alter the legal or moral nature of a relationship between two or more people by changing the assignment of claims and liberties. For example, I may have a claim to compensation if a motorist damages my bike, but I may choose to *waive* this claim and thereby unburden the motorist of the associated duty. A power also enables one to create new claims and liberties. For example, if I promise to provide my colleague with feedback on her paper, I thereby confer a claim (upon my colleague) and simultaneously acquire a duty. To take another example, if I tell my students that a particular assignment is optional, I thereby confer a liberty: I grant my students the freedom to either complete the assignment or not.

Finally, an *immunity* renders one invulnerable to attempts to alter one's assignment of claims, liberties, and powers in certain ways. For example, a mischievous colleague cannot oblige me to write a book defending the scientific validity of astrology simply by promising a publisher that I will do so. I am immune to having duties imposed upon me in this manner.

It is important to stress that many rights are examples of what Leif Wenar has called "molecular" rights.[7] What this means is that the rights in question are made up of *multiple* Hohfeldian incidents. As we saw in the cinema

---

6   Allen Buchanan, *The Heart of Human Rights* (New York: Oxford University Press, 2013), p. 59.

7   Leif Wenar, "The Nature of Rights", *Philosophy & Public Affairs*, vol. 33, no. 3, 2005, pp. 223–252, at pp. 229–230, pp. 233–234.

example above, when I book a specific seat, my right to sit in that seat incorporates both a liberty *and* a claim.

Having identified the four Hohfeldian incidents to which the phrase "a right" might refer, let us now distinguish between *artificial* rights and *moral* rights. Artificial rights are created and conferred by a social practice or institution (such as a legal system). For example, my liberty to sit wherever I please when watching a film is created and conferred by the rules of the cinema. If the cinema were to change its policy and require everyone to sit in a pre-assigned seat, then the liberty that I previously enjoyed would simply cease to exist. By contrast, moral rights exist prior to and independently of any institution. They are claims, liberties, powers, and immunities grounded in salient moral facts and identified by sound moral reasoning.[8] To illustrate, consider my right not to be punched. This right has both an artificial and a natural form. It has an artificial form because the law confers upon me a legal claim not to be punched, a claim which imposes legal duties on others. But suppose that the law were changed and that I were deprived of this legal claim. In this situation, there would continue to be compelling reasons to think that other people have a solely subject-grounded duty to refrain from punching me. This conviction is captured by saying that I have a moral claim not to be punched, a claim, that is, which does not depend for its existence upon institutional recognition.

Let us draw one final distinction, namely, that between *general* and *special* rights. For present purposes, I define a general right as a right possessed by everyone and a special right as a right possessed only by some subset of the population. My right to be paid by the university that employs me is a special right. It is a right possessed by me and by other university employees but by no one else. By contrast, it is reasonable to suppose that if the moral right not to be punched is possessed by anyone, it is possessed by everyone.

2.2 Understanding human rights

With these distinctions in hand, we are now in a better position to understand the nature of specifically *human* rights. As with rights more generally, there are both artificial and moral human rights. Artificial human rights are those enumerated in the major human rights documents, such as the Universal Declaration of Human Rights (1948), the International Covenant on Civil and Political Rights (1966), and the International Covenant on Economic, Social and Cultural Rights (1966). The two covenants are international treaties, and because international treaties constitute one of the primary sources of international law, these covenants create binding legal obligations. The Universal Declaration is not a treaty, but some jurists argue

---

8 Carl Wellman, *The Moral Dimensions of Human Rights* (New York: Oxford University Press, 2011), p. 10.

that many of the rights contained therein have now been accorded binding legal status by the second primary source of international law, namely, international custom. When a particular norm is repeatedly expressed in a consistent pattern of state behaviour and there is a widespread belief that this behaviour is legally required, the norm in question becomes international customary law.

According to the orthodox view of human rights, moral human rights are the moral rights that human beings possess simply in virtue of their humanity. As Carl Wellman has argued, the existence of these moral human rights is presupposed by the major human rights documents mentioned above.[9] The framers of the Universal Declaration assert that their aim is to *recognize* and *protect* human rights rather than to create new rights from scratch, and the two covenants maintain that the rights enumerated therein "derive from the inherent dignity of the human person". In a similar vein, the Preamble to the United Nations Charter declares that one aim of the members is to "reaffirm faith in fundamental human rights". In the recent past, those rights had been treated with "disregard and contempt", resulting in "barbarous acts which … outraged the conscience of mankind". These words were published in 1948 while the horror of the Nazi death camps remained vivid and untamed in the minds of their authors.

If human beings possess moral human rights, then one justification of corresponding legal human rights will appeal to the role that the latter play in instantiating the former in international law.[10] Moreover, the existence of moral human rights furnishes us with grounds to condemn existing institutional arrangements, and to campaign for reform or revolution, regardless of the content of national and international law.[11] If we possess a moral entitlement to a particular freedom, say, then the absence of a corresponding legal entitlement does nothing to vindicate a political regime that deprives us of that freedom. Rather, we can invoke our moral human rights – which exist independently of institutional recognition – in order to condemn that regime. As Wellman writes, "it is the independence of human rights from social practices that enables a social reformer to appeal to them to criticize the law and the other social institutions of any society".[12] (Whether, and how, the existence of moral human rights can be defended is the subject of the next section.)

Moral human rights (and some legal ones) take the form of Hohfeldian incidents. This can be illustrated with a series of examples. To begin with, the right not to be tortured is a claim-right, which imposes duties on others. It is worth noting that, like many others, this right generates *multiple* duties,

---

9   Ibid., p. 5, pp. 53–54, p. 56.
10 Ibid., p. 15.
11 Ibid., p. 8, p. 11.
12 Ibid., p. 11.

some of which are negative and some of which are positive. Most obviously, the right not be tortured imposes a negative duty to refrain from engaging in torture. But it also generates a duty to investigate suspected cases of torture and to pay one's share of the costs associated with enforcing the prohibition of torture and with punishing those who flout that prohibition.[13] To use Jeremy Waldron's phrase, rights generate "successive waves of duty".[14]

Some claim-rights generate duties that fall primarily, or even exclusively, on states. This is because there are some rights that states are uniquely placed to violate (e.g., the right of an arrestee to be informed of the reasons for her arrest and of any charges being brought against her). Moreover, even when we limit our attention to rights that can be violated by multiple kinds of agent, we see that states are capable of violating rights on an inordinately large scale.[15] By virtue of its various attributes – its monopoly on the means of violence, extensive bureaucracy, and effective revenue-raising, coordinative, and surveillance capabilities – the state is an exceptionally dangerous institution. On the other hand, and by virtue of the very same set of characteristics, the state is especially well positioned to provide individuals with the substance of their rights and also to protect them against violations.[16]

However, states are not the only entities upon which human rights impose duties. Human rights also impose duties upon international organizations (such as the United Nations, World Bank, and International Monetary Fund), non-governmental organizations (such as Amnesty International and Oxfam), multinational corporations (such as Nike, Coca-Cola, and ExxonMobil), and individual men and women. Individuals lack the capacities that make other entities especially effective at both realizing and violating human rights, but they nevertheless bear important responsibilities, especially when states and other institutions are derelict in their duties. (In the next chapter, we shall explore, among other things, the duties that individuals bear given pervasive institutional neglect of the world's poor.)

Having considered an example of a moral human claim-right, let us now turn to the remaining Hohfeldian incidents. An example of a moral human *liberty*-right is the right to freedom of expression. This right indicates that we lack a duty to refrain from expressing ourselves in various ways. I have no duty not to write this book and to thereby share with you a variety of controversial views, and none of us has any duty to refrain from criticizing governments, businesses, or any other institution that we might deem worthy of criticism. Of course, this right is not unlimited. Although I am at liberty to

---

13 Jeremy Waldron, *Liberal Rights: Collected Papers 1981-1991* (New York: Cambridge University Press, 1993), p. 25.
14 Ibid.
15 Wellman, *Moral Dimensions*, p. 34.
16 Ibid.

criticize the prime minister, for example, I may not engage in libel or slander. Another example of a moral human liberty-right is the right to resist those who attempt to violate one's other rights.[17] For example, if an assailant attacks me on the street, thereby violating my right to security, I am at liberty to defend myself, provided that certain conditions are satisfied.

An example of a moral human *power*-right is the right to freedom of association. I have no duty not to join or form a trade union, political party, or church. Exercising this right involves altering the moral relationship among oneself and others by changing the assignment of claims, duties, and liberties. For example, by joining a trade union, I thereby acquire a duty to pay a membership fee. Another example of a moral human power-right concerns the liberty to defend oneself that I mentioned in the previous paragraph. Under certain conditions, we possess the power to *transfer* our defensive rights to others.[18] For example, I may transfer my right of self-defence to my state, which may be able to protect my security more effectively than I can protect it myself. If, however, my state constitutes one of the primary threats to my security – if, for example, I am a member of a minority group that is viciously persecuted by the police and army – then I may transfer my defensive rights to *another* state, which, under certain conditions, may be morally permitted to intervene on my behalf.[19] (The limits of a state's right to defend its citizens and the citizens of other states will be explored at length in Chapters 9 and 10, where we shall address the issues of war and humanitarian intervention.)

Finally, a common example of a moral human *immunity*-right is the right against forced marriage. This right renders one invulnerable to attempts by others to alter one's moral situation in a particular way. When, for example, a young Afghan girl is forced into marriage by village elders, the husband does not thereby acquire any new moral rights vis-à-vis the girl.

One further conceptual point to make about human rights concerns their scope. As we noted earlier, moral human rights are possessed by all human beings simply in virtue of their humanity. This means that, to reuse the terminology introduced above, they are *general* rights. Some legal human rights have a narrower scope. This is because international treaties are binding only on those party to the agreement, and although international customary law is binding on all, it is likely that only a subset of the rights enumerated in the Universal Declaration are recognized as customary norms. This means that some legal human rights are best understood as special rights.[20]

---

17 Ibid., p. 24.
18 Cecile Fabre, *Cosmopolitan War* (Oxford: Oxford University Press, 2012), Ch. 2.
19 Ibid., Ch. 5.
20 Ibid., pp. 81–82.

2.3 Justifying human rights

The existence of moral human rights is controversial. As we have seen, these rights are said to exist independently of institutional recognition and to be possessed by all human beings simply in virtue of their humanity. Moreover, we have caught a glimpse of one issue that makes human rights particularly contentious. As I mentioned above, it is often thought that there is a human right against forced marriage. This is one example of how human rights can appear to conflict with the traditions of particular cultures. Later in this chapter, I will consider at some length how human rights can be defended against those who maintain that their promotion is unacceptably insensitive to cultural diversity. But before I turn to the task of defending moral human rights against common objections, I must attend to the task of providing a positive argument for their existence. That is the objective of the present section.

Why think that all human beings possess certain moral rights simply in virtue of their humanity? The standard answer to this question begins with the observation that, for all their differences, human beings share a variety of morally relevant characteristics. Although the many members of the human species differ considerably in various respects, they nevertheless retain a morally significant set of common needs, interests, and vulnerabilities.[21] To take the most obvious examples, all human beings will become hungry without food, dehydrated without water, and exhausted without rest; all are vulnerable to pain, exposure, trauma, fear, and anxiety; all are susceptible to illness and disease; all require adequate space in which to move around; and all need an adequate degree of mental stimulation, including interaction with others, without which they will incur psychological harm. These acute human vulnerabilities are common knowledge and are frequently instrumentalized by vicious individuals in a bid to bend others to their will. Moreover, these vulnerabilities are not specific to the members of a particular race or ethnicity: they are possessed by all human beings across the planet.

In an influential body of work, Martha Nussbaum has sought to frame human commonality in terms of a list of central human *capabilities*. The idea is that characteristic members of the human species possess certain innate capacities to function in particular ways. These "basic capabilities", if provided with adequate material and social support, can be transformed into "higher-level" capabilities that enable one to function in a manner that is distinctively human. Conversely, the basic capabilities can be deprived of nourishment, in which case their owner is denied the opportunity to realize his or her human potential.[22]

---

21 Simon Caney, *Justice Beyond Borders: A Global Political Theory* (Oxford: Oxford University Press, 2005), p. 36.

22 Martha Nussbaum, *Women and Human Development* (New York: Cambridge University Press, 2000) p. 83.

Given her focus on the concept of capabilities, rights language is used sparingly by Nussbaum. However, she explicitly states that her theory can be understood "as a species of the human rights approach".[23] Moreover, she notes that both approaches "play a similar role, providing an account of extremely important fundamental entitlements that can be used as a basis both for constitutional thought within a nation and for thinking about international justice".[24] It is therefore appropriate to invoke Nussbaum's arguments for our present purposes.

A pair of capacities that enjoy pride of place on Nussbaum's list of higher-level capabilities is what John Rawls has called "the two powers of moral personality".[25] These are the capacity for a sense of justice and the capacity for a sense of the good. Elaborating on the nature of these powers, Rawls notes that the former is "the capacity to understand, to apply, and normally be moved by" considerations of justice and that the latter is "the capacity to form, to revise, and rationally to pursue ... a conception of what we regard for us as a worthwhile human life".[26] In short, these are the abilities to be *reasonable* and *rational*.[27] Nussbaum identifies the capacity for a sense of justice as one part of what she calls the capability for *affiliation*, which includes the ability "to recognize and show concern for other human beings" and "to imagine the situation of another and to have compassion for that situation".[28] Nussbaum claims that these important capabilities suffuse the remaining items on her list, thereby rendering "their pursuit truly human".[29]

Other higher-level capabilities identified by Nussbaum, some of which can be understood as elaborations on the idea of a capacity for a sense of the good, include the ability "to imagine, think, and reason"[30]; to "use imagination and thought in connection with experiencing and producing self-expressive works and events of one's own choice"[31]; "to have attachments to things and people outside ourselves; to love those who love and care for us, to grieve at their absence"[32]; to engage in work in which one is "able to behave as a thinking being, not just a cog in a machine"[33]; "to laugh [and] to

---

23 Martha Nussbaum, *Frontiers of Justice: Disability, Nationality, Species Membership* (Cambridge, MA: Harvard University Press, 2006), p. 284.
24 Ibid.; Cf. Nussbaum, *Women and Human Development*, p. 97.
25 John Rawls, *Political Liberalism* (New York: Columbia University Press, 1993), pp. 301–302.
26 Ibid., p. 302.
27 Ibid.
28 Nussbaum, *Women and Human Development*, p. 79.
29 Ibid., p. 82.
30 Ibid., p. 78.
31 Ibid., p. 79.
32 Ibid.
33 Ibid., p. 82.

play"[34]; to pursue "opportunities for sexual satisfaction"[35]; and "to participate effectively in political choices that govern one's life".[36]

Nussbaum acknowledges that, in addition to having common capacities that enable the pursuit of a distinctively human existence, human beings are vulnerable to common threats and deprivations, some of which are referenced in the protections that she builds into her list of capabilities. Nussbaum observes that enabling people to develop, maintain, and exercise their capabilities requires, among other things, ensuring that they are "adequately nourished" and "have adequate shelter"[37]; that they are "secure against assault, including sexual assault, child sexual abuse, and domestic violence"[38]; that they are "protected by guarantees of freedom of expression" and "freedom of religious exercise"[39]; that they do not have their "emotional development blighted by overwhelming fear and anxiety, or by traumatic events of abuse or neglect"[40]; and that they "enjoy protections against discrimination".[41]

For present purposes, the most important aspect of Nussbaum's account is the idea that basic human capabilities, and their potential for development, specify the kind of life that is truly worthy of a member of our species. As human beings, we possess extraordinary moral powers that distinguish us from the other animals with whom we share the earth. When the development of these powers is arrested or we are denied the freedom or resources essential for their exercise, our human potential is wasted and there is something deeply regrettable about that. Nussbaum captures this idea by asking us to think "of a tragic character, assailed by fortune".[42]

> We react to the spectacle of humanity so assailed in a way very different from the way we react to a storm blowing grains of sand in the wind. For we see a human being as having worth as an end, a kind of awe-inspiring something that makes it horrible to see this person beaten down by the currents of chance – and wonderful, at the same time, to witness the way in which chance has not completely eclipsed the humanity of the person....[43]

---

34 Ibid., p. 80.
35 Ibid., p. 78.
36 Ibid., p. 80.
37 Ibid., p. 78.
38 Ibid.
39 Ibid., p. 79.
40 Ibid.
41 Ibid.
42 Ibid., p. 72.
43 Ibid., pp. 72–73.

And, of course, it is similarly horrible to witness a person beaten down not by chance but by the machinations of other people. It is worse, even, for harm inflicted by thinking beings is a manifestation of viciousness and malice. (Indeed, those who act with wickedness toward their fellows thereby expose their failure to adequately develop their own capacities, especially those for reason and empathy.) The sense of tragedy and anger that is engendered by the sight of a blighted human life "provide[s] us with strong incentives for protecting that in persons that fills us with awe".[44] As Nussbaum writes: "We see the person as having activity, goals, and projects – as somehow awe-inspiringly above the mechanical workings of nature, and yet in need of support for the fulfillment of many central projects".[45] In Nussbaum's account, it is the "awe-inspiring something" possessed by all human beings that grounds the range of entitlements that we commonly call human rights.

2.4 Cultural relativism

We now have at hand a rough sketch of the kinds of ideas to which one might appeal in order to defend human rights. Among these is the notion that all human beings have distinctive and remarkable capacities, the cultivation and exercise of which are essential for a fully human existence. The forgoing reflections can help to motivate some support for the existence of moral human rights and for the importance of creating corresponding legal entitlements. But these reflections are far from sufficient to dispel the scepticism about human rights that prevails in certain quarters. As I noted above, human rights are a contentious idea, and the practice of promoting human rights can appear to conflict with the customs and traditions of many cultures, especially in the non-Western world.

We have already encountered one example of this conflict. If there is a human right to freedom of association, then the practice of forced marriage must be regarded as morally subversive. Other examples of practices that conflict with widely endorsed human rights are female genital mutilation; the seclusion of women in certain Muslim and Hindu communities, which drastically limits women's opportunities for economic, social, and political participation; and ritual servitude, which is practised in certain parts of Africa and involves the sexual enslavement of young girls. Each of these practices violates a variety of fundamental rights, including rights to bodily integrity, sexual autonomy, and various basic freedoms. More generally, human rights advocacy clashes with patriarchal social norms – prevalent in certain parts of the world and among the adherents of certain religions – that emphasize the importance of servility, modesty, and obedience among women, and with the various instantiations of such norms in law.

---

44 Ibid., p. 73.
45 Ibid.

Most dramatically, it is sometimes said that human rights conflict with the values that predominate in large swathes of Asia. This claim has been made by several East Asian politicians – such as Lee Kuan Yew, the first prime minister of Singapore, and Mahathir bin Mohamad, the prime minister of Malaysia – who both maintain that Asian values attach comparatively little importance to the individual liberties prized in the West, while emphasizing order and discipline, familial loyalty, and obedience to the state. In recent years, it has become common to contrast Western conceptions of human rights with the "China Model", which expects "people [to] accept a very non-Western kind of civic bargain: political oppression in the public square in return for relative economic freedom and a rising quality of life".[46]

What troubles many people about the kinds of practices mentioned above is that they often appear not to be *deviant* activities, completely at odds with local mores (such as rape and murder in Britain, say), but rather manifestations of pervasive and deep-rooted cultural traditions. This perception has led some commentators to conclude that the kinds of entitlements enumerated in the Universal Declaration do not really correspond to anything that can be found in human nature but are instead reflections of a particularly Western outlook that has little purchase in other parts of the world. In the remainder of this chapter, I shall address the starkest version of this cultural critique, according to which the human rights movement represents a kind of neo-colonial enterprise that seeks to impose parochial Western values upon a diverse range of communities that have traditionally been governed by very different norms, and thereby objectionably stifles cultural pluralism. Because this critique comprises multiple strands, each of which requires separate examination, the discussion will range over several sections.

The cultural critique of human rights is sometimes built around the doctrine of *cultural relativism*. According to this doctrine, there can be no universal account of "right" and "wrong", appropriate for all human beings. Rather, each cultural community is governed by a distinct moral code, the content of which is determined not by abstract moral reasoning but by the norms and values internal to the community in question. In other words, morality is *conventional* and is, in that sense, comparable to etiquette. Different cultures have different greeting gestures, and we do not tend to think that one gesture is superior to any other; rather, in deciding which one to use, we defer to local custom.[47] According to those who believe that morality is similar to etiquette, deference to tradition is also the correct way of identifying standards of ethical conduct. In 1947, the Executive Board of the American Anthropological Association expressed misgivings about the proposed Universal Declaration, and their concerns were framed in relativist

---

46 Stefan Halper, *The Beijing Consensus: Legitimizing Authoritarianism in our Time* (New York: Basic Books, 2012), p. 3.

47 Caney, *Justice Beyond Borders*, p. 30.

terms. "Standards and values", the Board maintained, "are relative to the culture from which they derive". Consequently, "any attempt to formulate postulates that grow out of the beliefs or moral codes of one culture must to that extent detract from the applicability of any Declaration of Human Rights to mankind as a whole".[48]

What can be said in response to relativist concerns? Relativists standardly attempt to defend their position by pointing to the prevailing diversity of norms and practices and to the stubborn persistence of ethical disagreement. The first thing to say in reply is that a diversity of practices does not necessarily constitute evidence of disagreement about values. Rather, the fact that two societies have very different practices may simply reflect the fact that the two societies operate under very different circumstances. This point is made by James Griffin in relation to the observation that some societies have practised infanticide.

> [C]onsider the extreme case of life-threatening poverty. Tolerance of infanticide is an adaptation that most of us would make if forced to it by the direst poverty: say, if one were faced with the awful choice between the survival of one's newborn baby or one's young child. A plausible explanation of the disagreement over infanticide between a society of such abject poverty and one better off may not be a difference in evaluative frameworks but … a difference in material conditions.[49]

Griffin's suggestion is that some people have had to adapt to appalling material conditions that others have not had to endure and that such adaptation has involved making extremely difficult choices with which the more fortunate among us have not been faced. Implicit in Griffin's remarks is the thought that *had* we encountered such difficult decisions, it is not at all obvious that we would have chosen differently.

The first point, then, is that some apparent moral disagreements may turn out to be illusory. The second point to make in response to the relativist challenge concerns cases of genuine moral disagreement. From the fact that the members of different cultures disagree about what morality requires, it is not reasonable to infer that morality cannot be universal in scope. Rather than revealing that morality is culturally relative, ethical disagreement may arise because some people hold correct moral views while others (those with whom they disagree) hold incorrect moral views. (Alternatively, disagreement may arise because *all* parties to the dispute hold incorrect moral views.)[50]

---

48 Executive Board, American Anthropological Association, "Statement on Human Rights", *American Anthropologist*, vol. 49, no. 4, 1947, pp. 539–543, at p. 542.
49 Griffin, *On Human Rights*, p. 130.
50 Nickel, *Making Sense of Human Rights*, pp. 171–2.

If a colleague and I disagree about the best way to structure an article that we are co-authoring, we do not immediately conclude that there is no way of resolving the dispute. Rather, we each try to demonstrate that our preferred approach is the optimal one and that the other person has overlooked certain relevant considerations. We do not assume that our disagreement is comparable to a disagreement about etiquette and that neither approach is more justifiable than the alternative. Similarly, we should not assume that moral disagreement is comparable to disagreement about etiquette. Moreover, we should recognize the possibility that our moral judgements, like those that we make in other domains, can be defective. Our reasoning (and those of our opponents) can be distorted by a variety of considerations, including self-interest, emotion, pride, laziness, and ideology.[51] As James Nickel observes, "[d]isagreement does not show that reliable and rational methods of settling moral, political, and legal questions are unavailable or impossible". Rather, disagreement may persist because some people may be unaware of these methods "or they may be incapable of using them well because of bias, irrationality, or lack of knowledge about relevant facts".[52]

This last point is worth elaborating. Some critics of human rights ground their objections in dubious empirical premises. For example, Lee Kuan Yew is well known for claiming that political rights undermine prospects for economic development. According to Lee, Singapore's economic successes are attributable to its authoritarian form of governance. Yet experts have disputed this claim. In a response to Lee's assertions, the economist Amartya Sen notes that "Systematic empirical studies give no real support to the claim that there is a conflict between political rights and economic performance".[53] This is significant. If a particular culture, or some subset of its members, holds moral views that are grounded in faulty empirical premises, it would be odd to conclude that those views should not be regarded as inferior to those that emerge from a better account of empirical realities.[54] When moral disagreement arises because one or more of the parties are empirically misinformed, the fact that such disagreement exists provides no support for the thesis that morality is culturally relative.

It is likely that some people are drawn to cultural relativism because they deem it important to be tolerant of ways of life that differ from their own. We might worry that a commitment to human rights may impel one to be unduly hostile to unfamiliar cultures, and one might hope that a relativistic view will be more accommodating of cultural pluralism. However, if we think that tolerance is an important virtue, then we should be disturbed by the implications of cultural relativism. Remember that, according to the

---

51 Caney, *Justice Beyond Borders*, p. 48; Ibid.
52 Nickel, *Making Sense of Human Rights*, pp. 171–2.
53 Amartya Sen, *Human Rights and Asian Values* (New York: Carnegie Council on Ethics and International Affairs, 1997), p. 11.
54 Caney, *Justice Beyond Borders*, pp. 89–90.

relativist, each community is governed by a distinct moral code, the content of which is determined by its own traditions. An implication of this view is that acting intolerantly is morally justified if one is a member of an intolerant community. If we believe that it is important for one to be tolerant of others, irrespective of whether one's community recognizes tolerance as a virtue, then that is a reason to reject relativism, not to embrace it.[55] Of course, if tolerance is important, that may have significant implications for human rights doctrine. We may think that, because morality requires us to tolerate a wide variety of different cultures and customs, some of which endorse practices that sharply conflict with commonly recognized human rights, the list of human rights must in fact be shorter than it is often believed to be. I shall return to this concern in section 2.6. For now, the point to emphasize is that a commitment to the importance of tolerance should not lead one to embrace cultural relativism.

2.5 A Western imposition?

Even if the case for relativism is unpersuasive, it may nevertheless be objected that there is something unacceptably imperialistic about the contemporary human rights movement. After all, the objector might say, human rights are distinctively *Western* ideas, wielded by Western countries against the rest of the world. Regardless of their merits, these ideas are deeply alien to many non-Western cultures, and it is inappropriate to foist alien ideas upon unreceptive societies. Or so one might argue.

There are several points to be made here. First, let us assume that human rights originated in the West and that, for this reason, they can accurately be described as Western ideas. It is not obvious why this should be thought to have any implications for human rights advocacy. After all, the geographic origin of an idea need not constrain its applicability.[56] As Nussbaum reminds us, "[p]eople borrow things all the time, and the resourcefulness with which cultures make use of originally external materials is one of the most significant facts of human history".[57] Extending this thought, Wellman points out that "Many, perhaps most, of the concepts of the natural sciences originated in and were developed within Europe. But this does not imply that physics, chemistry and biology are inapplicable in distant lands".[58]

Second, the claim that human rights originated in the West is problematic. Although a variety of ideas closely associated with human rights can certainly be found in the history of Western thought, there is also clear

---

55 Nussbaum, *Women and Human Development*, p. 49; Nickel, *Making Sense of Human Rights*, p. 171.
56 Caney, *Justice Beyond Borders*, p. 87.
57 Nussbaum, *Creating Capabilities*, p. 102.
58 Wellman, *Moral Dimensions of Human Rights*, pp. 30–31.

evidence of such ideas in the thought of non-Western traditions. For example, Sen has described how the value of tolerance was extolled in the 3rd century BCE by the Buddhist emperor Asoka and in the 16th century by the Mughal emperor Akbar.[59] Asoka pronounced that "the sects of other people all deserve reverence"[60], and Akbar insisted that "No man should be interfered with on account of religion, and anyone [is] to be allowed to go over to a religion he pleased".[61] At roughly the same time that Akbar was writing these words, the Catholic authorities in Europe were busy executing heretics.[62]

Similarly, in the works of the Indian writer Kauṭilya, who lived in the 4th century BCE, Sen finds an endorsement of the value of individual freedom.[63] To be sure, Kauṭilya advocated freedom only for the upper classes, but, as Sen notes, "this limitation is not wildly different from the Greek concern with free men as opposed to slaves or women".[64] In short, Sen's claim is that some important elements of human rights thinking have deep roots in non-Western cultures.

A third point relates to the perception that Western states are eager to foist human rights upon others. Recall that some human rights are held specifically against the state, and one reason for this is that the state is a particularly dangerous institution. The point of some human rights – such as the right to a fair trial and the right against arbitrary detention – is to reduce the threat that the state poses to individual liberty. Now, of relevance here is the role that Western states have played in exposing other peoples to state institutions. As Nickel writes, "since the European colonial powers both developed and promoted the spread of the modern state, they have responsibilities to address its dangers. A recall of the product is not possible, but sharing the lessons about its dangers and remedies is".[65] The thought here is that Western states have a special duty to help to contain a danger they have contributed to creating and that therefore it is entirely appropriate for those states to take a lead in promoting human rights.

Fourth, human rights laws and norms are not used exclusively by the West to condemn transgressions in other parts of the world. Rather, these norms and laws are also invoked to criticize recalcitrant Western states. For example, during The Troubles in Northern Ireland, the European Court of Human Rights ruled that the UK had violated the European Convention. The decision related to the British military's use of interrogation techniques that the Court deemed "inhuman and degrading". Similarly, the US prison

---

59 Sen, *Human Rights and Asian Values*, pp. 19–20, 23–34.
60 Quoted in ibid., p. 19.
61 Quoted in ibid, p. 23.
62 Ibid., p. 24.
63 Ibid., pp. 20–22.
64 Ibid., p. 22.
65 Nickel, *Making Sense of Human Rights*, p. 173.

camp at Guantanamo Bay has been repeatedly criticized by human rights experts at the UN and by human rights organizations such as Amnesty International.

Finally, it should be noted that human rights have inspired individuals who played instrumental roles in the dismantling of Western empires. For example, the ideals embodied in human rights were embraced by Gandhi and Nehru, who led the Indian struggle for independence from British colonial rule.[66] If these ideals were Western exports – along with oppression and brutality – then they were subsequently weaponized and used against their progenitors.

2.6 Toleration and respect

As I mentioned earlier, the appeal of cultural relativism can perhaps be explained, at least in part, by the perception that relativism supports a tolerant moral outlook. Similarly, a concern for toleration is likely to be one of the factors motivating the complaint that human rights reflect a form of Western imperialism. As we have seen, relativism is in fact no friend of toleration, and prominent concerns relating to the relationship between human rights and the West can be adequately addressed. Nevertheless, we cannot pretend that cultural diversity does not exist. The various cultural communities that comprise our world are regulated by a diverse plurality of values, and nothing that has been said so far demonstrates that a human rights ethic is sufficiently accommodating of that diversity. Of course, it is not a criticism of human rights to point out that, in many societies, the values they embody are very far from being adequately respected. An account of moral human rights identifies liberties and goods to which we are morally entitled, not those which are actually universally enjoyed. Similarly, legal human rights specify standards that governments should strive to meet; they do not aim to describe the ways that governments actually behave. Nevertheless, we might worry that the bar – the moral threshold – has been set too high. Some communities are governed by norms and values that are very different from those expressed in the major international human rights documents, and it might be said that at least some of these cultures are worthy of toleration and respect; indeed, that they are entitled to toleration as a means of expressing respect. Moreover, it might be argued that by criticizing traditional and hierarchical communities that fail to satisfy the liberal standards it proposes, the human rights movement fails to treat these communities with the respect that they are rightfully owed.

In response to this argument, a number of points can be made. First, although it is of course true that our world exhibits considerable cultural

---

66 Nussbaum, *Women and Human Development*, pp. 38–39; Nussbaum, *Creating Capabilities*, p. 105.

diversity, it should be borne in mind that there is also considerable diversity *within* cultures. The histories, texts, and traditions of any particular culture will contain a variety of different (and potentially conflicting) elements, and there will often be disagreement (either private or public) among the culture's members about which of these elements are central and which are peripheral.[67] For example, Nussbaum notes that some Indian Muslim women "have urged other women to ask what is really important in the tradition, and whether the really important features justify seclusion and veiling".[68] Moreover, to the extent that there is a dominant interpretation of the culture, this will typically reflect the views and interests of those within the culture who wield most power. The views of those who have traditionally been denied power – such as women, minorities, and the poor – are commonly neglected.[69] These observations are pertinent because whether we treat an individual with respect by tolerating a culture in which she is enveloped will depend upon whether that culture is one that she identifies with and regards as truly her own. We clearly do not respect someone by refusing to criticize or challenge a culture that systematically neglects her interests and that she experiences as thoroughly oppressive. Furthermore, it will often be very difficult to establish whether a particular individual endorses the culture that surrounds her unless she has opportunities to shape, criticize, and leave that culture, opportunities that will not be available in the absence of various rights.[70]

Second, when we encounter individuals whose views differ from our own, it is not obvious that the most respectful course of action is always to remain silent.[71] Suppose that you express a moral view that I believe to be mistaken, a view that reflects your cultural background. In this situation, I can either share with you the grounds for my belief or keep those grounds to myself. If I take the former option, I thereby provide you with reasons that you may previously have overlooked and grant you the opportunity to evaluate those reasons. By contrast, if I take the latter option, I thereby withhold information that you may regard as valuable and that may have prompted you to revise your views. This withholding of information can be disrespectful for a number of reasons. To begin with, it might reflect a negative judgement of your character. For example, I might withhold the information because I think you lack the fortitude to handle challenges to your worldview or because I think you have insufficient intelligence to adequately process the information I possess. These are clearly disrespectful, infantilizing judgements.

In addition, regardless of my motive, withholding the information should be regarded as disrespectful because we all have a strong interest in holding

---

67 Nussbaum, *Women and Human Development*, p. 47, p. 49.
68 Ibid., p. 46.
69 Nussbaum, *Creating Capabilities*, pp. 106–107.
70 Caney, *Justice Beyond Borders*, pp. 88–89.
71 Simon Caney, "Cosmopolitanism and the Law of Peoples", *Journal of Political Philosophy*, vol. 10, no. 1, 2002, pp. 95–123, at pp. 107–108.

true or reasonable beliefs and in acting in accordance with the requirements of morality. If we discover that, for extended periods of our lives, we have acted in ways that we subsequently realize are morally wrong, this will be a cause for deep regret. By withholding considerations and arguments that I deem important for moral reasoning, I may thereby deny you a chance to abandon a path that, were you better informed, you would regard as ethically misguided (and that you may still come to repudiate later in life, albeit much later than you ideally would have liked).

In addition to having a strong interest in holding, and acting in accordance with, reasonable beliefs, we each have a strong interest in correctly identifying those things that are good for us and to which we are morally entitled. This is because understanding our entitlements can have important implications for our quality of life. Nussbaum notes that a number of the Indian women whom she interviewed as part of her research did not appreciate the value of various important goods and often did not view their own disadvantage as in any way unjust.[72] These women accepted wage discrimination at work; failed to recognize that they were severely malnourished; did not lament the absence of clean water; had no desire for the education that had been withheld from them; and regarded abuse as "a part of women's lot in life, just something women have to put up with".[73]

Should outsiders respect these women's judgements and refuse to criticize or challenge the social arrangements that have produced their disadvantage? Should we even decline to regard them as disadvantaged? This would be unwarranted, for it is not difficult to identify factors that can be expected to deform these women's preferences. As Nussbaum remarks, people's preferences are often "manipulated by tradition and intimidation".[74] Moreover, a lack of education, and of exposure to alternative views, means that the disadvantaged often lack the intellectual resources with which to properly evaluate their situation. (A dearth of encounters with competing viewpoints is especially likely in societies where the right to freedom of expression is not adequately respected.)

Relatedly, Jon Elster has explained that people often "adapt" their preferences, adjusting their desires and aspirations in accordance with what appears realistically attainable.[75] The phenomenon of adaptive preferences is captured by the fable of the fox and the grapes: realizing that they are out of his reach, the fox convinces himself that the grapes are sour and that he does not want them anyway. The general point is well made by Nussbaum:

> If someone who has no property rights under the law, who has had no formal education, who has no legal right of divorce, who

---

72 Nussbaum, *Women and Human Development*, pp. 109–110, pp. 112–113.
73 Ibid., p. 112.
74 Ibid., p. 115.
75 Jon Elster, *Sour Grapes: Studies in the Subversion of Rationality* (Cambridge: Cambridge University Press, 1983).

will very likely be beaten if she seeks employment outside the home, says that she endorses traditions of modesty, purity, and self-abnegation, it is not clear that we should consider this the last word on the matter.[76]

Importantly, when disadvantaged individuals are introduced to goods that they were previously denied and in which they previously showed little interest, they often quickly recognize the value of those goods. For example, Nussbaum tells us "that women who have become literate find literacy valuable and even delightful, [and] that they report satisfaction with their new condition".[77] In addition, Nussbaum notes that "in just a few weeks [deprived] women [who participate in self-help groups] learn to want employment rights, property rights, [and] clean water".[78]

In short, respect does not require us to refrain from engaging in criticism. When we encounter individuals who are dismissive of human rights (either their own or those of others), it can be appropriate – and even respectful – to challenge their views and to share with them our reasons for regarding their views as mistaken.

2.7 Rawls on toleration

The issue of toleration cannot be set aside just yet, for this ideal has played a prominent role in the influential work of John Rawls. Best known for his liberal-egalitarian theory of domestic justice, Rawls has also defended a much more minimalist account of justice for the international realm. This is not the place to undertake a full-scale examination of Rawls's view – and, for the reader's sake, I shall set aside much of Rawls's idiosyncratic terminology – but it will be worth our while to consider some of its key details.

Rawls presents a very short list of human rights and argues that, in order to be deserving of toleration, a state need not respect any of the many additional rights enumerated in the major human rights documents. The rights included on Rawls's list are

> the right to life (to the means of subsistence and security); to liberty (to freedom from slavery, serfdom, and forced occupation, and to a sufficient measure of liberty of conscience to ensure freedom of religion and thought); to property (personal property); and to formal equality as expressed by the rules of natural justice (that is, that similar cases be treated similarly).[79]

---

76 Nussbaum, *Women and Human Development*, pp. 42–43.
77 Ibid., p. 152.
78 Ibid., p. 161.
79 John Rawls, *The Law of Peoples* (Cambridge, MA: Harvard University Press, 1999), p. 65.

A number of important rights are conspicuous by their absence. Omitted from Rawls's list are the rights to democratic political participation, freedom of expression, freedom of association, and the right to education. Moreover, Rawls's interpretation of the right to freedom of religion is very limited: there may be an established religion, and the members of "other religions, though tolerated, may be denied the right to hold certain [political] positions".[80] Although Rawls acknowledges that a state which respects only this truncated list of rights "does not treat its own members reasonably or justly",[81] he nevertheless maintains that such a state can be worthy of toleration.

Toleration, on Rawls's account, is a demanding concept. To tolerate a particular set of states "means not only to refrain from exercising political sanctions – military, economic, or [even] diplomatic – to make [these states] change [their] ways" but also to recognize the states in question "as equal participating members in good standing" of the international community.[82] Moreover, when a state is worthy of toleration, liberal states must refrain from offering that state incentives to reform in a liberal direction.[83]

If states that fail to respect the vast majority of rights enumerated in the major human rights documents are nevertheless worthy of recognition "as equal participating members in good standing", it is natural to suppose that Rawls is right to insist that the list of "real" or "genuine" human rights is much shorter than commonly believed. Let us examine Rawls's view in more detail.

It is important to note that although Rawls thinks that a state which respects only his meagre list of human rights can be worthy of toleration, he maintains that it must also satisfy a number of additional conditions. Most importantly, although it need not be organized democratically, it must offer its members some opportunities for political participation. Rawls suggests that a non-democratic state can do this by implementing what he calls a "consultation hierarchy", whereby government officials are required to consult with appointed representatives of the various groups that comprise society.[84] Moreover, alert to the danger that some "members of society, such as women, who may have long been subjected to oppression and abuse", will not be adequately represented, Rawls recommends that a majority of the

---

80 Ibid., fn. 2.
81 Ibid., p. 83.
82 Ibid., p. 59.
83 Ibid., pp. 84–85.
84 Ibid., pp. 71–78.

representatives of "the (previously) oppressed be chosen from among those whose rights have been violated".[85]

This recommendation is less progressive than it might seem, as "oppression is here defined as the violation of human rights".[86] Since Rawls fails to recognize many of the human rights listed in major human rights documents, individuals who suffer violations of these rights, and who can plausibly be regarded as oppressed in virtue of those violations, will not be so regarded by Rawls. Nevertheless, it should be clear that the non-democratic states that Rawls deems worthy of toleration, which he calls "decent hierarchical societies", are considerably more benign than at least the vast majority of non-democratic states that we find in our world. Rawls does not provide any real-world examples of "decent" hierarchical societies, and it is not clear that he thinks any actually exist.[87]

However, it is worth considering whether "decent" hierarchical societies have a strong claim to be tolerated. According to Rawls, liberal states are committed to tolerance by reasons of consistency. At the domestic level, Rawls notes, liberal societies tolerate the existence of various illiberal groups and this is believed to be an important requirement of liberal values. For example, liberal societies permit authoritarian religious organizations, and refusing to allow the members of such groups to live in accordance with their own beliefs would be regarded as contrary to a liberal outlook. By parity of reasoning, Rawls maintains that, at the international level, liberal states should tolerate societies that organize themselves in a hierarchical manner and deny various liberal rights to their members (provided that they meet the minimal requirements of decency that Rawls specifies).[88]

What should we make of this argument? Although liberal thinkers do believe that the state should tolerate illiberal groups domestically, they do not believe that such groups should be tolerated in the particular way that Rawls argues "decent" hierarchical societies should be tolerated. Liberalism permits illiberal domestic groups to organize their lives in a hierarchical fashion and to champion illiberal principles, but liberalism does not allow such principles to be incorporated into society's political arrangements. In other words, liberals do not allow domestic political institutions to be (re)designed in a manner that accommodates illiberal values. Yet this is exactly what Rawls proposes internationally. According to Rawls, an adequately tolerant international society is one that jettisons key liberal rights that cannot be accepted by "decent" hierarchical societies.[89]

---

85 Ibid., p. 75.
86 John Tasioulas, "From Utopia to Kazanistan: John Rawls and the Law of Peoples", *Oxford Journal of Legal Studies*, vol. 22, no. 2, 2002, pp. 367–396, at p. 384.
87 Rawls, *Law of Peoples*, p. 75.
88 Ibid., 59–60.
89 Kok-Chor Tan, "Liberal Toleration in Rawls's Law of Peoples", *Ethics*, vol. 108, no. 2, 1998, pp. 276–295, at pp. 282–283; Nussbaum, *Frontiers of Justice*, pp. 251–252.

There is another important difference between liberal toleration of illiberal groups domestically and the kind of toleration that Rawls advocates internationally. In the domestic case, members of illiberal groups have viable exit options. For example, they can choose to leave their church and join a different one or to abandon religion altogether. By contrast, exiting an illiberal *society* is likely to be much more difficult.[90] Rawls insists that, in order to count as "decent" and thus be worthy of toleration, a society must allow (and even assist) its members to emigrate.[91] But the freedom to emigrate is worthless without the freedom to immigrate, and there is no guarantee that those looking to leave hierarchical societies will find other states that are willing to take them in. (Remember that Rawls's truncated list of human rights does not feature a right to education, so the members of hierarchical societies may well lack the skills that democratic states often look for when deciding whom to admit.)

If there are good reasons why liberals should favour the kind of international society that Rawls envisions, it should now be clear that these cannot be reasons of consistency: liberals can tolerate illiberal groups domestically while also reasonably refusing to tolerate "decent" hierarchical societies. Before moving on, one final point should be made, a point which relates to the fact that rights should be seen as interconnected. Rawls's approach assumes that rights can be mixed-and-matched, that a society can adequately protect one set of rights while disregarding another. But there is evidence to suggest that there are limits to how far this holds true. Importantly, Sen's research demonstrates that rights to democratic participation play an important role in preventing economic and social disasters, such as famines, which pose a serious threat to people's most basic entitlements.[92] As Sen notes:

> Political and civil rights give people the opportunity to draw attention forcefully to general needs and to demand appropriate public action. The response of a government to acute suffering often depends on the pressure that is put on it, and this is where the exercise of political rights (voting, criticizing, protesting, and so on) can make a real difference.[93]

If political rights are necessary to protect the more basic rights that Rawls affirms, then he cannot justify excluding the former from his list.[94] In fact, Rawls essentially concedes this point. In a footnote, he acknowledges that

---

90 Nussbaum, *Frontiers of Justice*, pp. 253–254.
91 Rawls, *Law of Peoples*, p. 74.
92 Sen, *Human Rights and Asian Values*, pp. 12–13.
93 Ibid., p. 12.
94 Andrew Kuper, "Rawlsian Global Justice: Beyond The Law of Peoples to a Cosmopolitan Law of Persons", *Political Theory*, vol. 28, no. 5, 2000, pp. 640–674, at pp. 663–664.

"some writers maintain that full democratic and liberal rights are necessary to prevent violations of human rights. This is stated as an empirical fact supported by historical experience. I do not argue against this contention, and indeed it may be true".[95]

2.8 Diversity

I want to conclude this chapter with a comment on diversity. If the human rights movement is successful, various cultural practices that fail to adequately respect human rights will cease to exist. Some will be outlawed while others will wither and die as they are abandoned by the individuals whose interests they neglect. For this reason, there may be less cultural diversity in the world than exists at present. In order to ascertain whether this should be a cause for regret, we should consider what reasons we have to value diversity.

The value of diversity is most apparent when we know that we have the freedom to choose among the variety of options constitutive of that diversity. For example, a diverse restaurant menu is desirable because it is more likely to provide options that I feel like eating on any given occasion. But the diversity provided by cultural practices that violate human rights is not experienced in this way. A world with both liberal and authoritarian communities is in one sense more diverse than a world containing only liberal communities: it is more diverse when viewed from the perspective of the universe. But it is not more diverse when viewed from the perspective of disadvantaged people forced to live their lives subject to the arbitrary power of others. The existence of authoritarian communities does not provide these people with additional life options to choose from, but rather coercively imposes one particular mode of living.

It might be pointed out that a world with both liberal and authoritarian communities provides those born in *liberal* communities with additional options, insofar as they may choose to move from the former to the latter, but, for obvious reasons, very few people choose to avail themselves of this opportunity. Perhaps it will also be said that some people living in liberal communities take some gratification from the knowledge that there are also illiberal communities in the world, communities that differ in remarkable ways from their own. But to the degree that those communities frustrate the ability of their members to live fully human lives, any preference on the part of outsiders for their continued existence should be regarded as perverse and as generating no claim to satisfaction.

The final point to make is that while human rights rule out some social practices, they play an invaluable role in protecting many others.[96] Human

---

95 Rawls, *Law of Peoples*, p. 75, fn. 16; cf. p. 79.
96 Caney, *Justice Beyond Borders*, p. 91.

rights to freedom of thought, expression, association, and religion enable people to form and pursue their own conception of the good life, provided that, in doing so, they do not violate the rights of others. It is precisely this crucial freedom that is denied by the kinds of authoritarian communities that the human rights movement rightly condemns.

3 POVERTY

Since the end of the Cold War, it has become less common to speak of a Third World. When the Berlin Wall fell, so did the Second World with which we had previously contrasted the Third and the First. In the new millennium, we often speak instead of a single "global village".[1] This new terminology has its virtues: it reflects the economic, cultural, and political integration that constitutes contemporary globalization. But it also has a downside. It obscures a reality that the older nomenclature made more vivid, a reality in which the least advantaged people on the planet live lives far removed from those enjoyed by the richest. In the poorest parts of our "global village", 766 million people survive each day on less than what could be purchased in the US for $1.90.[2] Almost 6 million children die before reaching the age of five, and nearly half of these children lose their lives because they do not have enough food.[3] Between 2014 and 2016, 795 million people experienced chronic hunger.[4] Roughly 880 million people live in slums and almost 700 million of these lack adequate sanitation.[5] Approximately 156 million young people in poor countries are classed as "working poor". This means that they are in paid employment but also live in extreme poverty (on less than $1.90 a day) or in moderate poverty (on no more than $3.10 a day).[6]

Some victims of extreme poverty die because they cannot get enough to eat, whereas others are killed by diseases which, if they exist at all, are rarely fatal in rich parts of the world – diseases such as malaria, measles, and

---

1   This term was coined in Marshall McLuhan, *The Gutenberg Galaxy: The Making of Typographic Man* (London: Routledge and Kegan Paul, 1962).
2   *The Human Development Report 2016: Human Development for Everyone* (New York: United Nations Development Programme: 2016), p. 29.
3   Ibid, p. 30; Cf. Lucia Hug, David Sharrow, and Danzhen You, *Levels and Trends in Child Mortality (2017)* (New York: United Nations Children's Fund, 2017), p. 3.
4   *Human Development Report*, p. 30
5   Ibid., p. 32.
6   Ibid., p. 34.

diarrhoea.[7] Those who survive poverty often have their lives blighted by debilitating yet easily treatable conditions such as cataracts or obstetric fistulas. A fistula is an injury incurred during childbirth whereby the tissue between the mother's vagina and bladder or rectum is broken. The condition is caused by the pressure the foetus's head exerts against the mother's pelvic bone during prolonged, obstructed labour. In poor countries, adequate medical assistance is often unavailable, and the sustained pressure of the foetus's head creates a hole, through which urine or faeces leak. Those with fistulas are often shunned by their husbands and communities. According to the Worldwide Fistula Fund, about two million women and girls are afflicted with this "disease of poverty".[8]

There are important gender differences in the way that poverty is distributed. In the 25- to 34-year-old age group, for every 100 men living in poor households, there are 120 women.[9] In 16 countries in sub-Saharan Africa, "[f]emale poverty rates are between 5 and 20 percentage points higher than male poverty rates".[10] Poverty exposes women to increased risks of violence and sexual exploitation and undermines their ability to leave abusive relationships.[11]

If extreme poverty were administered as a punishment for the worst crimes, our penal system would be condemned as barbaric and inhumane. In reality, the "crime" that extreme poverty punishes is the act of being born in the wrong place at the wrong time. Yet the persistence of extreme poverty does not seem to unduly trouble the typical citizen of the First World. Commitments to the global poor rarely feature among the campaign pledges of politicians eager to win office in North America or Western Europe, and the dominant view held by the relatively affluent is that contributing to poverty relief – by, say, donating to Oxfam or UNICEF – is morally optional. The purpose of this chapter is to consider whether this dominant view is defensible or whether extreme poverty is in fact a problem that we are morally obligated to address.

3.1 Peter Singer and the drowning child

Contemporary ethical reflection on global poverty often centres on the work of the Princeton philosopher Peter Singer and his famous thought experiment about a drowning child. Suppose that your journey to work each day

---

7 Peter Singer, *The Life You Can Save: Acting Now to End World Poverty* (London: Picador, 2009), pp. 4–5.
8 http://worldwidefistulafund.org/fistula-faqs.aspx
9 Ana Maria Munoz Boudet (et al.), *Gender Differences in Poverty and Household Composition Through the Life-Cycle: A Global Perspective* (Washington, DC: World Bank Group, 2018), p. 12.
10 Ibid.
11 For a discussion of the gendered character of global injustice, see Heather Widdows, *Global Ethics: An Introduction* (Durham: Acumen, 2011), Ch. 11.

takes you past a shallow pond. One morning, you notice that a very young child has fallen into the pond and is struggling to remain above the surface. If you wade in to help the child, you will muddy your nice clothes and be late for work. But there is no one else around, and it is clear that if you do not assist the child, she will drown.[12] It seems obvious enough that what you ought to do is wade in and rescue the child. It also seems obvious that you are *morally required* to do this. If, instead of providing assistance, you ignore the child and walk on, you will not simply decline an opportunity to do something good; you will have acted monstrously. It is hard to imagine anyone dissenting from this view.

What grounds our conviction that we are morally required to rescue the drowning child? Two considerations seem relevant: first, the death of a child is a very bad thing; second, we can prevent the child's death at little cost to ourselves. If these are the two considerations that we deem relevant when we conclude that we ought to rescue the child, we seem to be committed to something like the following principle: if it is within our power to prevent something very bad from happening and we can do so at little cost to ourselves, we ought, morally, to do so. This principle, combined with the two considerations I just mentioned, appears to be the most straightforward way of accounting for our conviction that we ought to wade into the pond and assist the child.

But this principle seems to have much more wide-ranging implications. One such implication appears to be that, if you are an adequately well-off individual living in an affluent society, you are morally required to assist the global poor. After all, extreme poverty is a very bad thing, and research suggests that you can alleviate the plight of the world's poorest at little cost to yourself: $50 could restore the sight of an impoverished individual blinded by cataracts[13]; $250 could provide rehydration therapy to a child who otherwise would die from diarrhoea[14]; a donation of between $100 and $450 could cover the cost of repairing an obstetric fistula[15]; and $820 could save a life by funding the provision of anti-malarial bed nets. Small donations can save and transform the lives of impoverished people without having much of an effect on the bank balance of the donor.

At this point, it is worth pausing to consider the nature of the argument that I have just sketched. I began by identifying a judgement that I imagine all readers of this book will confidently endorse, namely, that we should rescue the drowning child. Next, I formulated a general moral principle that can be used to explain our endorsement of this judgement. This principle

---

12 Singer, *The Life You Can Save*, pp. 3–5.
13 Ibid., p. 101.
14 Ibid., pp. 88–89.
15 Ibid., pp. 102–103.

holds that if it is within our power to prevent something very bad from happening and we can do so at little cost to ourselves, we ought, morally, to do so. Having identified this principle by reflecting on a situation in which it has an uncontroversial application (the drowning child scenario), I moved to a context in which we have much less confidence in our ethical judgements (global poverty). Applied to this new context and combined with certain empirical assumptions about the ease with which we can assist the global poor, the principle yields the conclusion that we are morally required to contribute to the alleviation of global poverty. If we are unhappy with this conclusion, we might revise the principle that produced it, but if we revise that principle we risk sweeping away the moral basis of the conviction with which we began (and in which we had so much confidence), namely, that we ought to rescue the drowning child. If we wish to hold on to that conviction – which, presumably, we do – we may have to accept that we are also morally required to assist the world's poor. The argument I have sketched employs a familiar philosophical strategy, one that seeks to bring our moral judgements and moral principles into what John Rawls called "reflective equilibrium".[16]

As I have said, the drowning child example was originally formulated by Peter Singer, and it is what most people remember of his work.[17] But the thought experiment actually plays a surprisingly marginal role in his overall argument. As we saw, the drowning child case can be used to support the principle that we ought to prevent very bad things from happening when we can do so at little cost to ourselves. But Singer actually favours a different principle, and it is that principle, rather than the drowning child example, which is the fulcrum around which his argument turns. According to Singer's preferred principle, "if it is in our power to prevent something bad from happening, *without thereby sacrificing anything of comparable moral importance*, we ought, morally, to do it".[18]

After introducing this principle, Singer notes that one of its implications is that we ought to rescue the drowning child. He then points out that the principle also has the more controversial implication that we are all required to make drastic sacrifices in order to combat world poverty. We should donate large sums of money to charity, and we should keep giving until we reach the point at which, by giving more, we would be imposing upon ourselves burdens comparable in severity to those we are trying to alleviate. Given that the burdens associated with extreme poverty are very large, this implies that we should be giving away almost all of our wealth. Singer writes:

---

16 John Rawls, *A Theory of Justice*, Revised Edition (Cambridge, MA: Harvard University Press, 1999), pp. 18–19, 42–45.

17 The example originally appeared in Singer's classic article "Famine, Affluence, and Morality", *Philosophy and Public Affairs*, vol. 1, no. 3, 1972, pp. 229–243.

18 Ibid., p. 231 (emphasis added).

> Suppose you have just sent $200 to an agency that can, for that amount, save the life of a child in a developing country who would otherwise have died. You've done something really good, and all it has cost you is the price of some new clothes you didn't really need anyway. Congratulations! But don't celebrate your good deed by opening a bottle of champagne, or even going to a movie. The cost of that bottle or movie, added to what you could save by cutting down on a few other extravagances, would save the life of another child. After you forgo those items, and give another $200, though, is everything else you are spending on as important, or nearly as important, as the life of a child? Not likely! So you must keep cutting back on unnecessary spending, and donating what you save, until you have reduced yourself to the point where if you give any more, you will be sacrificing something nearly as important as a child's life ...[19]

Now, if Singer's claim were that our duty to rescue the drowning child could be explained *only* by the principle he advocates, then he would have provided us with a good reason to accept that principle and also the radical conclusions it entails. But this is not what Singer says, and such a claim is clearly implausible, for our duty to rescue the drowning child can also be explained by far less demanding principles that lack the extreme implications of Singer's. (As we have already seen, it can be explained by the principle that we ought to prevent very bad things from happening when we can do so at little cost to ourselves.)

In his later work, Singer appeals to a different example, one which he borrows from the philosopher Peter Unger and which takes us closer to the principle he favours. The example runs as follows:

> Bob is close to retirement. He has invested most of his savings in a very rare and valuable old car, a Bugatti, which he has not been able to insure. The Bugatti is his pride and joy. Not only does Bob get pleasure from driving and caring for his car, he also knows that its rising market value means that he will be able to sell it and live comfortably after retirement. One day when Bob is out for a drive, he parks the Bugatti near the end of a railway siding and goes for a walk up the track. As he does so, he sees that a runaway train, with no one aboard, is rolling down the railway track. Looking farther down the track, he sees the small figure of a child who appears to be absorbed in playing on the tracks. Oblivious to the runaway train, the child is in great danger. Bob can't stop the train, and the child is too far away to hear his warning shout, but

---

19 Singer, *The Life You Can Save*, p. 18.

> Bob can throw a switch that will divert the train down the siding where his Bugatti is parked. If he does so, nobody will be killed, but the train will crash through the decaying barrier at the end of the siding and destroy his Bugatti. Thinking of his joy in owning the car and the financial security it represents, Bob decides not to throw the switch.[20]

In this case, the cost of saving the child's life is much greater than it was in the pond example. If he were to save the child, Bob would not merely muddy his clothes and be late for work; rather, he would lose a cherished possession and surrender his financial security. Nevertheless, even with full information about Bob's motivations and everything he stood to lose from throwing the switch and diverting the train, it is tempting to condemn Bob's inaction. Many people will feel that Bob was morally required to throw the switch even though he could not do so without incurring a sizeable personal cost. And that judgement takes us beyond the fairly minimal principle we began with, according to which we ought to prevent very bad things from happening when we can do so at little cost to ourselves. Bob *cannot* prevent something very bad from happening at little cost to himself; he can save the child's life only by making a very *large* sacrifice. If we want to say that Bob ought to make that sacrifice, then we will need a principle that is closer to the more demanding alternative favoured by Singer; that is, we will need a principle that requires us to prevent very bad things from happening even when doing so carries a significant cost. And if we embrace such a principle, our obligations to the world's poor will become considerably more demanding; an implication of such a principle is that we are required to donate large sums of money to aid organizations even when doing so significantly diminishes our own financial wellbeing.

3.2 Alternatives to Singer's view

It is important to be clear about exactly what Singer is and is not saying. He is not claiming that poverty can be eradicated only if each affluent individual makes enormous sacrifices. On the contrary, he suggests that if each person "did their bit", the burden that would have to be borne by each individual would be relatively small. Nor is Singer claiming that the best way to eradicate poverty involves some people doing a lot while others do nothing or very little. Rather, Singer's claim is that since many people are *not* doing their bit, others are required to "pick up the slack".[21]

Notice that we can ask two different questions about our duties to the world's poor. We can ask what would be required of us in a world where

---

20 Ibid., pp. 13–14; Peter Unger *Living High and Letting Die* (New York: Oxford University Press, 1996).
21 Singer, *The Life You Can Save*, p. 39.

everyone complies with the requirements of an optimal (just and efficient) scheme of poverty eradication. And we can ask what would be required of us in a world where some people refuse to comply with the requirements of such a scheme. Singer is offering an answer to the second question. His claim is that when some people fail to discharge their duties to the world's poor, those duties are transferred to the rest of us; we all acquire extra "remedial" duties that we would not have in a world where everyone does their bit. These remedial duties may be very demanding, but that is not a reason to dismiss them or to deny their status as genuine duties. Sometimes, morality *is* very demanding; that fact is illustrated by our intuitive response to the story about Bob and his Bugatti.

However, there is a further complication that has to be addressed. It is true that morality can sometimes be very demanding, and we cannot deny the authenticity of its imperatives – we cannot deny that they *really are* moral imperatives – simply on the grounds that complying with them requires considerable sacrifice. But there is a notable difference between Bob's relationship to the child on the railway track and our own relationship to the global poor, a difference which is not captured by reflecting on the demandingness of providing assistance. The difference is that Bob is the only person in a position to save the child whereas you and I are not the only people in a position to assist the world's poor. On the contrary, there are countless affluent people who could all contribute to alleviating severe poverty, and if they all helped out, our own obligations would be quite manageable.

Why is this difference relevant? Suppose we agree that Bob has a duty to sacrifice his Bugatti in order to save the child. There is nothing in the story to suggest that Bob's duty assumes this very demanding character only because someone else has failed to make their contribution to the child's rescue. By contrast, if Singer is right that we have very demanding duties to assist the world's poor, we have those duties only by virtue of the fact that other people have failed to do their bit. When we say that Bob ought to throw the switch and divert the train, we are not suggesting that people have a duty to pick up the large amount of slack created by third parties failing to play their part. But that is exactly what Singer suggests when he argues that we must make endless sacrifices for the global poor. Singer's argument rests on a principle that requires us to do more when others do less, and some philosophers have deemed that to be unacceptable.

Liam Murphy has argued that, in order to be plausible, a moral principle requiring us to promote good outcomes should not impose greater demands on us as compliance with that principle shrinks; the requirements such a principle places on us when we are the only ones complying with it should be no more arduous than they are when compliance is widespread. Murphy suggests that Singer's principle treats conscientious people *unfairly* by expecting them to perform the tasks that less diligent individuals have allowed to pile up. He writes: "We should do our fair share, which can amount to a great sacrifice in certain circumstances; what we cannot be required to do is other people's shares as well as our own".[22] An implication of Murphy's argument is that what we owe the world's poor is what we would owe them under an optimal scheme of poverty eradication that distributed responsibilities equitably among the affluent. If we discharge the duties that we would be allocated by such a scheme, then we have done enough. The fact that such a scheme is not actually in place, and other people are not actually doing what it would require of them, does not affect the content of our obligations.

Before proceeding, we should note that although Murphy's view is less demanding than Singer's, it is still more demanding than conventional morality. Two aspects of Murphy's view challenge the status quo. First, Murphy believes that we are *morally required* to assist the poor – not just that it is morally good to assist them. Second, however we define a "fair share", it is quite apparent that the majority of people living in affluent countries are not doing enough. But how plausible is Murphy's view? One objection that is often levelled at Murphy's account is that it generates unpalatable conclusions.

Consider the following variation on the pond case, which was suggested by Elizabeth Ashford.[23] Imagine that there are ten children drowning in the pond and that there are five adults who could provide assistance. It seems natural to suppose that each adult should rescue two children; this would be the fairest way to distribute responsibility. But suppose that all but one of the five adults refuse to help. The one conscientious adult who is willing to provide assistance hauls two children out of the pond, and then notices that the other four adults have walked off. An implication of Murphy's view is that the conscientious adult has no duty to rescue the remaining eight children, even if she can do so at little cost to herself. She has done her fair share and that is all that can be demanded of her. But can that be right? Most of us will surely baulk at such a conclusion.

One possible response to this objection runs as follows. It is true that Murphy's account has some unwelcome implications, but we should not infer from that fact that Murphy's account must be rejected. Rather, we should ask whose account has more overall plausibility, Murphy's or Singer's. After all, Singer's view *also* has unwelcome implications: it commits us to making endless sacrifices for the sake of the global poor. So, before we write off Murphy's account, we should ask how it fares in comparison with Singer's. As Murphy writes: "We must keep in mind the problems facing all other possible principles ... and make a judgment of overall relative plausibility".[24]

Now, if we make the relevant comparison, it is not obvious that Murphy's account will come out on top. After all, the extreme demands identified by

---

22 Liam B. Murphy, "The Demands of Beneficence", *Philosophy & Public Affairs*, vol. 22, no. 4, 1993, pp. 267–292, at p. 278.

23 Elizabeth Ashford, "The Demandingness of Scanlon's Contractualism", *Ethics*, vol. 113, no. 2, 2003, pp. 273–302, at p. 286.

24 Murphy, "Demands of Beneficence", p. 290, fn. 41.

Singer's account may simply reflect the extremity of our situation. While we do not often think of them as such, the circumstances in which we live are really quite extraordinary. As Singer observes:

> we are living in the midst of an emergency in which [thousands of] children die from avoidable causes every day... And millions of women are living with repairable fistulas, and millions of people are blind who could see again. We can do something about these things.[25]

What makes our circumstances extraordinary is not the degree and severity of suffering but the fact that the suffering is remediable and that so few people who are able to help actually do anything. Singer's account, then, may provide an extreme morality for an extreme age.[26]

However, we should bear in mind that we do not necessarily have to choose between Singer's account and Murphy's. Perhaps there is an alternative that is preferable to both. I suggested that Murphy's account is endangered by its refusal to countenance a duty to exceed one's fair share, even when one can do so at little cost to oneself. But this shortcoming does not compel us to retreat from Murphy's view to Singer's; rather, it suggests a position that falls somewhere between the two. The view I have in mind departs from Murphy's inasmuch as it accepts that we can be required to do more than our fair share when we can do so at little cost to ourselves, but it falls short of Singer's view in the following sense: it claims that we cannot be expected to keep picking up the slack when doing so will be excessively burdensome. The thought underlying this view is articulated by Kwame Anthony Appiah when he writes: "If so many people in the world are not doing their share – and they clearly are not – it seems to me I cannot be required to derail my life to take up the slack".[27] Doing our fair share will require us to do more than many affluent individuals are currently doing, and we can be required to exceed our fair share when doing so will not involve unduly large burdens. But we may deny that the selfishness of others can impose upon us a duty to make very large sacrifices.

On this view, then, the fairness-based considerations that Murphy invokes have some weight, but they are not decisive. The fact that performing a particular act would involve doing more than your fair share is not sufficient to free you from an obligation to perform that act. Similarly, the fact that performing a particular act is very demanding is not sufficient to

---

25 Singer, *The Life You Can Save*, p. 149.
26 Cf. Ashford, "Demandingness of Scanlon's Contractualism", pp. 292–293; and Elizabeth Ashford, "Obligations of Justice and Beneficence to Aid the Severely Poor", in Patricia Illingworth, Thomas Pogge, and Leif Wenar (eds.), *Giving Well: The Ethics of Philanthropy* (New York: Oxford University Press, 2011), p. 39.
27 Kwame Anthony Appiah, *Cosmopolitanism* (New York: Norton, 2006), pp. 164–165.

free you from an obligation to perform that act. But if performing a particular act is very demanding *and* that act is not part of your fair share, it is plausible to think that you lack an obligation to perform. Even Murphy acknowledges that the view I have just described appears to be a "particularly strong" alternative to his own.[28]

These considerations might tempt us to say that concerns about fairness are sometimes outweighed by the needs of others. When the costs of unfairness are small and the needs of others are great, fairness must be set aside. The burdens associated with tackling severe poverty may be distributed unfairly, but fairness is not all that important. However, before we decide to frame the argument in these terms, we should bear in mind that it is not just the case for *limiting* our duties to the global poor that appeals to considerations of unfairness. When we propose the existence of demanding duties to assist the global poor, considerations of unfairness will often be at the forefront of our minds. After all, the victims of severe poverty are not just very badly off, but very badly off through no fault of their own. And that is immensely unfair. (Remember that 6 million children die before reaching their fifth birthday. How could these children possibly be responsible for their plight?) Moreover, affluent individuals have benefitted enormously from the good fortune of being born into a rich part of the world. And that, too, is unfair. Thus, when we assist the world's poor, we are acting to reduce unfairness.[29] And when we pick up the slack created by affluent individuals who refuse to do their bit, we are contributing more than our fair share to a project that is motivated (in part) by a commitment to fairness.

3.3 Symptoms and institutions

Despite their differences, all of the accounts I have discussed so far converge on the conclusion that relatively affluent members of the "global village" should be donating substantial sums of money to poverty-relief agencies. But it is sometimes said that these accounts have a common shortcoming: they all focus on symptoms rather than on the underlying causes of the problem that we are trying to address; they recommend giving money to organizations that aim to mitigate the worst effects of poverty rather than challenging the practices and institutions that are responsible for creating poverty in the first place. In a critical discussion of Singer's work, Andrew Kuper writes: "Children starve, suffer, and die because of political and economic arrangements ... [U]nless attention is paid to transforming these deep institutional

---

28 Murphy, "Demands of Beneficence", p. 287, fn. 37.
29 Ashford, "Demandingness of Scanlon's Contractualism", p. 291. Richard J. Arneson, "Moral Limits on the Demands of Beneficence?", in Deen K. Chatterjee (ed.), *The Ethics of Assistance: Morality and the Distant Needy* (Cambridge: Cambridge University Press, 2004), p. 38.

factors, aid agencies will have only limited victories in a losing battle against the sources of poverty".[30]

I will turn to consider some possible causes of poverty in a moment, but before I do, it is worth considering whether Kuper's critique hits the mark. It is surely true that a sustainable, long-term solution to severe poverty requires the transformation of political and economic structures and not just a series of donations from conscientious individuals. But in the absence of such a transformation – and without a clear understanding of how to bring it about – what is required of us? Surely, we should be acting to reduce the suffering that occurs under existing institutional arrangements. If a doctor lacks the means to cure her patient's illness, she does the next best thing: she alleviates his symptoms. And if she did not, we would conclude that she had neglected her duties. Singer makes a similar point by appealing to the efforts of the German industrialist Oskar Schindler, who was portrayed by Liam Neeson in the Steven Spielberg film *Schindler's List*. Singer writes:

> When we can't make deep structural changes, it is still better to help some people than to help none. When Oskar Schindler protected Jews who would otherwise have been murdered, he had no impact on the structure of the Nazi genocide, but he did what he could, and he was right to do so. One can only wish that more Germans had done the same.[31]

Global justice undoubtedly requires institutional reform, but until such reform is achieved, it is hard to deny that we have duties to counter the worst effects of extant unjust structures if and when we can.

3.4 Is poverty caused by local or global factors?

So far, I have spoken exclusively about our duties to *assist* victims of severe poverty. I have written as though the most salient aspect of our relationship to the world's poor is the fact that we are in a position to help them. Indeed, I have assumed that our relationship to the poor is similar to our relationship to the drowning child and the other imperilled children in the various thought experiments described above. If severe poverty persisted independently of our conduct – in the same way that the drowning child sinks beneath the surface independently of our conduct – this would be an appropriate assumption. But if, instead, the persistence of severe poverty is attributable to our actions, then our relationship to the world's poor and our

---

30 Andrew Kuper, "Facts, Theories, and Hard Choices: Reply to Peter Singer", *Ethics and International Affairs*, vol. 16, no. 1, 2002, pp. 125–126, at p. 125.
31 Peter Singer, "Achieving the Best Outcome: Final Rejoinder", *Ethics and International Affairs*, vol. 16, no. 1, 2002, pp. 127–128, at p. 128.

relationship to the drowning child are very different. And if severe poverty persists not just because we fail to provide assistance but because we *actively sustain it*, then our relationship to the world's poor is more like our relationship to a drowning child whom we have *pushed in* to a pond.

Now, most citizens of affluent countries believe that severe poverty exists independently of their actions. They think that poverty has its roots in the institutions and practices of the poor countries themselves. This view is expressed by John Rawls, who suggests that when a country fails to develop,

> the problem is commonly the nature of the public political culture and the religious and philosophical traditions that underlie its institutions. The great social evils in poorer societies are likely to be oppressive government and corrupt elites.[32]

For Rawls, severe poverty has as its source factors that are native to the countries it afflicts. The view that severe poverty has domestic or local causes is certainly a common one, but can it withstand critical scrutiny?

At the beginning of this chapter, I noted that, since the end of the Cold War, it has become less common to think of poor countries as comprising a distinct "Third World" and increasingly common to speak of a single "global village". I said that one virtue of this new terminology is that it reflects the economic interdependencies of contemporary globalization. Today, countries exist not in isolation but as constituent elements of a global economy governed by a complex system of rules. When Rawls asserts that poverty is caused entirely by factors native to the countries it affects, he thereby denies that the rules of the global economy are implicated in its persistence. But is this denial plausible?

Some familiar aspects of the international economic order raise some doubts. It is well known that the international trade regime – which is governed by the World Trade Organization (WTO) – permits certain practices that hurt the interests of the poor. When it comes to selling goods on the world market, certain products are especially important to poor countries. These countries have an abundance of low-paid manual workers and this means that they have a competitive edge (or comparative advantage) in the production of labour-intensive goods. But, in order to protect their own interests, rich countries have imposed inordinately high tariffs on labour-intensive imports. This raises the price of the goods that poor countries are trying to sell and makes those countries less competitive. Douglas Irwin, an economist, writes:

> In the case of manufactured goods, developed countries have low tariffs on average but much higher tariffs on labor-intensive manufactures, particularly textiles and apparel. These are

---

32 John Rawls, "The Law of Peoples", in Stephen Shute and Susan Hurley (eds.), *On Human Rights* (New York: Basic Books, 1993), p. 77.

precisely the goods in which developing countries have a comparative advantage... In the United States, for example, the exports of Mongolia, Bangladesh, and Cambodia, among the poorest countries in the world, faced an average tariff of about 15 percent. Meanwhile, the exports of Norway, France, and Singapore faced an average tariff of 1 percent.[33]

Rich countries also pay lavish subsidies to their farmers. This enables rich-country farmers to "dump" their products – that is, sell them below the cost of production – on world markets and outcompete their poorer rivals. Martin Wolf, another economist, writes:

perhaps the greatest of all the scandals remains the treatment of agriculture. In this area, one of comparative advantage for many developing countries, they have hardly managed to raise their share of world exports.... What stops the developing countries is the staggering scale of rich-country subsidies... Some argue that such dumping can be beneficial to developing countries that are net food importers. With very few exceptions, this is not so. In most developing countries, farmers are not just the majority of the population, but the overwhelming majority of the poor. Thus the dumped products benefit an urban minority at the expense of the rural majority... [I]t is virtually certain that developing countries would gain hugely from the elimination of current farm policies in the high-income countries. The World Bank has estimated the annual welfare losses to developing countries at $20 billion a year...[34]

So, rich countries maintain practices that serve their own ends while disadvantaging the world's poor, and the rules of the global economy permit them to do so. This is hardly surprising given that it is the rich countries that write those rules. The trade negotiators of wealthy nations have used their superior bargaining power to design a trade regime that favours the affluent citizens they represent while undermining the interests of the poor.

Still, although global institutions may have some adverse effects on the economic prospects of poor countries, it might be said that those effects are insignificant when compared with those generated by local factors. We all know that many poor countries are blighted by civil wars and ruled by corrupt and authoritarian governments, and it seems reasonable to hold that

---

33 Douglas A. Irwin, *Free Trade Under Fire*, Third Edition (Princeton, NJ: Princeton University Press, 2009), p. 203.
34 Martin Wolff, *Why Globalization Works* (New Haven, CT: Yale University Press, 2005), pp. 215–216.

until these problems are remedied, severe poverty will inevitably persist. Indeed, it might seem "far-fetched, even preposterous, to blame the global economic order for the persistence of severe poverty in countries that are ruled by obvious thugs and crooks".[35]

Now, it is certainly true that corruption, authoritarianism, and civil wars are endemic throughout many poor regions and that these maladies play a significant role in sustaining severe poverty. But an important possibility that is often overlooked is that these local dysfunctionalities may themselves be stimulated by global institutions. This is a central thesis of the Yale philosopher Thomas Pogge. Why do poor countries often have corrupt and authoritarian governments? Why are they frequently marred by civil conflicts and coup attempts? Pogge argues that these problems are produced, at least in part, by key aspects of the global economic order that were put in place, and are maintained to this day, by the world's richest countries.[36]

In order to understand this argument, we need first to consider a phenomenon known as the "resource curse". Economists have observed that countries endowed with an abundance of natural resources such as oil, gas, and minerals are often very poor. Given that we are inclined to think of natural resources as a key to prosperity, this is somewhat puzzling. It would not be especially surprising to learn that an abundance of natural resources is not *sufficient* for a country to prosper, but what *is* surprising is the discovery that resource wealth actually seems to be implicated in the persistence of severe poverty.

Resource wealth is thought to contribute to the problems that undermine the economic prospects of developing countries in a number of different ways. First, resource wealth creates incentives for insurrection. Ruthless individuals know that if they can topple their government and seize power, they will gain access to the country's resources and to the riches they can acquire from selling them. Eager to appease potential insurrectionists, vulnerable governments often direct state funds toward military officers who could easily stage a coup if displeased with the status quo. Second, natural resources constitute a source of funds for insurgents waging insurrectionary wars and thus sustain such conflicts beyond the point at which they could otherwise have ceased. Third, authoritarian rulers can use the revenues they derive from resource sales to pay for weapons and soldiers and thereby reinforce their power. As they are not dependent on popular support, these rulers have little incentive to improve the livelihoods of their people.[37]

You might be wondering what all this has to do with the global economy. Am I not describing problems created entirely by nature and by

---

35 Thomas Pogge, "'Assisting' the Global Poor", in Deen K. Chatterjee (ed.), *The Ethics of Assistance: Morality and the Distant Needy* (Cambridge: Cambridge University Press, 2004), p. 268.

36 Thomas Pogge, *World Poverty and Human Rights*, Second Edition (Cambridge: Polity Press, 2008).

37 Ibid., pp. 119–120; Leif Wenar, "Property Rights and the Resource Curse", *Philosophy & Public Affairs*, vol. 36, no. 1, pp. 2–32, 2008, at pp. 3–4.

residents of the Third World? To see why that is an overly simplistic view, ask yourself this: who buys the resources that authoritarian regimes and insurgents are selling? Who provides the revenue that these actors need to sustain themselves? Typically, the resources are bought by the rich countries' corporations, which then pass their acquisitions on to affluent consumers. It is these consumers who are the ultimate source of demand. What's more, these sales do not take place on the black market; on the contrary, they are entirely above board. More specifically, they are permitted by the international trade regime's customary rule for establishing who has the right to sell a country's resources, a rule which Pogge calls the "resource privilege".[38] According to this rule,

> all that is necessary for a group to acquire the legal right to sell off a territory's resources is the power to inflict violence on the territory's people. Whoever can maintain coercive control over a country's population (or in the case of civil warriors, over part of a population) is recognized internationally as legally authorized to sell off that country's resources.[39]

The resource privilege is a key aspect of the global economic order that the rich countries have designed, and it is the resource privilege that makes resource wealth a curse for so many of the world's poorest people. As Leif Wenar writes:

> The resource curse is not a curse that falls on poor countries because they have abundant resources. Natural resources are by definition valuable. The "curse" results from a defect in the rules that allocate control over these resources. The fault is not in nature, but in human institutions, here specifically markets... The blessing of resources turns into a curse when tyrants and insurgents are allowed to sell off a country's resources while crushing popular resistance, and to use the proceeds in ways that make the people worse off.[40]

Observers of international relations know that the rich countries sometimes suppress democracy directly by orchestrating the overthrow of democratically elected leaders such as Salvador Allende and by propping up dictators like Mobutu, Suharto, and Pinochet. But these observers often overlook the fact that the rich countries also suppress democracy indirectly, and more systematically, by maintaining a global institutional architecture that

---

38 Pogge, *World Poverty and Human Rights*, p. 119.
39 Wenar, "Property Rights and the Resource Curse", p. 12.
40 Ibid., pp. 8–9.

perpetually undermines the prospects of democratic governance – with dire consequences for the world's poorest people.

Another central feature of the global economy that appears to militate against the interests of the poor is the "borrowing privilege". Irrespective of how a government acquires and exercises power, it enjoys the legal right to borrow in the country's name. Like the resource privilege, the borrowing privilege incentivizes coup attempts and provides despotic rulers access to the funds that they need to maintain power in the face of widespread opposition.[41] In addition,

> when the yoke of dictatorship can be thrown off, the international borrowing privilege saddles the country with the often huge debts of the former oppressors. It thereby saps the capacity of its fledgling democratic government to implement structural reforms and other political programs, thus rendering it less successful and less stable than it would otherwise be.[42]

Once important features of the global economic order like the resource and borrowing privileges are brought into focus, an analysis of world poverty that concentrates exclusively on domestic factors loses its appeal. Of course authoritarian governments and corrupt elites contribute to the persistence of severe poverty. But, as Pogge notes,

> this analysis is nevertheless ultimately unsatisfying, because it portrays the corrupt social institutions and corrupt elites prevalent in the poor countries as an exogenous fact: as a fact that explains, but does not itself stand in need of explanation... An adequate explanation of persistent global poverty must not merely adduce the prevalence of flawed social institutions and of corrupt, oppressive, and incompetent elites in the poor countries but must also provide an explanation for this prevalence.[43]

If the analysis offered by Pogge and Wenar is sound, it follows that it is a mistake to think of our duties to the world's poor purely in terms of assistance. If the institutions we impose are implicated in the creation and maintenance of severe poverty, then we are failing the world's poor not (or not merely) by neglecting our *positive* duties to aid but by refusing to honour our *negative* duties to refrain from inflicting harm. Pogge concludes: "most of us do not merely let people starve but also participate in starving them".[44]

---

41 Pogge, *World Poverty and Human Rights*, pp. 120–121.
42 Ibid., p. 121.
43 Ibid., pp. 117–118.
44 Ibid., p. 220; cf. p. 182.

We might think that this is an unfair accusation. We might say: "I accept that the rules of the global economy harm the poor, but I did not design those rules or campaign for their implementation. Nor did I oppose attempts to rewrite them. If a politician promised to, say, reform the resource privilege, I would vote for her. How, then, can you say that I am responsible for harms inflicted by the global economy?"

Pogge mentions a number of ways in which ordinary citizens may unwittingly collaborate in the imposition of an unjust social order. They may collaborate by contributing their labour to the society's economy, by paying taxes to its government, and by conferring legitimacy through their participation in its political and legal institutions.[45] Does this mean that we must emigrate or risk imprisonment by refusing to pay our taxes? Pogge suggests a less burdensome alternative: we should offset the damage we have caused by donating money to poverty relief organizations.[46] Although this recommendation resembles Singer's, Pogge emphasizes that we are required to give not in order to *assist* the world's poor but in order to *compensate* them for the harms that we have inflicted.

Pogge's analysis reveals an additional reason to give to the poor. Even if you are sceptical of the claim that you bear personal responsibility for the harms that the global order inflicts, you nevertheless *benefit* from that order. You benefit, for example, from the fact that access to reasonably priced oil is not conditional on our corporations being able to find a minimally decent regime to buy from. You pocket gains from a system that redistributes wealth from the poor to the rich, and you are duty-bound to disgorge yourself of those gains, irrespective of whether you contribute to the maintenance of that system.[47] If a computer error resulted in my life savings accidently being deposited into your bank account, you would clearly wrong me if you failed to return them. And you would wrong me not by failing to provide assistance but by unjustly sustaining a harm that has befallen me. The same is true when we refuse to relinquish gains that an unjust economic system has extracted from the world's poor.

3.5 Is the global order really harming the poor?

One major difference, then, between the approach taken by people like Singer, on the one hand, and the approach favored by Pogge and his followers, on the other, is that the former emphasizes positive duties to assist the poor whereas the latter emphasizes negative duties to refrain from inflicting harm. Pogge actually assumes – for the sake of argument – that there are *no* positive duties to assist the poor and argues that our duties to alleviate

---

45 Ibid., pp. 72, 141, 151.
46 Ibid., pp. 26, 142, 150.
47 Pogge, "'Assisting' the Global Poor", pp. 278–279.

poverty can be understood entirely in terms of the negative duty not to cause harm (and the associated duty to compensate for harms that we have already caused). One consideration that motivates Pogge's approach is the fact that citizens of affluent countries are often very dismissive of positive duties. Pogge writes:

> Inviting people, in positive-duty style, to help overcome a moral disgrace is unlikely to work... [C]itizens of wealthy countries have (deliberately or unconsciously) developed highly effective ways of organizing their lives to make physically distant misery mentally distant as well. The vast majority of them ignore positive-duty arguments and contribute nothing or very little to charities that fight chronic poverty abroad. The conduct of these people will not be changed by lamenting the mere failure to change the rules in order to "help" the global poor ...[48]

The dominant moral view of our age is that, although assisting the needy is morally optional, we have very stringent and grave duties to refrain from causing harm. We might seek to challenge the dominant view, as Singer has done, by arguing that we in fact have demanding and weighty positive duties to provide assistance. Or we might accept the dominant view but contend that this view has unexpected implications. If Pogge is right to claim that severe poverty is largely attributable to institutional arrangements that we uphold, the dominant view yields the unexpected conclusion that we have stringent and grave duties to alleviate such poverty.

Pogge's view, unlike Singer's, relies on a particular account of what causes severe poverty. For Singer, the causes of poverty are largely irrelevant. What matters is that many people are suffering and that we have the capacity to alleviate their suffering without incurring burdens nearly as significant as those we would be reducing. These considerations are sufficient to ground duties to the world's poor. Pogge's argument, by contrast, rests on the proposition that severe poverty is attributable to global institutions that we uphold. If this proposition is false, then the specific argument Pogge advances will not succeed. (To be sure, Pogge sets aside positive duties for the sake of argument; he does not *deny* the existence of such duties.[49] But positive duties arising independently of harms inflicted by the global order play no role in his account of what is owed to the world's poor.)

---

48 Thomas Pogge, "Response to the Critics", in Alison M. Jaggar (ed.), *Thomas Pogge and his Critics* (Cambridge: Polity Press, 2010), p. 179.

49 Thomas Pogge, "Severe Poverty as a Human Rights Violation", in Thomas Pogge (ed.), *Freedom from Poverty as a Human Right: Who Owes What to the Very Poor?* (New York: Oxford University Press, 2007), p. 20.

Now, the widespread view that global poverty is caused *entirely* by factors native to the countries it affects – the view that Pogge calls the "Purely Domestic Poverty Thesis"[50] – is surely false. But it is possible to reject this view without endorsing Pogge's rival claim that global poverty is largely attributable to the global order. One can adopt an intermediate position which holds that whereas *some* global poverty is caused by the global order, *some* global poverty has a different provenance.[51] Pogge is open about the fact that the available evidence does not conclusively support his stronger view, although he does think that his view is supported by the preponderance of existing evidence.[52] Part of the problem here is that social scientists have neglected the questions that would have to be answered in order to either prove or disprove Pogge's hypothesis. As Pogge observes:

> There is much work, by economists, historians, and others, on the causes of poverty. Nearly all of it examines how poverty has evolved in various countries and regions, seeking to determine which of the internationally diverse local factors explain relative successes and failures.[53]

In other words, the existing literature does not adequately examine the role of the global order in the maintenance of world poverty. Pogge suggests that the narrow focus of social scientists may reflect the fact that they "feel emotionally more comfortable, and careerwise more confident, with work that traces the persistence of severe poverty back to local causes rather than to global institutions we are involved in upholding".[54] But he notes that

> there is also a good methodological reason for the research bias toward national and local causes: There being only this one world to observe, it is hard to obtain solid evidence about how the overall incidence of poverty would have evolved differently if this or that global factor had been different. By contrast, solid evidence about the effects of national and local factors can be gleaned from many poor countries that differ in their natural environment, history, culture, political and economic system, and government policies.[55]

---

50 Pogge, "'Assisting' the Global Poor", p. 265.
51 See Joshua Cohen, "Philosophy, Social Science, Global Poverty", in Jaggar (ed.), *Thomas Pogge and his Critics*; Simon Caney, "Cosmopolitanism and Justice", in Thomas Christiano and John Christman (eds.), *Contemporary Debates in Political Philosophy* (Malden, MA: Blackwell, 2009), pp. 393–394.
52 Pogge, "Response to the Critics", p. 181.
53 Pogge, *World Poverty and Human Rights*, p. 16.
54 Pogge, "'Assisting' the Global Poor", p. 267.
55 Ibid., p. 268.

Because there are not multiple global orders, the particular global order we inhabit (and the effects it produces) cannot be compared to different orders with different designs.

Pogge stresses that, whatever explains the dearth of social-scientific research into the relationship between severe poverty and the global order, we "should not confuse absence of evidence with evidence for absence of our responsibility for world poverty".[56] Moreover, Pogge suggests that, until more conclusive evidence arrives, we should err on the side of caution and act as though the institutions we uphold are indeed deeply implicated in the persistence of severe poverty. After all, "the consequences of underestimating the harm we do to the global poor are far graver for them than the consequences of overestimation would be for us".[57] Pogge illustrates this point with an analogy: "It would be gravely immoral ... to continue operating a lead smelter when there is merely a preponderance of evidence for its emissions causing serious mental retardation among the children of the nearby village".[58] Similarly, it would be gravely immoral to continue imposing a global economic order while we await conclusive evidence for the claim that it is in fact doing what it appears to be doing, namely, perpetuating severe global poverty.

3.6 Conclusion

As Singer observes, we are living in the midst of an emergency, an emergency in which millions of people endure crippling poverty throughout the duration of their lives. Thomas Pogge's work forces those of us living in wealthy parts of the world to confront a disturbing possibility, namely, that we are not mere bystanders to this poverty but active accomplices in its maintenance. Perhaps Pogge is wrong about this. Perhaps poverty's causes are not of our making. But even if we are not responsible for *creating* poverty, it does not follow that we lack a responsibility to fix it. As Singer and others have helped to show, we may have stringent duties to assist the world's poor, irrespective of whether we have caused their predicament. These duties may not require the extremely high level of self-sacrifice advocated by Singer, but they are likely to be demanding nonetheless and may well require more than simply doing one's fair share.

---

56 Pogge, "Response to the Critics", p. 181.
57 Ibid., p. 182.
58 Ibid.

4 INEQUALITY

It is often said that the rich can and should do more to end severe poverty worldwide. In the previous chapter, we saw how this claim is supported by robust philosophical argument. But even if world poverty were eradicated, some people would remain considerably worse off than others; the end of global poverty would not mean the end of global *inequality*. The aim of this chapter is to consider whether and why global inequality matters.

4.1 Cosmopolitanism

Within the advanced societies of the First World, concerns about *domestic* inequality go in and out of fashion. During the New Labour years in the UK, for example, such concerns disappeared from the political agenda, but they resurfaced in the second decade of the 21st century when activist movements like Occupy attacked the concentration of income and wealth in the hands of the richest 1%. These popular concerns mirror strands of an academic debate in which some of the most influential political theorists in the Western world have defended "egalitarian" principles of distributive justice. A principle of distributive justice tells us how goods like income and wealth should be allocated, and an "egalitarian" distributive principle instructs us to reduce or eliminate inequalities in the distribution of those goods. (The word "egalitarian" is derived from the French word "égalité", which means "equality".)

Egalitarianism comes in different varieties, and it does not necessarily condemn any and every inequality. An egalitarian principle may condemn only certain types of inequality, or inequalities that exceed a certain size, or that have a particular kind of source (such as the bad luck of the worse-off). When inequalities are small or when they are traceable to choices made by the disadvantaged, some egalitarians are willing to tolerate them. Moreover, egalitarianism may require the *eradication* of (certain types of) inequality, or, more modestly, it may require simply its *reduction*.

The largest inequalities exist not within societies but among them. The inequality between a typical citizen of the US and a typical citizen of

Bangladesh is far greater than the inequality that exists among members of the first group. The typical American has opportunities for a flourishing life that the typical Bangladeshi simply lacks (and this would continue to be true even if all Bangladeshis were able to escape from crippling poverty). To be sure, the inequality that exists among the richest and poorest Americans is sizeable and problematic, but it is dwarfed by the inequality between members of the First and Third Worlds. Many people find international inequality especially troubling, and a number of political theorists have argued that we should aim for a more egalitarian world order.

Those who advocate global egalitarianism often describe themselves as *cosmopolitans*. The "cosmos" refers to the universe, and the term "cosmopolitan" has its origin in the Greek word "kosmopolites", meaning a citizen of the world. For global egalitarians, "we are all citizens of the world in the sense that we should all be included within a common scheme of [egalitarian] distributive justice".[1] World citizenship entitles us to membership in a global community committed to realizing our socioeconomic rights.

However, it is important to distinguish between different types of cosmopolitanism. Global egalitarianism is what we might call a *strong* instantiation of that ideal, a substantive political morality with a determinate and demanding content. Strong cosmopolitanism contrasts with a more foundational moral idea, an idea which we might call *basic* cosmopolitanism.[2] Basic cosmopolitanism is not a substantive political doctrine but a view about the general way in which policies and institutions are to be defended or criticized. When we decide which institutions to establish, maintain, reform, or abolish, basic cosmopolitanism holds that we must consider, impartially, the claims of each person who will be affected.[3] Underlying this recommendation is the thought that each human being is an *equal* subject of moral concern. This idea can be interpreted in different ways, but at the very least it implies that "the various good and bad things that can happen to people should be valued in the same way no matter who those people are and where in the world they live".[4] Elaborating on this idea, David Miller notes: "A world in which there is a starving peasant in Ethiopia is to that extent as bad as a world in which there is a starving peasant in Poland, all else being equal".[5]

---

1   Simon Caney, "Cosmopolitanism and Justice", in Thomas Christiano and John Christman (eds.), *Contemporary Debates in Political Philosophy* (Malden, MA: Blackwell, 2009), p. 389
2   Cf. the distinction between "strong" and "weak" cosmopolitanism in David Miller, *National Responsibility and Global Justice* (Oxford: Oxford University Press, 2007), p. 27ff.
3   Charles R. Beitz, "Cosmopolitan Liberalism and the States System", in Chris Brown (ed.), *Political Restructuring in Europe: Ethical Perspectives* (London: Routledge, 1994), p. 124; Charles R. Beitz, "Social and Cosmopolitan Liberalism", *International Affairs*, vol. 75, no. 3, 1999, pp. 515–529, at p. 519.
4   Miller, *National Responsibility and Global Justice*, p. 28.
5   Ibid., p. 28.

Another thought underlying the basic cosmopolitan emphasis on the impartial consideration of all affected interests is the notion that each human being is an *ultimate* unit of moral concern.[6] Our evaluation of different policies and institutions must be based on considerations about the interests of individuals rather than the interests of collectives. This is because, from the perspective of morality, the interests of individuals are what ultimately matter. The interests of collective entities – such as nations, churches, families, and ethnic communities – matter only *derivatively*: they matter to the extent that they promote the interests of individuals. To say that we should adopt a particular policy because it is, say, good for the nation (taken as a whole) is not appropriate. We need to consider how that policy bears on the interests of each affected person.

Although this should be reasonably clear from what has just been said, it is worth emphasizing that cosmopolitan claims about the ultimate status of individual human beings as units of moral concern are intended to convey the moral priority of individual human interests over those of collective or corporate entities only; such claims do *not* imply that human interests always take precedence over those of non-human animals. Cosmopolitans can (and often do) recognize that practices which conduce to the interests of human beings can nevertheless be thoroughly unjust by virtue of the way in which they ride roughshod over the interests of non-human animals.[7] Factory farming is an obvious example of such a practice. In this connection, it is worth noting that Peter Singer, whose cosmopolitan views we encountered in the previous chapter, provided the philosophical inspiration for the animal liberation movement.[8]

Unlike strong versions of cosmopolitanism such as global egalitarianism, basic cosmopolitanism is widely (though not universally) endorsed among political theorists. In fact, some political theorists have suggested that the widespread endorsement of basic cosmopolitanism has rendered the label superfluous. Matthias Risse claims that the term "has outlived its usefulness for matters of distributive justice". He continues: "We have learned the basic cosmopolitan lesson: moral equality is an essential part of any credible theory of global justice. We live on a 'cosmopolitan plateau'".[9]

What should we make of Risse's claim? Although all contemporary contributors to the global justice debate recognize that each human being is, in some sense, an *equal* subject of moral concern, a number of high-profile

---

6   Thomas Pogge, *World Poverty and Human Rights*, Second Edition (Malden, MA: Polity Press, 2008), p. 175.

7   Cf. Brian Barry, "Statism and Nationalism: A Cosmopolitan Critique", *Nomos*, vol. 41, 1999, pp. 12–66, at p. 37.

8   See, for example, Peter Singer, *Animal Liberation* (London: Pimlico, 1995). For another example of a cosmopolitan thinker defending the interests of non-human animals, see Martha Nussbaum, "Beyond 'Compassion and Humanity': Justice for Nonhuman Animals", in C. Sunstein and M. Nussbaum (eds.), *Animal Rights: Current Debates and New Directions* (New York: Oxford University Press, 2004).

9   Mathias Risse, *On Global Justice* (Princeton, NJ: Princeton University Press, 2012), p. 10. Cf. Miller, *National Responsibility and Global Justice*, pp. 27–28.

theories fail to acknowledge that they are also *ultimate* subjects of moral concern.[10] In this sense, these theories fail to be cosmopolitan in even a basic sense. Moreover, what Risse calls "the basic cosmopolitan lesson" has surely not been learned by many of our fellow citizens and political representatives. On the contrary, this lesson is frequently ignored. It is ignored, for example, when we insist on trade rules that benefit our compatriots while harming the world's poor and when we refuse to adequately curb greenhouse gas emissions that will exacerbate immiseration abroad. In these ways and others, the moral equality of our fellow humans is not taken seriously. It is thus surely an exaggeration to claim that the basic cosmopolitan label "has outlived its usefulness for matters of distributive justice". Many political theorists may reside on a "cosmopolitan plateau", but countless members of the rich world have chosen to settle elsewhere.

Nevertheless, the primary focus of this chapter is not the *moral* equality of persons that is emphasized by basic cosmopolitanism but the *distributive* equality advocated by the egalitarian version of strong cosmopolitanism. Our main question is whether we have reason to tackle the large inequalities of opportunity that exist at the global level.

4.2 The case for global equality

We can start to address our question by considering why we might want to reduce inequalities at the *domestic* level (i.e., *within* states rather than among them). In his famous book *A Theory of Justice*, the late Harvard philosopher John Rawls identified a number of reasons to support the egalitarian principles that he believed should be implemented at the level of the state. Rawls noted that less egalitarian alternatives, which preserve the inequalities generated by the free market, sanction distributions of income and wealth that are unduly influenced by factors that are "arbitrary from a moral point of view".[11] The morally arbitrary factors that Rawls had in mind were social class, family background, and good fortune in what Rawls called the "natural lottery".[12] Some members of society are better off than others simply because they were lucky enough to be born into wealthier families, to be sent to expensive private schools, or to inherit natural abilities and talents that are more highly valued by the market. These factors are "morally arbitrary" in the sense that they are things for which people cannot be held morally responsible: our social class, family background, and genetic endowments are each a product of brute luck.[13]

---

10 On this point, see Caney, "Cosmopolitanism and Justice", p. 390.

11 John Rawls, *A Theory of Justice*, Revised Edition (Cambridge, MA: Harvard University Press, 1999), p. 14.

12 Ibid., p. 64.

13 This was not Rawls's official argument for the egalitarian principles he favoured, but it is the one that many of his readers found most compelling. See Will Kymlicka, *Contemporary Political Philosophy: An Introduction* (New York: Oxford University Press, 2002), pp. 67–69.

Rawls's discussion was about specifically domestic inequality, but a similar argument can be applied at the global level. If inequality is unjust when it is the product of morally arbitrary factors – factors for which the disadvantaged are not morally responsible – then global inequality is at least as troubling as domestic inequality. After all, no one is morally responsible for being born and raised in one country rather than another; no one chooses to be born in, say, Sudan rather than Sweden: where we are born is a simple matter of brute luck. As Thomas Pogge has written:

> It does not really matter whether one is born in Kansas or in Iowa, and so there is not much to justify, as it were. On the other hand, it matters a great deal whether one is born a Mexican or a U. S. citizen, and so we do need to justify to a Mexican why we should be entitled to life prospects that are so much superior to hers merely because we were born on the other side of some line – a difference that, on the face of it, is no less morally arbitrary than differences in sex, in skin color, or in the affluence of one's parents.[14]

If global inequalities cannot be justified, then a strong case can be made for the claim that they must be eliminated or at least drastically reduced.

It may be said that disadvantaged individuals can leave their country of birth and move to a more prosperous nation. But frequently this is not a viable option. Many disadvantaged individuals lack the resources needed to move from one country to another, and those who are able to make the journey are often forcibly excluded or expelled by border guards. The rich, eager to preserve their privileged status, are often unwilling to open their doors to those who wish to share the benefits that luck has bestowed upon them.

Some disadvantaged individuals may be reluctant to leave the poor countries into which they were born even if the opportunity presents itself. They may feel bound to their country of birth by family ties, a sense of cultural belonging, or obligations to their compatriots. But even if they choose to stay for these reasons, it remains true that they have been disadvantaged by morally arbitrary factors. As Cecile Fabre points out, we are no more responsible for becoming emotionally attached to our country of birth than we are for being born there in the first place.[15] Being burdened with the choice of remaining poor in the country that we regard as our home or pursuing the psychologically onerous task of seeking a better life in an alien land is just

---

14 Thomas Pogge, "An Egalitarian Law of Peoples", *Philosophy & Public Affairs*, vol. 23, no. 3, 1994, pp. 195–224, at p. 198. The same line of argument is presented in Caney, "Cosmopolitanism and Justice", pp. 394–395.

15 Cecile Fabre, "Global Distributive Justice: An Egalitarian Perspective", *Canadian Journal of Philosophy*, vol. 35, supp. 1, 2005, pp. 139–164, at pp. 146–148.

one further disadvantage suffered by those unlucky enough to be born in the Third World.

Some affluent individuals counter the claim that they have benefitted from good luck with the assertion that they have worked hard for their wealth. But notice that working hard is entirely compatible with being a beneficiary of good luck. In many cases, hard work and luck both play a role in determining how well one fares. The way in which effort and luck interact to generate extraordinary benefits for the members of affluent countries can be illustrated with an analogy. Consider a game show in which contestants compete for a cash prize by answering a series of questions. Each time a contestant answers a question correctly, the size of the prize increases. If, at the end of the show, there are no winners, the prize "rolls over" to the next episode, when another set of contestants are given a chance to compete for it. The longer this process continues, the bigger the prize becomes, and the larger the sum of money that the eventual winner takes home. Now, consider a scenario in which this process continues for a considerable period of time. Week after week, there are no winners, and the size of the prize becomes very large. What should we say about the determinants of the eventual winner's takings? It is true that the successful contestant has "worked" for her winnings: she answered questions correctly (which might reflect her past research into a variety of subjects), and she performed better than her rivals. But the *amount* of money that the winner takes home has little to do with her own efforts. The size of the prize is determined, in large part, by the efforts of the previous contestants. The winner benefits from the good fortune of participating later in the show's run, after a series of earlier contestants has driven up the size of the reward. It is true that the winner has made a contribution to the size of the prize and that she would not have won the money if she had exerted no effort whatsoever. But the extent of her contribution is dwarfed by the cumulative efforts of the previous contestants: the large size of the reward is attributable largely to the labours of others.

Something similar can be said about the rewards reaped by those of us who live in advanced, industrial societies and, more specifically, about the income we earn by providing various goods and services in the market. No one denies that we work for our income, but the size of the reward we receive is largely determined by the efforts of past generations, by the contributions our ancestors made to the development of legal, political, and socioeconomic institutions from which we benefit enormously.

Lots of affluent individuals like to think of themselves as in some sense "self-made". They point to their modest upbringing and deny that they received any kind of head start in life. But compared with those who were born into impoverished regions of the world, they clearly *did* have a head start, and a pretty massive one at that. We have benefitted from basic security, economic and political stability, an advanced legal system, free education, robust healthcare, and much else besides. In the absence of these things, which were already in place when we were born, all of our hard work would count for little. We were lucky enough to be born into a society in which opportunities for economic wellbeing abound. The denizens of the Third World typically work much harder than members of the First. They work for longer hours and in more gruelling conditions. But the pay-off for their efforts is often meagre because the prerequisites for economic advancement are either absent or underdeveloped.

It is also important to stress that the degree to which one generation is able to secure advantages for its descendants is greatly influenced by factors beyond its control. Many social scientists believe that a country's economic prospects are affected by the nature of its geography. To take two examples, landlocked countries with dysfunctional or antagonistic neighbours have lacked opportunities to participate in the world economy, and malaria can undermine the economic prospects of countries located in tropical and subtropical regions where malarial parasites are able to complete their growth cycle.[16]

If what I have said so far is correct, much of the global inequality that currently exists is attributable to morally arbitrary factors. Countless individuals are disadvantaged by the bad brute luck of being born into the "wrong" countries, while the affluent benefit massively from simple good fortune. If the unequal global distribution of valuable opportunities is morally arbitrary, it looks like we should deem that distribution unjust.

However, some philosophers have argued that although global inequalities are indeed morally arbitrary, it does not follow that these inequalities are unjust. According to these philosophers, the special presumption against morally arbitrary inequality arises only under special conditions. Moreover, they claim that these conditions exist within states but not among them. Thus, egalitarian duties extend only to the borders of our state and no further. In the remainder of this chapter, I will analyze the various reasons that some philosophers have given to support these claims and I will consider whether they can withstand theoretical scrutiny. My conclusion will be that they cannot and that the case for global equality therefore remains unanswered.

4.3 The case against global equality: The Coercion argument I

Our current task, then, is to examine the arguments of those who claim that morally arbitrary inequalities at the global level do not demand rectification. One thing to bear in mind here is that some critics of global egalitarianism accept basic cosmopolitan claims about the equal and ultimate moral status of all human beings and the impartial consideration to which each person is entitled. Their claim is that we can accept basic cosmopolitan tenets without committing ourselves to the strong cosmopolitan view that we are required

---

16 Caney, "Cosmopolitanism and Justice", pp. 393–394.

to reduce or eliminate global distributive inequality. Thus, Michael Blake, an influential critic of global egalitarianism, writes:

> My argument is that a globally impartial liberal theory is not incompatible with distinct principles of distributive justice applicable only within the national context. This is true, however, not because we care more about our fellow countrymen than we do about outsiders, but because the political and legal institutions we share at the national level create a need for distinct forms of justification... What a principle demands changes depending upon the context in which it is applied; that we owe distinct things to fellow nationals need indicate not partiality toward those nationals, but rather a more sophisticated understanding of what impartiality really demands.[17]

In order to establish whether this kind of strategy can succeed – to see whether basic cosmopolitan premises can be reconciled with an approach to global justice that rejects distributive equality – we will have to look more closely at the arguments employed by its proponents.

If morally arbitrary inequalities are unjust within states but not among them, there must be an important difference between the domestic and global realms that can explain this fact. What might that difference be? There are two common types of answer to this question. The first appeals to the allegedly distinctive form of *coercion* that states impose on their citizens, whereas the second invokes the allegedly distinctive kind of *cooperation* in which co-citizens engage. I will consider coercion-based arguments in this section and the next. I will consider a cooperation-based argument in section 4.5.

Blake begins his critique of global egalitarianism with the observation that states coerce their citizens. The coercive nature of the state is most explicit in its administration of the criminal law, in its punishment of criminal offenders. But the state coerces its citizens in other ways, too: by enforcing contracts and property rights, for example, and by levying taxes. As Blake notes, "All the forms of legal rules we use are ultimately backed up with coercive measures … [L]aw is a web of coercion … [E]very judicial act is an act of implicit violence, whether that act is the imprisonment of a criminal or the adjudication of a property dispute".[18]

The next move in Blake's argument is to point out that coercion is disrespectful because it invades individual autonomy. Autonomous individuals are "part authors of their own lives"; they are "able to develop and pursue self-chosen goals and relationships".[19] But coercion undermines our auton-

---

17 Michael Blake, "Distributive Justice, State Coercion, and Autonomy", *Philosophy & Public Affairs*, vol. 30, no. 3, 2002, pp. 257–296, at pp. 257–258.
18 Ibid., pp. 278–279.
19 Ibid., p. 267.

omy. It is "designed to replace the chosen option [of an individual] with the choice of another…"[20] Blake claims that because coercion undercuts our autonomy in this way, it is "presumptively wrong".[21] What he means by this is that coercive practices are guilty until proven innocent. When assessing coercive actions or institutions, the burden of proof lies with their defenders. If I shove you to the ground, you will probably be pretty annoyed. And unless I can provide a justification for my actions (maybe I was pushing you out of harm's way), it is reasonable for you to condemn my behaviour – and to insist that I not do it again. Likewise, unless the state's coercive practices can be justified, they should be abolished.

How might state coercion be justified? Blake claims, plausibly enough, that state coercion is justified if no one can reasonably reject it.[22] But what conditions would have to be satisfied in order to ensure that state coercion cannot be reasonably rejected? Blake points out that in order to ensure that state coercion cannot be reasonably rejected, the institutions it maintains must be acceptable to the least advantaged individuals subject to it.[23] If coercive measures are used to maintain a laissez-faire capitalist economy in which large morally arbitrary inequalities are allowed to metastasize, those measures will be liable to reasonable rejection by the least advantaged. Therefore, in order to ensure that state coercion can be justified, we must ensure that the institutions it maintains permit inequality only when inequality works to the advantage of the worst-off members of society. This is the very point of egalitarian social policy: to justify coercive state practices that would otherwise be intolerable.

With the foregoing argument, Blake develops a particular account of the *grounds* of egalitarian justice. He tells us why equality is important and why it is something that individuals can demand. But Blake claims that this account also has implications for the *scope* of egalitarian justice. If the point of egalitarian redistribution is to justify state coercion, then it seems to follow that although such redistribution is required within state borders, it is not needed beyond them. Blake argues that equality cannot be required at the global level since at the global level there is no state coercion to justify.[24] In the absence of a global state, there can be no demand for global egalitarian justice.

What should we think of Blake's argument? Does it succeed in demonstrating that we should reject global egalitarianism? Those of us who wish to defend global equality can respond to Blake's challenge in a number of ways. First, we might concede Blake's claim that the point of equality is to justify state coercion, but resist Blake's inference that equality is not required

---

20 Ibid., p. 272.
21 Ibid., p. 278.
22 Ibid., p. 281.
23 Ibid., pp. 282–284.
24 Ibid., pp. 287–288.

globally. In other words, we could accept Blake's premise about the *grounds* of egalitarian justice but reject his conclusion about the *scope* of egalitarian justice. (To use the terminology introduced in Chapter 1, this strategy aims to show that Blake's argument is a *non sequitur*.)

One version of this strategy starts by noting that some of the wealthiest states in the world once maintained extensive empires and imposed upon their foreign subjects the same kind of coercion that they inflicted upon their citizens. Individual men and women in the colonies were ensnared in the same "web of coercion" as those in the Mother Country. If a state has egalitarian duties of distributive justice to its citizens, and if it has those duties because it imposes upon them a coercive regime of a particular kind, then it must also have egalitarian duties of distributive justice to the members of its colonies, for they are subject to the self-same regime. This means that, contrary to what Blake maintains, the demands of egalitarian justice do not necessarily terminate at the borders of the state; rather, these demands sometimes extend internationally.[25]

Now, one might wonder whether these observations have any contemporary relevance. After all, the age of empire is long behind us; the imperial apparatus that once linked colonies and colonizers has been dismantled. Or has it? Some critics maintain that the process of decolonization was rigged, that it was "engineered in such a way as to lock in the relations of economic dependency" that it was ostensibly supposed to extinguish.[26] According to these critics, the decolonization process created "a new 'comprador' class with a vested interest in [existing relations of dependency] and then transferr[ed] formal power to those indigenous elites".[27] If this critique is accurate, then there is a sense in which ex-colonial powers remain implicated in the coercive regimes currently imposed on their former subjects.

But even those who are sceptical about the existence of such "neo-colonialism" will struggle to deny that the official history of imperialism retains contemporary relevance. This is because, to put it lightly, colonial powers cannot be said to have discharged any egalitarian obligations that they had to their foreign subjects. And although they may have subsequently severed relations with their former colonies, any unspent obligations did not simply disappear. By severing relations, colonial powers may have ensured that they would not incur any *additional* obligations, but they did not thereby divest themselves of the obligations that they had already acquired. We do not think that a father can relinquish responsibility for his child simply by leaving the mother. Similarly, we must deny that a colonial power can unburden itself of unspent obligations simply by extricating itself from the relationships that generated those obligations. Ex-colonial powers remain *in*

---

25 Lea Ypi, Robert E. Goodin, and Christian Barry, "Associative Duties, Global Justice, and the Colonies", *Philosophy & Public Affairs*, vol. 37, no. 2, 2009, pp. 103–135.

26 Ibid., p. 118.

27 Ibid.

debt to their former subjects. And they can settle that debt only through egalitarian redistribution.[28]

So far, I have assumed that Blake's premise about the point of egalitarian social policy is correct. I have suggested that even if Blake is right to claim that demands for equality are grounded in facts about state coercion, we can reject his claim that such demands are reasonable only when they arise within state borders. But now I want to question whether Blake's premise is actually defensible. To do so, it will be helpful to start by introducing a common distinction between *necessary* and *sufficient* conditions. To illustrate this distinction with some everyday examples: eating a bowl of cereal is sufficient to satisfy my appetite at breakfast time; by eating the cereal, I *do enough* to satiate my hunger. But eating the cereal is not necessary to satisfy my appetite, for I could have satisfied my appetite by eating a slice of toast instead. By contrast, whereas turning the steering wheel of your car is necessary to manoeuvre around a corner, doing so is not sufficient. It is not sufficient since, in addition to turning the wheel, you also have to press the accelerator pedal.

Notice that Blake's claim is that state coercion is *necessary* to ground egalitarian duties. Blake maintains that, in the absence of state coercion, legitimate demands for equality cannot arise. But is this really true? To challenge Blake's claim, Andrea Sangiovanni has offered the following thought experiment:

> Imagine an internally just state. Let us now suppose that all local means of law enforcement – police, army, and any potential replacements—are temporarily disarmed and disabled by a terrorist attack. Suppose further that this condition continues for several years. Crime rates increase, compliance with the laws decreases, but society does not dissolve at a stroke into a war of all against all. Citizens generally feel a sense of solidarity in the wake of the attack, and a desire to maintain public order and decency despite the private advantages they could gain through disobedience and noncompliance; this sense of solidarity is common knowledge and sufficient to provide assurance that people will (generally) continue to comply with the law. The laws still earn most people's respect: the state continues to provide the services it always has; the legislature meets regularly; laws are debated and passed; contracts and wills drawn up; property transferred in accordance with law; disputes settled through legal arbitration, and so on.[29]

---

28 Ibid., pp. 122–133.
29 Andrea Sangiovanni, "Global Justice, Reciprocity, and the State", *Philosophy & Public Affairs*, vol. 35, no. 1, 2007, pp. 3–39, at pp. 10–11.

In short, Sangiovanni asks us to imagine a society very much like the ones we are familiar with but in which the state has been deprived of its coercive capacities by a terrorist attack. If Blake is right that state coercion is a necessary condition for egalitarian principles to arise, then, in Sangiovanni's hypothetical society, distributive equality is not a requirement of justice. Demands for equality are appropriate prior to the attack, but after the attack they lose their legitimacy. But, as Sangiovanni notes, this implication of Blake's account seems oddly arbitrary. After all, the "state continues to do all the things it did before the attack (except coerce those subject to it): contracts are drawn up; taxes are paid; benefits collected, and so on. Why should the principles of distributive justice we use to evaluate the political system be any different?"[30] Sangiovanni's question is intended rhetorically. There appears to be *no* good reason why the principles we endorse after the attack should be any different from those we endorsed before.

What should we infer from this? We might say that although state coercion could be *sufficient* to generate egalitarian demands, Blake is wrong to suggest that it is *necessary*. This would be one further way to open up the possibility of extending to the global realm the egalitarian principles that Blake sought to contain within the borders of states. We could accept that state coercion can ground egalitarian principles, acknowledge that state coercion does not exist at the global level, but maintain that there are *other* considerations that also ground egalitarian principles and that *are* applicable at the global level. However, I want now to suggest that state coercion is *not even sufficient* to generate egalitarian demands. Contrary to what Blake suggests, egalitarian justice is not grounded in state coercion.

To see this, we should start by asking why Blake does not recommend simply *abolishing* coercive state institutions. If state coercion "demonstrates an attitude of disrespect, of infantilization"; if it expresses "contempt for the individual coerced"[31] (as Blake maintains), why not bring it to an end? When Blake turns his attention to coercive practices that exist at the global level, he suggests that, instead of attempting to reform them and ensure that they are justified, we should simply pursue their abolition.[32] Well, why not take the same attitude to the coercive practices that operate in the domestic realm?

Blake's answer to this question is that although state coercion constrains our autonomy in certain ways, it also promotes it.[33] State coercion prevents others from violating our property rights, compels our associates to honour their contractual obligations, guarantees our security, secures funds with which to provide healthcare and education, and so forth. In all these ways, state coercion fosters and preserves our capacity to function as autonomous

---

30 Ibid., p. 11.
31 Blake, "Distributive Justice, State Coercion, and Autonomy", p. 268.
32 Michael Blake, "Coercion and Egalitarian Justice", *The Monist*, vol. 94, no. 4, 2011, pp. 555–570, at pp. 566–569.
33 Blake, "Distributive Justice, State Coercion, and Autonomy", p. 265, p. 282.

beings. If coercive state practices were disassembled – if we were to revert to a state of nature – our prospects for living autonomous lives would be drastically diminished.

With these observations in mind, we are in a good position to question Blake's claim that state coercion grounds principles of egalitarian justice. If coercive state practices perform the valuable role of maintaining our autonomy, it is reasonable to ask why that fact alone is not enough to justify their coerciveness. Why think that state coercion would be liable to reasonable rejection in the absence of distributive equality? It is hard to see how this question could be satisfactorily answered. State coercion seems to provide its own justification, without any need for egalitarian redistribution. If an individual questions why she should accept coercive state practices, we can point to the great, autonomy-enhancing benefits that those practices deliver.[34]

To be clear, the claim being made here is not that distributive equality is *not* a requirement of justice but rather that Blake is mistaken about *why* it is such a requirement. The claim is that Blake's account of the grounds of egalitarian justice is false. And if this account is false, we need not accept any implications that it might have for the scope of egalitarian justice. Blake's attempt to refute global egalitarianism is unsuccessful.

4.4 The case against global equality: The Coercion argument II

We have seen that Blake's coercion-based account of the grounds and scope of distributive equality is vulnerable to attack from multiple angles. However, we cannot dismiss the coercion account just yet. Before we can do that, we need to consider a variant of the coercion account that has been developed by the moral philosopher Thomas Nagel. Like Blake, Nagel argues that egalitarian principles apply exclusively within state borders. Inequalities that exist at the global level may be morally arbitrary but they are not unjust. Nagel also follows Blake in explaining the different status of domestic and global inequalities by appealing to the coercive nature of state institutions. But in addition to this, Nagel emphasizes the fact that citizens of a state are expected to participate in the maintenance of state institutions. Nagel identifies this as the key reason why legitimate demands for equality can arise within states but not among them. He writes:

---

34 Ryan Pevnick, "Political Coercion and the Scope of Distributive Justice", *Political Studies*, vol. 56, 2008, pp. 399–413, at pp. 401–403; Gabriel Wollner, "Equality and the Significance of Coercion", *Journal Of Social Philosophy*, vol. 42, no. 4, 2011, pp. 363–381, at p. 369; Andrea Sangiovanni, "The Irrelevance of Coercion, Imposition, and Framing to Distributive Justice", *Philosophy & Public Affairs*, vol. 40, no. 2, 2012, pp. 79–110, at p. 91.

> A sovereign state is not just a cooperative enterprise for mutual advantage. The societal rules determining its basic structure are coercively imposed: it is not a voluntary association. I submit that it is this complex fact – that we are both putative joint authors of the coercively imposed system, and subject to its norms, i.e., expected to accept their authority even when the collective decision diverges from our personal preferences – that creates the special presumption against arbitrary inequalities in our treatment by the system.
>
> Without being given a choice, we are assigned a role in the collective life of a particular society. The society makes us responsible for its acts, which are taken in our name and on which, in a democracy, we may even have some influence; and it holds us responsible for obeying its laws and conforming to its norms, thereby supporting the institutions through which advantages and disadvantages are created and distributed. Insofar as those institutions admit arbitrary inequalities, we are, even though the responsibility has been simply handed to us, responsible for them, and we therefore have standing to ask why we should accept them. This request for justification has moral weight even if we have in practice no choice but to live under the existing regime. The reason is that its requirements claim our active cooperation, and this cannot be legitimately done without justification – otherwise it is pure coercion.[35]

In short, Nagel's claim is that, as citizens of a state, we are expected to accept and uphold a system that coercively shapes our life prospects, and such an expectation can be legitimate only if the system in question ensures that we are not disadvantaged by morally arbitrary factors. This is an account of the grounds of egalitarian justice: it seeks to explain why demands for distributive equality are sometimes legitimate. But, like Blake's, this account also has implications for the scope of egalitarian justice. States may sometimes coerce outsiders – e.g., by preventing would-be migrants from entering their territory – but because those outsiders are not expected to support state institutions – because they are not "joint authors of the coercively imposed system" – their coercive treatment cannot give rise to legitimate demands for equality.[36] The conditions that ground egalitarian principles exist exclusively within state borders.

---

[35] Thomas Nagel, "The Problem of Global Justice", *Philosophy & Public Affairs*, vol. 33, no. 2, 2005, pp.113–147, at pp. 128–129.

[36] Ibid., pp. 129–130.

Nagel's view is complex but his core idea is quite straightforward and can be illustrated with an analogy. Suppose that you and I are in a band together. Suppose that we have finished writing a new song but that you have now decided to add an extra verse, which expresses controversial political views from which I dissent. Given that I am a "joint author" of the song (it will be released "in my name") and that I will be expected to contribute to live performances of it, I can reasonably demand that you excise the new lyrics. By contrast, this demand cannot reasonably be made by people who have no connection to the band. Similarly, given that citizens are expected to contribute to the socioeconomic regime created by their state – given that it is constructed "in their name" – they can reasonably demand that it satisfy certain requirements. But these demands cannot reasonably be made by outsiders because the state does not act on their behalf. Or so Nagel claims.

Nagel's view is vulnerable to a powerful objection. Nagel wants to draw a sharp distinction between a state's relationship with its citizens, on the one hand, and a state's relationship with outsiders, on the other. Both relationships may be coercive, but the former, unlike the latter, is not based on *sheer* coercion. Rather, the state "acts in the name" of its citizens; it expects their "active cooperation". But now the question arises: what about states that *do not* act in the name of their citizens? What about states that expect not cooperation but mere submission? Does Nagel's view lead us to the absurd conclusion that dictatorships are bound by less demanding distributive requirements than democracies?

Nagel considers a similar objection and attempts to deflect it by adopting a "broad interpretation" of what it means for a citizen to be a joint author of the law. He considers the case of a colonial or occupying power and suggests that when such a regime

> claims political authority over a population, it purports not to rule by force alone. It is providing and enforcing a system of law that those subject to it are expected to uphold as participants, and which is intended to serve their interests even if they are not its legislators. Since their normative engagement is required, there is a sense in which it is being imposed in their name.[37]

But Nagel's suggestion invites an obvious reply. What about states that plainly *do* rule by force alone? What about states that impose a legal system that is clearly *not* intended to serve the interests of its subjects? Consider the slave states of antebellum America. It cannot plausibly be claimed that these states served the interests of the slave population.[38] But this means that, in

---

37 Ibid., p. 129, fn. 14.
38 A. J. Julius, "Nagel's Atlas", *Philosophy and Public Affairs*, vol. 34, no. 2, 2006, pp. 176–192, at p. 183.

Nagel's view, they were not constrained by the dictates of egalitarian justice. As Arash Abizadeh writes, "the perverse implication of [Nagel's view] is that a tyrant can exempt himself from the demands of justice by relying solely on pure coercion … The closer a tyrant's rule approaches pure slavery, the less it can be criticized for being unjust".[39] To use the terminology introduced in Chapter 1, Nagel's view is a *reductio ad absurdum*. It must be rejected on account of the absurd conclusions that it generates.

4.5 The case against global equality: Cooperation

At the beginning of this chapter, I made the case for extending egalitarian principles to the global level. I then considered two objections to global equality. The first invoked the coercive nature of the state, whereas the second emphasized the fact that coercive state institutions demand the active cooperation of their citizens. We saw that both of these objections miss their target. I shall finish the chapter by considering a further challenge to global egalitarianism, a challenge which sets aside facts about state coercion and focuses exclusively on the (allegedly) distinctive form of social cooperation in which co-citizens engage.

According to Sangiovanni, the duty to eliminate morally arbitrary inequality within the state arises from the requirement to give our fellow citizens a fair return for what they have given us. More specifically, Sangiovanni argues that redressing morally arbitrary inequality is how we reciprocate for the contribution our fellow citizens have made to the provision of basic collective goods that enable us "to develop and act on a plan of life".[40] The goods Sangiovanni has in mind are security, access to a legally regulated market, and enforceable property rights.[41] Our fellow citizens contribute to the provision of these goods by cooperating to uphold state institutions. They do this by paying taxes, complying with the law, and engaging in various types of political activity.[42] By participating in a cooperative endeavour to maintain and reproduce the state, our fellow citizens ensure that we possess "the individual capabilities to function as citizens, producers, and biological beings".[43]

Like Blake and Nagel, Sangiovanni argues that his account of the grounds of egalitarian justice has implications for the scope of egalitarian

---

39 Arash Abizadeh, "Cooperation, Pervasive Impact, and Coercion: On the Scope (not Site) of Distributive Justice", *Philosophy & Public Affairs*, vol. 35, no. 4, 2007, pp. 318–358, at p. 352.
40 Andrea Sangiovanni, "Global Justice, Reciprocity, and the State", p. 20.
41 Ibid.
42 Ibid.
43 Ibid., p. 21.

justice. If egalitarian redistribution is a way of reciprocating for the provision of basic collective goods, and if those goods are produced exclusively by our fellow citizens, then egalitarian redistribution is not something that we owe to outsiders.[44]

The core idea at the heart of Sangiovanni's argument is intuitive enough. If someone makes sacrifices in order to benefit you in significant ways, it is natural to think that you owe them something in return, and one way in which you might discharge that duty is by helping them to shoulder certain burdens. Suppose a friend lends you a large sum of money to help you to get your business off the ground. If, later in life, your friend finds herself experiencing financial difficulties, it is plausible to hold that you should do what you can to assist her. Similarly, given that our fellow citizens have provided the goods that we need to develop and act on a plan for life, we might think that we have duties to shield them from morally arbitrary disadvantage.

How can defenders of global equality reply to Sangiovanni's claims? One possible response has the same form as the first argument that we offered in reply to Blake's account: we can accept Sangiovanni's premise about the grounds of egalitarian justice but reject his conclusion about its scope. More specifically, we could concede that the point of distributive equality is to reciprocate for the provision of basic collective goods, but resist Sangiovanni's inference that egalitarian principles apply only among compatriots. We could do this by arguing that, contra Sangiovanni, it is not only our fellow citizens who provide the basic collective goods that enable us to develop and act on a plan for life: foreigners also make a contribution.

Consider the good of security. There are a number of ways in which the members of other states contribute to our enjoyment of this good. Chris Armstrong has made this point using the example of nuclear alliances. He writes:

> Nations share nuclear technology, base missiles and early-warning devices on each others' territory, and sign pacts agreeing to mutual defense. This is the provision of the collective good of physical security at the transnational level via relations of reciprocity and interdependence. It is genuinely collective provision in the sense that the nature of the provision is significantly conditioned by its being a joint project; individual states working alone could not produce an equivalent system.[45]

---

44 Ibid., pp. 21–22.
45 Chris Armstrong, "Coercion, Reciprocity, and Equality Beyond the State", *Journal of Social Philosophy*, vol. 40, no. 3, 2009, pp. 297–316, at p. 310.

Members of other states also contribute to our security via international trade. In a variety of different ways, the international trade regime enhances our security by reducing the probability of military conflict. For example, the trade regime makes the use of force less appealing by facilitating the establishment of valuable economic relations that conflict would disrupt; it reduces incentives to engage in wars of conquest and plunder by offering more efficient means of promoting economic growth; and it cultivates cosmopolitan identities that supplant more antagonistic nationalist sentiments.[46] Given that the trade regime is maintained not only by our fellow citizens but also by members of other states, it follows that members of other states contribute to our security. Thus, if egalitarian duties are owed to those who contribute to the provision of the basic collective goods that Sangiovanni identifies, then egalitarian duties are owed to outsiders.[47]

Consider now another response to Sangiovanni's argument. Defenders of global equality can point out that Sangiovanni's account is *incomplete*. Sangiovanni argues that egalitarian duties are owed among compatriots because compatriots participate together in a cooperative endeavour that produces the basic goods that each individual needs in order to pursue his or her life plan. The cooperative scheme in which citizens engage yields material benefits, and, because of the contributions they have made, each citizen can stake a claim to a share of those benefits. But consider this: the cooperative scheme to which citizens contribute does not just output material benefits; it also relies on a variety of material *inputs*. The cooperative fire requires fuel to burn. One implication of this is that we cannot say that citizens have exclusive claims to the benefits produced by the cooperative scheme unless we know that they also had exclusive claims to the resources that were used as inputs.[48]

Consider an analogy. If a group of people pool the artworks they own in order to exhibit them at a show, then each member of the group has a fairness-based claim to a proportionate share of the revenue derived from ticket sales. But if it turns out that some of the paintings were *stolen*, then a portion of their earnings must be surrendered. Similarly, if some of the benefits derived from a national cooperative enterprise were generated using resources that the participants did not rightfully own, then the participants have no claim to those benefits.

A theory of justice will not be complete if it specifies entitlements to the outputs of a cooperative process only; it must also specify entitlements to inputs. But Sangiovanni's account tells us only how to distribute outputs.

---

46 Patrick J. McDonald, "Peace through Trade or Free Trade?", *Journal of Conflict Resolution*, vol. 48, no. 4, 2004, pp. 547–572.

47 James Christensen, *Trade Justice* (Oxford: Oxford University Press, 2017), pp. 139–140.

48 Simon Caney, "Humanity, Associations and Global Justice: A Defence of Humanity-Centred Cosmopolitan Egalitarianism", *The Monist*, vol. 94, no. 4, 2011, pp. 506–534, at pp. 516–517.

Thus, a global egalitarian could agree with Sangiovanni that the outputs of national cooperative schemes should be distributed equally among citizens, but insist that the inputs should be distributed equally around the globe. This might involve, for example, a globally egalitarian distribution of the world's natural resource wealth. So, Sangiovanni's argument fails to undermine the case for global equality.

4.6 Conclusion

In this chapter, we have seen that considerations which lead political thinkers to condemn domestic inequality should also lead us to condemn inequalities that arise at the global level. We have seen that attempts to show that legitimate concerns about morally arbitrary disadvantage arise only within the borders of states do not succeed. In the next chapter, we will see how the case for global equality is challenged, but ultimately strengthened, by an encounter with the political morality of nationalism.

5 NATIONALISM

In the previous chapter, we considered the case for extending egalitarian principles to the global domain. We also encountered several (unsuccessful) objections to such an extension. These objections were each built around an attempt to identify a morally relevant distinction between the claims of foreigners and those of our compatriots. In this chapter, we shall examine several further attempts to identify such a distinction. However, whereas the arguments in Chapter 4 appealed to allegedly significant features of *states* (and, in particular, to their coercive and cooperative natures), the arguments to be addressed here focus on allegedly significant features of *nations*. In other words, this chapter considers whether the conception of global justice that we have been constructing can survive an encounter with the political morality of *nationalism*. We will ask whether that conception is compatible with nationalist ideals and, if it is not, which should yield: nationalism or our conception of global justice.

5.1 Nations and nationality

In popular discourse, the words "state" and "nation" are often used interchangeably, but they actually have different meanings. According to one well-known definition, a state is a political institution that claims a monopoly on the legitimate use of force within a particular territory.[1] A nation, by contrast, is a cultural entity. Some nations ("nation-states") have borders that map neatly onto those of a state, but others do not. In some cases, multiple nations exist within the boundaries of a single state (a "multinational state"), whereas in others a single nation is spread across multiple states. A (contested) example of a multinational state is the Kingdom of Spain, which incorporates Galicia, Catalonia, the Basque Country, and several other autonomous communities that are regarded by some as constituting distinct

---

[1] Max Weber, "Politics as a Vocation", in H. H. Gerth and C. W. Mills (eds.), *From Max Weber* (London: Routledge and Kegan Paul, 1970), p. 78.

nations. An example of a nation that spans several states is Kurdistan, the territory of which is divided among Turkey, Syria, Iraq, and Iran.[2]

In addition to distinguishing between nations and states, we should take care to differentiate, from the outset, between nationality and ethnicity. Whereas ethnicity is defined in terms of biological descent, nationality, as already mentioned, can be defined in terms of a common culture. Many nations are "multi-ethnic" in character (the US, to take an obvious example, comprises Italian-Americans, Irish-Americans, Latino-Americans, and various other ethnic groups), and many ethnic groups (Jews, for example) are dispersed across multiple nations. So, nationalist movements that seek to promote the interests of their members need not assume the worryingly racist character that they often possess in practice.[3]

Nevertheless, nationalism is a doctrine about which many progressively minded people are often wary. Many associate it with mindless, flag-waving deference to one's own country and a chauvinistic disregard for people of different countries and cultures. In its most despicable guises, nationalism fuelled the maniacal, industrial-scale slaughter of Jews under the Third Reich, the Rwandan genocide, and the vicious ethnic conflicts that engulfed the former Yugoslavia after the dissolution of the Soviet Union. But nationalism comes in different forms, and, as with all thought systems, the most tenable versions are not discredited by the mere existence of regressive alternatives. Albert Einstein's description of nationalism as an infantile disease, "the measles of the human race", certainly applies to some kinds of nationalism, but other instantiations are entitled to a hearing.[4] The particular variety of nationalism that I will focus on here is the distinctively liberal version defended by David Miller, a political theorist based at the University of Oxford.

Before we can evaluate nationalist ideals, we must acquire a firmer understanding of the concept of a nation and the related concept of nationality. I have said what a nation is not, but more needs to be said about what a nation is. I mentioned that a nation is cultural in nature, but so is an Andrei Tarkovsky appreciation society. What is distinctive about a nation? The first point to note is that nations have a *territorial* component. Whereas Andrei Tarkovsky fans may be scattered across the world (and their interactions may take place exclusively within online fora), the members of a nation are bound to a particular parcel of land; they identify with a particular part of the planet that they think of as their home.[5]

---

2   David Miller, *On Nationality* (Oxford: Oxford University Press, 1995), pp. 18–19; Simon Caney, *Justice Beyond Borders: A Global Political Theory* (Oxford: Oxford University Press, 2005), p. 14.

3   Miller, *On Nationality*, pp. 19–21; Caney, *Justice Beyond Borders*, pp. 14–15.

4   Quoted in Helen Dukas & Banesh Hoffmann (eds.), *Albert Einstein: The Human Side* (Princeton, NJ: Princeton University Press, 1979).

5   Miller, *On Nationality*, pp. 24–25.

Second, while co-nationals need not share the same ethnicity, they will inevitably have certain common characteristics. As Miller remarks, the members of a nation cannot be understood "as people who merely happen to have been thrown together in one place and forced to share a common fate, in the way that the occupants of a lifeboat, say, have been accidentally thrown together".[6] Rather, in order for a group of individuals to constitute a nation, it must be the case that those individuals "belong together by virtue of the characteristics that they share".[7] However, as Miller immediately goes on to acknowledge, identifying the kinds of characteristics that can bind the members of a nation together is not an easy task. He suggests that the "public culture" that unifies a nation may be conceived of as a general

> set of understandings about how a group of people is to conduct its life together. This will include political principles such as a belief in democracy or the rule of law, but it reaches more widely than this. It extends to social norms such as honesty in filling in your tax return or queueing as a way of deciding who gets on to the bus first. It may also embrace certain cultural ideals, for instance religious beliefs or a commitment to preserve the purity of the national language. Its range will vary from case to case ...[8]

So, singling out the types of characteristics that define a nationality is not straightforward. But the extent of the problem that this represents is kept in check by a third feature of national communities, namely, the way in which they are "constituted by belief".[9] Elaborating on this idea, Miller observes that "nations exist when their members *recognize one another as compatriots*, and *believe* that they share characteristics of the relevant kind".[10] He adds:

> it is a mistake to begin from the position of an outside observer trying to identify nations by looking to see which people have common attributes such as race or language. On the one hand, we may find people who share one or more such attributes, and yet do not constitute a nation because they do not think of themselves as forming one (Austrians and Germans, for instance). On the other hand, if we take those peoples who do by the test of mutual recognition and shared beliefs form nations, there is no one characteristic (such as race or religion) that each of them has in common.[11]

---

6 Ibid., p. 25.
7 Ibid.
8 Ibid., p. 26.
9 Ibid., p. 22.
10 Ibid. (emphasis added).
11 Ibid.

One further aspect of nations that should be highlighted is their *historical* nature. A nation is typically conceived as exhibiting a distinctive character that extends back through time, while its members think of themselves as inheriting an identity that has been shaped by their ancestors and that bears the imprint of significant past events.[12] Importantly, the popular histories that inform a nation's public culture will often contain a considerable degree of fiction; the stories that nations tell themselves about their own pasts invariably depart from reality to a greater or lesser extent.[13]

5.2 National self-determination

Now, according to nationalist doctrine, nations have a strong claim to enjoy control over the territory that they identify as their homeland. In other words, they have an important interest in being *self-determining*, an interest that others should respect.[14] Some nationalists hold that self-determination can be achieved only through independent statehood – by transforming the nation into a nation-state – whereas others are willing to settle for the establishment of sub-state political institutions (such as a regional parliament).[15] Regardless of the favoured institutional arrangement, the underlying commitment is to collective control of national affairs. Importantly, nationalists hold that, over a wide range of issues, a nation's political institutions should be authoritative. Over "those matters that are the primary concern of its members"[16], the nation must enjoy *sovereignty*, where this means that the nation must not be subject to a higher power with the capacity to overturn its decisions; the authority the nation yields with regard to these decisions must be *ultimate*. The nation may, of course, choose to delegate certain decision-making powers to supranational institutions (such as the European Union [EU]), but it cannot be required to do so, and it must always have the right to take back powers that it previously surrendered.[17]

National self-determination, and the sovereignty that it is thought to require, is said to be valuable for a number of reasons. One argument for the value of national self-determination appeals to the value of national culture and the important role that national political institutions can play in its preservation. Miller suggests that a national culture is valuable because it "not only gives its bearers a sense of where they belong and provides an historical identity, but also provides them with a background against which

---

12 Ibid., pp. 23–24.
13 Ibid., pp. 31–41.
14 Ibid., p. 81.
15 Ibid.
16 Ibid.
17 Ibid., p. 101.

more individual choices about how to live can be made".[18] The thought is that our national identity orients us in the world and enables us to develop and act upon a plan for life. National culture helps us to make sense of our social environment and makes available a range of options from which we can draw our conception of the good.

The standing of a nation's demand for self-determination will depend on how that nation defines the range of "matters that are the primary concern of its members". If, for example, it believes that its racial superiority and interest in *lebensraum* grant it exclusive rights to the territory and resources of its neighbours, then, clearly, its demands will be unacceptable. But if the nation takes seriously basic cosmopolitan ideas about the moral equality of human beings, then it will recognize that the legitimate scope of its authority is constrained by the interest that *other* nations have in self-determining *their* internal affairs. This point is explicitly acknowledged by Miller, who stresses that the principle of national self-determination that he favors has a "reiterative" character: it ascribes claims to each and every nation.[19] If each nation is to have an autonomous sphere in which it can be self-directing, then the autonomous spheres of other nations must by necessity be limited in scope. Miller writes: "in justifying my own country's claim to be an independent political unit, I am also justifying the corresponding claims of others".[20]

But this point may have wider implications than my *lebensraum* example implies. In the run-up to the 2016 British referendum on whether Britain should remain a member of the EU, those encouraging a Leave vote campaigned under the slogan "take back control". This slogan expressed a widespread view that supranational institutions usurp legislative powers that rightly belong in the hands of nations. But how plausible is this view about where power belongs? The view's credibility is challenged by the fact that many of the decisions over which national communities have traditionally been sovereign can have seriously adverse implications for outsiders. For example, a country's policies for regulating (or not regulating) the emission of greenhouse gases have consequences not only for its own inhabitants but for humans (and non-humans) more generally. Similarly, a country's willingness to accept refugees for resettlement influences the size of the burden that must be borne by third parties, and the degree to which it taxes its corporations affects the ability of other governments to tax theirs.

These facts reveal that it is highly problematical to claim that national sovereignty should remain as extensive as it has been in the past. Why, it is natural to ask, should a nation be permitted to exercise control over matters that bear so heavily on the important interests of foreigners? Why should traditional definitions of "matters that are primarily the concern of its

---

18 Ibid., pp. 85–86.
19 Ibid., pp. 99–100.
20 Ibid., p. 100.

members" go unchallenged? Why should we not redraw the boundaries of national autonomous spheres and transfer certain powers to democratically structured supranational institutions? After all, doing so would ensure that all affected parties can be represented in decision-making fora.[21]

Nationalists might say that the externalities generated by the kinds of national decisions that I have mentioned are not explicable as threats to national self-determination as they conceive of that ideal. The appropriate response to this claim, if true, is that national self-determination is not all that we care about. If worries about cross-border pollution, refugee burden-sharing, and corporate regulation are better framed as, say, *cosmopolitan* concerns, then what we should say is that cosmopolitan concerns take priority. National self-determination is valuable when and because it serves the well-being and agency interests of individuals. When national self-determination and the interests of individuals pull in different directions, it is the former that must yield. This will mean reducing the scope of national sovereignty and investing certain powers in democratically structured supranational institutions.

5.3 National self-determination and international redistribution

Notwithstanding what has just been said, cosmopolitans should perhaps not be too hasty in their dismissal of nationalist principles, for some may contain ideas that can be mobilized for cosmopolitan purposes. More specifically, certain nationalist principles might bolster the case for international redistribution. Indeed, this could be true of national self-determination. It has been argued that although some degree of political independence is necessary for national self-determination, this is not sufficient; if nations are to be self-determining, certain *economic* conditions must also be satisfied. Indeed, Miller himself suggests that nations "cannot exercise any sort of collective autonomy unless they have a sufficient resource base to be economically viable".[22] He infers from this that, if we take seriously a nation's claim to be self-determining, we must be committed to ensuring redistribution from the resource-rich to the resource-poor. He writes: "resource transfers should be made so as to allow each national community to reach a threshold of viability, giving it an economic base from which national self-determination can meaningfully be exercised".[23]

These redistributive commitments that Miller extracts from the principle of national self-determination are fairly minimal and are considerably less

---

21 For a more in-depth discussion of these and related issues, see Caney, *Justice Beyond Borders*, pp. 156–160.

22 Ibid., p. 105.

23 Ibid., p. 106.

demanding than those favoured by strong cosmopolitans. But it has been argued that Miller underestimates the redistributive consequences that follow from taking the principle of national self-determination seriously, and that this principle in fact yields robustly egalitarian conclusions. For example, Kok-Chor Tan has argued that economic inequalities translate into inequalities of power and that those inequalities weaken the capacity of the worse-off to be self-directing. His claim is that even if a nation is not poor in an *absolute* sense, if it is poor*er* than others (i.e., if it is poor in a *relative* sense), then it will be vulnerable to coercion and domination and such vulnerability will clearly undermine its prospects for self-determination.[24] If Tan is right, then, given their commitment to national self-determination, nationalists should favour greater reductions in global inequality: nationalists and strong cosmopolitans should converge on the same conclusion.

But is Tan's argument persuasive? It should be noted that some of the arguments that Tan uses to support his claim rely on contingent facts about the way in which the global institutional order is currently structured. For example, Tan points out that within the International Monetary Fund (IMF), voting rights are distributed according to wealth: the richer a country is, the more extensive the set of voting rights it is granted. One consequence of this is that economic inequalities are transformed into political ones: states that are worse off in financial terms wield less influence within an important international organization.[25] But this is a result of current IMF rules, not an inevitable upshot of international inequality. If the rules were changed, this particular problem would go away, even if economic inequality persisted. Thus, nationalists could argue that all Tan has shown is that they should oppose the current distribution of voting power within the IMF; he has not shown that they should be committed to global equality.

A similar point applies to a related argument that Tan makes about the World Trade Organization (WTO). Tan gestures toward the asymmetric capacities of rich and poor members to ensure that their trading partners comply with WTO rules.[26] Although rich countries can keep others in line by threatening to limit access to their valuable markets, similar threats made by poor countries are ineffectual: their markets are too insignificant for the prospect of reduced access to incentivize compliance among the rich. This appears to be another way in which economic inequality translates into a political inequality that undermines poorer nations' capacities for self-determination. But, again, the power differentials in question are attributable to the way in which international institutions are currently structured – and, more specifically, to WTO rules governing dispute settlement: they do not flow directly from international inequality. If WTO rules

---

24 Kok-Chor Tan, *Justice Without Borders: Cosmopolitanism, Nationalism, and Patriotism* (Cambridge: Cambridge University Press, 2004), 116–121.
25 Ibid., p. 119.
26 Ibid., pp. 119–120.

were changed – if, for example, poorer members were permitted to *collectively* withhold market access from uncooperative wealthy states or to nominate countries with larger markets to retaliate against rich rule-breakers on their behalf[27] – then, even if economic inequality were not eliminated, the particular problem under consideration would be resolved. Nationalists could acknowledge that their commitment to self-determination entails opposition to existing WTO rules without feeling bound to sign up to global egalitarianism.

But now let us ask why the institutional revisions that I have just recommended have not actually been made. The answer is surely that the status quo is beneficial to wealthy nations and that those nations have used the superior bargaining power that their greater wealth affords to preserve it and to block proposals for reform. Thus, notwithstanding the comments made in the previous two paragraphs, one might still argue that respecting the interests that nations have in self-determination involves securing distributive equality: if countries are to negotiate on an equal footing within international fora, wealth disparities must be radically reduced. Interestingly, Michael Blake has voiced support for the view that promoting national self-determination requires the equalization of material holdings. In his early contributions to the global justice debate, Blake argued *against* global equality, as we saw in the previous chapter. But in more recent work, Blake claims that although equality is not valuable "for its own sake", it plays an important instrumental role in securing "the democratic self-government demanded by justice".[28] He concludes that the policy proposals recommended by his analysis will be "markedly similar" to those favoured by strong cosmopolitans.[29]

Why, then, do many nationalists remain sceptical about global egalitarianism? Nationalists have advanced a number of arguments against pursuing distributive equality beyond national borders, and the remaining sections of this chapter will be devoted to their evaluation.

5.4 National self-determination and global egalitarianism

Two nationalist arguments against global equality appeal directly to the value of national self-determination. According to the first of these arguments, while egalitarian redistribution might promote the self-determination of

---

27 Robert E. Hudec, "Broadening the Scope of Remedies in WTO Dispute Settlement", in Friedl Weiss and Jochem Wiers (eds.), *Improving WTO Dispute Settlement Procedures* (Folkestone: Cameron May Publishers, 2000).

28 Michael Blake, "Coercion and Egalitarian Justice", *The Monist*, vol. 94, no. 4, 2011, pp. 555–570, at p. 567. It is worth noting that, in work published subsequent to that cited above, Miller has also expressed sympathy for this line of argument. See David Miller, *National Responsibility and Global Justice* (Oxford: Oxford University Press, 2007), pp. 75–77.

29 Ibid., p. 569.

currently disadvantaged nations, such redistribution will undermine the self-determination of the better-off. Global egalitarianism recommends taking from the rich and giving to the less fortunate, but this policy reduces the capacity of wealthy nations to be self-directing. And, according to some nationalists, that is unacceptable.[30]

This argument suffers from a number of problems. First, as we have already seen, egalitarian redistribution enhances capacities for self-determination among the currently disadvantaged; it moves us from a world in which those capacities are concentrated in the hands of the wealthy to a world where those capacities are more evenly shared. From a nationalist perspective that emphasizes the importance of self-determination, it is not at all obvious why the former world should be preferred to the latter.[31]

Second, if we take seriously the case for global equality made in the previous chapter, claiming that redistribution from richer to poorer nations compromises the former's self-determination amounts to saying that after a fair distribution of goods has been established, nations that previously benefitted from an unfair distribution have fewer resources with which to do as they please. But, when stated in this way, it becomes unclear why this complaint should be thought to carry any weight whatsoever. A thief has fewer resources with which to do as he pleases after the state returns the goods he stole to their rightful owners; the thief's self-determination is diminished by the state's intervention. But nobody thinks that this fact tells against the state's actions. The thief's misappropriation of other people's property enhances his capacity to be self-directing but that enhanced capacity is not something to which he is entitled; thus, he has no legitimate grievance when the state's enforcement of property rights reduces that capacity. Similarly, wealthy states that benefit from an unjust distribution of resources have no complaint when egalitarian measures redistribute the goods that they currently possess.[32]

Now, it might be said that, unlike a thief, wealthy nations have not *stolen* the resources at their disposal. Setting aside the point that some wealthy nations *have* stolen (with brazen and brutal audacity) goods to which they clearly had no right, the most relevant point here is that if our theory of justice implies that these nations are *not entitled* to the resources in their possession, then those resources are *morally akin* to stolen goods, regardless of whether or not they were actively *taken*. If these nations resist calls for international redistribution, they act like an unscrupulous neighbour who refuses

---

30 Samuel Black, "Individualism at an Impasse", *Canadian Journal of Philosophy*, vol. 21, no. 3, 1991, pp. 347–377, at pp. 360–362, 373–377.

31 Simon Caney, "Global Equality of Opportunity and the Sovereignty of States", in Tony Coates (ed.), *International Justice* (Aldershot: Ashgate, 2000), p. 135.

32 For related considerations, see ibid., pp. 134–135; Tan, *Justice Without Borders*, pp. 100–101.

to return my lawn chairs after a strong wind blows them into her yard (the major difference being that the resources in question are considerably more important than mere garden furniture).

The nationalist argument that we have just considered (and rejected) claims that global egalitarianism objectionably limits the self-determination of wealthy nations. According to a second nationalist argument, global egalitarianism reduces the self-determination of *poor* nations. The thought is that some poor nations may be less efficient at managing their affairs than external agencies, and that when this is the case, global egalitarianism will recommend intrusive interference in the nation's internal affairs. This argument is made by Miller, who suggests that global egalitarians are compelled "to take seriously the case for benevolent imperialism".[33]

How should we respond to this argument? One possible reply is to make the concessive point that global egalitarians can and ought to endorse a *pluralistic* moral outlook that recognizes the importance of a variety of different values. In other words, we should, according to this line of reasoning, acknowledge that distributive equality is but one of several goods that we should seek to promote. In addition to valuing equality, we should care about a number of other ideals, including liberty, community, democracy, and, most relevantly for present purposes, self-determination. And we should concede that when these different values come into conflict, equality will not always be the one to which we ought to defer: sometimes other goods should take priority. Thus, when global equality can be further promoted only by intrusively intervening in the internal affairs of disadvantaged nations, we ought to concede that sometimes equality should be sacrificed for the sake of self-determination.[34]

An alternative to thinking of equality as one good among many is to incorporate a respect for pluralism into an egalitarian outlook. When I initially set out the egalitarian ideal in the previous chapter, I couched it in terms of equalizing opportunities for a flourishing life. Since then, I have written almost exclusively about equalizing wealth. But, as all but the most miserly individuals will acknowledge, money is not the only thing that one requires in order to flourish. If we think, plausibly enough, that self-determination is one of the things that contribute to a flourishing existence, then opportunities for self-determination should be among the bundle of goods that we seek to equalize. Framed in this way, global egalitarianism does not conflict with respecting the self-determination of disadvantaged nations; rather, the importance of self-determination is acknowledged from *within* an egalitarian perspective.[35]

---

33 Miller, *On Nationality*, p. 77.

34 Cecile Fabre, "Global Egalitarianism: An Indefensible Theory of Justice?", in Daniel A. Bell and Avner de-Shalit (eds.), *Forms of Justice: Critical Perspectives on David Miller's Political Philosophy* (Lanham, MD: Rowman & Littlefield, 2002), p. 318, pp. 327–328.

35 Caney, "Global Equality of Opportunity and the Sovereignty of States", p. 139.

5.5 Global egalitarianism and special duties to compatriots

We have just encountered two versions of the nationalist worry that global egalitarianism unduly restricts the scope of national self-determination. A related concern is that the pursuit of equality at the global level would leave no space for the special obligations that we owe to our fellow nationals. This objection starts from the premise that co-nationals have special duties to each other by virtue of the special relationship in which they stand. Indeed, Miller maintains that such duties are *constitutive* of nationality: part of what it *means* to recognize an individual as a co-national is to acknowledge special duties toward her; failure to acknowledge such duties would be a failure to properly understand the relationship.[36] The problem with global egalitarianism is said to be that it proscribes the exercise of these duties. If we are required to ensure that nationality is not a source of inequality, it is hard to see how exercising special duties to co-nationals could be permissible, for an inevitable consequence of discharging such duties will surely be that co-nationals are made better off than foreigners. Thus, if we are to take nationality seriously, we must abandon aspirations for global equality.

One way to respond to this objection is simply to reject the claim that nationality entails special duties to co-nationals. We can accept that special duties are constitutive of *some* relationships (families and friendships, for example) but deny that this is true of nationality. A friend who fails to acknowledge special duties toward you is clearly no friend at all, and a parent who recognizes no (or only minimal) duties to his children obviously has an impoverished conception of parenthood: special duties are central to these kinds of relationships. But why think that this is also true of nationality? The relationship we share with our fellow nationals – the vast majority of whom are complete strangers to us – does not obviously belong in the same category as our relationships with our families and friends. Although Miller expresses various doubts, it seems quite "possible to value national identity in the sense of taking pleasure in the various cultural features and cultural activities that one shares with one's fellow countrymen, while thinking that this has no ethical significance" and no consequences for the scope of one's duties.[37] Miller suggests that this is not how "we" actually experience our national identities,[38] but this seems to beg the question by simply assuming a nationalist outlook.

Another way to respond to the nationalist objection currently under scrutiny is to argue that even if we were to concede that nationality entails special duties to compatriots, this would not pose a challenge to global

---

36 Miller, *National Responsibility and Global Justice*, p. 40; cf. pp. 35–36.
37 Ibid., p. 40.
38 Ibid.

egalitarianism, for, contrary to what nationalists such as Miller have claimed, global egalitarianism is in fact *compatible* with such duties. Recall the point, made right at the start of the previous chapter, that egalitarianism comes in different varieties and different strengths. Recall, in particular, the observation that egalitarianism might require either the *eradication* or *reduction* of inequality. These considerations reveal how global egalitarianism can be reconciled with special duties to co-nationals. An advocate of global egalitarianism could hold that while justice requires the mere *reduction* of inequality at the global level, our special relationship with our co-nationals grounds a special duty to *eradicate* inequality domestically. In other words, our recognition of special duties to fellow nationals is expressed in our adoption of a stronger version of egalitarianism at the national level.[39]

5.6 Global egalitarianism and national responsibility

Earlier, we addressed the nationalist claim that global egalitarianism will license unwarranted interference in the affairs of disadvantaged nations. A rather different nationalist complaint is that global egalitarians will insist on the provision of *undeserved assistance* to such nations. To illustrate this misgiving, Miller asks us to consider two pairs of fictional nations: (1) Affluenza and Ecologia and (2) Procreatia and Condominium. Affluenza rapidly expends the resources at its disposal in a myopic quest for immediate gain, whereas Ecologia adopts a policy of conservation. Meanwhile, Procreatia encourages large families whereas Condominium carefully regulates population growth. One upshot of the divergent policies pursued by the two pairs of countries is that the members of Ecologia and Condominium ultimately end up with a larger share of resources than those of Affluenza and Procreatia. Now, Miller suggests that an implication of global egalitarianism is that Affluenza and Procreatia are entitled to resource transfers from Ecologia and Condominium. But this, Miller objects, is unfair: the flip side of national self-determination is national responsibility; reckless nations should bear the burdens of the decisions that they make, and their prudent counterparts should not be required to bail them out.[40]

The first point to note about Miller's hypothetical cases is that they have limited applicability to the world in which we actually live. As has been noted several times already in this book, many of the burdens borne by less advantaged nations appear to be attributable not to choices that they have

---

39 This argument draws on considerations advanced in Chris Armstrong, "National Self-Determination, Global Equality and Moral Arbitrariness", *Journal of Political Philosophy*, vol. 18, no. 3, 2010, pp. 313–334, at pp. 322–323.

40 Miller, *National Responsibility and Global Justice*, pp. 68–72. For a similar argument, see John Rawls, *The Law of Peoples* (Cambridge, MA: Harvard University Press 1999), pp. 117–118.

made but to factors beyond their control: poorer countries are disadvantaged by geography and by harmful features of the global institutional order. Therefore, even if we think that it would be unfair to redistribute to Miller's fictional disadvantaged nations (which are responsible for their own plight), it does not follow that it would be unfair to redistribute to the disadvantaged nations that actually exist.

A second point to note is that even when national communities *do* make poor decisions, the nature of the consequences that attach to those decisions is influenced by the character of the institutional environment in which they are made. As Thomas Pogge observes, "the burdens typically arising from unfortunate decisions are much larger under some designs of the institutional order than under others", even in the absence of straightforward redistributive measures that essentially nullify the decisions in question.[41] Pogge illustrates this point with a domestic example. He notes that, at the societal level, we might choose to permit debt bondage. If we did, and I found myself unable to repay a loan that I had taken out, bearing the full consequences of my actions would involve slaving away for my creditor. But in decent societies, the legal system outlaws debt bondage, so although I will still incur certain burdens by defaulting on my loan repayments, I will not be reduced to virtual slavery.[42] Similarly, how the international order is structured affects the nature of the costs that flow from poor decisions at the national level. Pogge writes:

> The international order can be so structured that the rules of the world economy reflect the bargaining power of the various states [which in turn reflects their relative wealth], effectively preventing poorer societies from achieving rates of economic growth that are easily available to richer ones – or this order can be structured so that, regardless of the distribution of power, it maintains fair and open markets that actually make it easier for poorer than for richer societies to achieve high rates of economic growth.[43]

Under the first design of the international order – which is the one that is currently in place – the consequences of poor decisions are much graver than they would be under the less punitive alternative that Pogge describes. Under the current order, poor decisions that reduce a nation's wealth, and thereby its bargaining power, also reduce its capacity to secure equitable trading rules and the economic opportunities that such rules could provide. The crux of Pogge's argument is that even if Miller is right to say that nations should bear

---

41 Thomas Pogge, "Do Rawls's Two Theories of Justice Fit Together?", in Rex Martin and David A. Reidy (eds.), *Rawls's Law of Peoples: A Realistic Utopia?* (Oxford: Blackwell, 2006), p. 215.
42 Ibid.
43 Ibid.

the consequences of their decisions, we will still have to decide, when designing our social institutions, precisely what those consequences will be. The claim that one should bear the consequences of one's choices is often heard in debates about both domestic and global politics. That the consequences which flow from our decisions are not a fixed product of nature but a labile outcome of social choice is an important insight that we would all do well to keep in mind.

A further problem with the "undeserved assistance" argument is that it is unfair to individuals.[44] This unfairness arises from the fact that the argument treats the nation as a single entity with a unified will rather than as a collection of independent persons. When we say that "the nation" spent profligately or that "the nation" pursued a path of sustainable development, what we typically mean is that *some subset* of the nation's members chose these policies. The corollary of this is that some *other* subset of the nation's members did *not* choose them. When the adverse consequences of "national" decisions are dispersed throughout the national community, burdens are inevitably borne by individuals who played no part in creating them. This is especially problematical in autocratic states in which ordinary citizens lack formal opportunities to influence the conduct of their government; when governments choose poorly, it is non-culpable citizens who pay the price. A related problem with expecting national communities to bear the consequences of imprudent decisions is that those decisions will often have long-term effects. But this is unfair to those who were still children when the decisions were taken and to those who were not yet born. Why, it is natural to ask, should future generations be expected to bear the costs of choices made by their forebears? In short, then, the nationalist claim that global egalitarianism insists upon the provision of undeserved assistance is off the mark.

5.7 The limits of human motivation

Let's consider another nationalist objection to global egalitarianism. It is sometimes said that the case for global equality rests on an unrealistic conception of human nature. When thinking about what justice requires, we should be sensitive to the limits of human motivation, and, according to this line of reasoning, global egalitarians fail to take those limits seriously. More specifically, they fail to recognize that although individuals can be motivated to contribute to the wellbeing of their fellow nationals, with whom they share common characteristics and common bonds, they cannot reliably be motivated to make sacrifices for those outside of their community.

---

44 Charles R. Beitz, "Social and Cosmopolitan Liberalism", *International Affairs*, vol. 75, no. 3, 1999, pp. 515–529, at pp. 526–528; Simon Caney, "Cosmopolitanism and Justice", in Thomas Christiano and John Christman (eds.), *Contemporary Debates in Political Philosophy* (Malden, MA: Blackwell, 2009), pp. 400–401.

To bolster this argument, Miller appeals to the historical character of nations that I mentioned earlier and, in particular, to the mythical elements that typically infuse a national community's preferred account of its own past. He suggests that national myths "perform a moralizing role, by holding up before us the virtues of our ancestors and encouraging us to live up to them".[45] By promulgating these myths, nations can ensure that their members' "sense of solidarity with and obligation to their compatriots [is] increased".[46] More generally, Miller suggests that when it comes to identifying the right conception of justice, it is not enough to show that a particular conception is supported by rationally compelling arguments; rather, the correct account of justice must track our natural dispositions. It must accommodate the fact that there are certain sentiments that we naturally feel toward members of our community but not toward outsiders.[47] Although there may be "a small number of heroic individuals who are genuinely able to govern their lives by considerations of pure principle", the vast majority are not capable of doing this, and our moral theorizing should reflect that fact.[48]

One might try to support Miller's claims by pointing to the paltry amounts that affluent individuals actually donate to charities supporting the foreign needy or to the fact that so many wealthy individuals voice opposition to foreign aid programmes. But there are multiple problems with this strategy. First, reluctance to give unilaterally (i.e., even when others are not giving) is not the same as reluctance to contribute to a cooperative endeavour in which many people participate. As Peter Singer writes, "our sense of fairness makes us less likely to give when others are not doing so, [and] the converse also holds: we are much more likely to do the right thing if we think others are already doing it".[49] Unwillingness to give may sometimes be grounded in an aversion to making sacrifices that are not being made by others, rather than in a lack of concern for those who would benefit from one's giving. We may baulk at being expected to contribute when others are doing nothing, or very little, but be happy to contribute when we can see that others are doing their fair share.

Second, although the belief that foreign aid programmes are too generous is widespread, so too is ignorance about the size of foreign aid budgets; people consistently overestimate how much our governments spend. Singer notes:

> In four different surveys that asked Americans what portion of government spending ... goes to foreign aid, the median answers ranged from 15 percent to 20 percent. The correct answer is less

---

45 Miller, *On Nationality*, p. 36.
46 Ibid.
47 Ibid., pp. 57–58.
48 Ibid., p. 58.
49 Peter Singer, *The Life You Can Save: Acting Now to End World Poverty* (London: Picador, 2009), p. 64.

> than 1 percent... A majority of people in these surveys also said that America gives too much aid – but when they were asked how much America should give, the median answers ranged from 5 percent to 10 percent of government spending. In other words, people wanted foreign aid "cut" to an amount five to ten times greater than the United States actually gives![50]

Third, we cannot identify the right thing to do simply by looking at what people are already doing. If we could, moral and political philosophers like me would be out of a job. But that would be the least of our worries. If we thought we could work out how we ought to act by simply observing common patterns of behaviour, then, in other times and places, we would have had to conclude that slavery, feudalism, and various other barbarous practices were actually morally acceptable. Moreover, we would be compelled to endorse a number of contemporary practices that Miller and other nationalists wish to condemn, such as the exploitation of weak states by the more powerful.

A more general response to Miller's view is that if it is indeed "heroic" to act in solidarity with those who are not members of one's own community, then there must be a lot of heroes out there. Consider the fact that in the UK alone there are over one and a half million vegetarians, many of whom are motivated by a desire to avoid contributing to the abuse and exploitation of non-human animals. These people are willing to forego widely available benefits for the sake of individuals beyond their community – indeed, beyond their species. The suggestion that they are acting in a "heroic" capacity is flattering but clearly absurd. The dispositions that Miller regards as exceptional are actually held by large numbers of people, and this fact undermines the claim that global egalitarianism fails to respect the limits of human motivation.[51]

A second general response to Miller's argument, and an especially important one, is that we should not think of human motivation as static or as unamenable to change. From the premise that humans currently tend to be less concerned about outsiders than about their co-nationals, we cannot infer that they are bound to remain that way. Nor should we conclude that we have no choice but to simply wait for them to change. After all, as Tan has argued, nation-building projects that seek to stimulate the emergence of communal bonds among co-nationals are themselves expansionary in character; their aim is to bring within our sphere of concern those who were previously regarded as mere strangers. As Tan notes, "the purpose of a common nationality ... is to enable citizens to transcend the local and parochial bonds and ties of family, kin, and tribe, and to extend the scope of their

---

50 Ibid., p. 35.
51 For a similar argument, see Caney, *Justice Beyond Borders*, p. 133.

moral universe to also encompass strangers".[52] If nationalists are right to suggest that these nation-building endeavours have been largely successful, why terminate our efforts at the boundaries of our nation? "[W]hy not capitalize on this 'expansionary momentum' to expand the scope of our moral concern beyond conationals to include also foreigners?"[53]

At one stage in his argument, Miller claims that one advantage of nationalist theories over cosmopolitan alternatives is that the obligations associated with the former, unlike those associated with the latter, need not stand in tension with our own personal projects. He writes: "to the extent that I really do identify with the group or community in question, there need be no sharp conflict between fulfilling my obligations and pursuing my own goals and purposes. The group's interests are among the goals that I set myself to advance".[54] By contrast, Miller argues, fulfilling the global obligations defended by strong cosmopolitans "involves driving a wedge between ethical duty and personal identity".[55] This is because, when it comes to grounding these duties, no "considerations about who I am, where I have come from, or which communities I see myself as attached to" can play a role.[56]

But Miller's claims are vulnerable to a number of powerful objections. First, the national culture that we identify with might have an *inter*nationalist (or cosmopolitan) character. To illustrate, notice that when Donald Trump announced a reduction in the number of refugees who would be admitted into the US, many of his critics objected to this policy on the grounds that it was un-American. They pointed to the country's tradition of welcoming displaced people and condemned Trump for departing from that tradition. Those who protested against Trump's policies appealed to sentiments expressed in "The New Colossus", the poem inscribed on the Statue of Liberty, which reads, in part: "Give me your tired, your poor, your huddled masses yearning to be free". The former British prime minister, Gordon Brown, pursued a similar strategy when he campaigned for Britain to remain in the EU. In a speech titled "Lead not Leave", Brown cast Britain as a country that had played a leading role in promoting a culture of human rights throughout Europe. He noted the important role that Britain played in liberating Nazi concentration camps and in resisting Soviet expansionism.

The relevant point here is this: to the degree that Britain and the US have internationalist traditions – traditions which emphasize our moral obligations to outsiders – it is simply false to claim that no "considerations about who I am, where I have come from, or which communities I see myself as attached to" can play a role in motivating support for cosmopolitan ends. We

---

52 Tan, *Justice Without Borders*, p. 104.
53 Ibid., pp. 104–105. Cf. Charles R. Beitz, "Rawls's Law of Peoples", *Ethics*, vol. 110, no. 4, 2000, pp. 669–696, at p. 683.
54 Miller, *On Nationality*, p. 66.
55 Ibid., p. 57.
56 Ibid.

do not have to drive "a wedge between ethical duty and personal identity" since our personal identity is shaped by a national culture that embraces cosmopolitan values.

Now, it might be said that Brown gave an unduly romanticized account of British history, an account which conveniently ignores the many instances where Britain has chosen to trample over the rights of other peoples. But, as we have seen, nationalists also present romanticized versions of our history, and thinkers like Miller suggest that it is appropriate to do so when this promotes the achievement of moral goals.

A second objection to Miller's argument is made by Gillian Brock, who points out that driving a wedge between ethical duty and personal identity is a common demand of a moral life and that there is nothing unusual or unacceptable about the requirement to do so. As Brock writes: "In the usual course of our ethical deliberation, we are constantly asked to set aside feelings of attachment that stem from personal identity".[57] For example, if we are interviewing applicants for a job, and a family member or close friend is among the shortlisted candidates, it is uncontroversial to believe that we must set aside our personal ties and make an impartial decision. "We must get used to doing such things if we aim to justify our actions".[58]

It is also worth mentioning that if the pursuit of national projects aligns closely with our own personal interests, we have a reason to subject those projects to especially careful moral scrutiny. As Brock writes,

> we should be suspicious of relying heavily on what human sentiment makes so easy and obvious. It is precisely because helping members of our own group is so fulfilling and beneficial that we must be very careful; we may need help (especially from more cosmopolitan theories) to check that we are not merely rationalizing what we are inclined to do anyhow.[59]

Miller assumes that it is a virtue of nationalism that it tracks our natural sentiments. But one must be wary of the fact that nationalism may appear to be an appealing morality *simply because* it chimes with our self-interested preferences and independently of whether there are good reasons to endorse it.

5.8 The value of natural resources

We have seen that many nationalist objections to global egalitarianism miss their target. Before this chapter is concluded, one final objection should be considered, one which targets the feasibility of the egalitarian claim that

---

57 Gillian Brock, *Global Justice: A Cosmopolitan Account* (Oxford: Oxford University Press, 2009), pp. 261–262.
58 Ibid., p. 262.
59 Ibid.

resource-rich countries should compensate the less advantaged. A common egalitarian claim is that resource-rich nations should be taxed according to their holdings and that the funds generated by this tax should be transferred to nations with a smaller resource endowment.[60] But some nationalists have objected that we cannot compare the relative worth of resources located in different territories, for the level of value attributed to a particular set of resources will vary from one national community to the next: we lack a common metric with which to make authoritative comparisons. Miller illustrates this point with a number of examples. A tract of land well suited to the cultivation of vineyards will be ascribed greater value in a wine-drinking society than in a society in which the consumption of alcohol contravenes the edicts of the dominant religion. Similarly, oil discovered beneath Mecca would have less value for the Saudis, presuming that they would be unwilling to extract it, than it would for those outsiders who do not regard the site as sacred and inviolable.[61] But if there is disagreement about the value to assign to resources, implementing egalitarian justice will be less than straightforward; indeed, it may not always be clear which of two nations is endowed with greater resource wealth.

It is important, however, not to exaggerate the difficulties involved. After all, there is considerable disagreement about the value of resources *within* national societies, yet we do not think of this as an insurmountable obstacle to securing distributive justice at the domestic level. This point is made by Daniel Weinstock.

> In Canada, for example, entire "forms of life" have emerged out of industries concerned with the extraction of various natural resources. For inhabitants of fishing villages of Newfoundland, of the farmlands of the Prairies, or of the logging villages of British Columbia, the resources that they harvest represent more than just fungible goods, the full value of which might be fully expressed in monetary terms or traded off against other goods. Rather, they are laden with meaning and symbolic value, as befits the resources around which a community has organized its life. The situation with respect to these resources is completely different, say, for urban dwellers within the same country. It is much more likely that they will have a more pragmatic dollars and cents approach to these resources.[62]

Weinstock observes that these examples "reveal that national communities are often bitterly divided over the correct meaning to ascribe to different

---

60 For a discussion of different versions of this proposal, see Paula Casal, "Global Taxes on Natural Resources", *Journal of Moral Philosophy*, vol. 8, no. 3, 2011, pp. 307–328.
61 Miller, *National Responsibility and Global Justice*, p. 59.
62 Daniel M. Weinstock, "Miller on Distributive Justice", in Daniel A. Bell and Avner de-Shalit (eds.), *Forms of Justice*, p. 277.

kinds of resources and of the relative weight they ought to be granted ..."[63] These intra-national disagreements about how resources should be valued create problems when it comes to resolving distributional conflicts domestically. Is it permissible to liberalize domestic markets, and reap the benefits of free trade, even if this means allowing certain industries to buckle under the weight of foreign competition, provided that we compensate the losers with financial payments? Or are such payments incommensurate with other values that are lost when the industries in question collapse? These questions are not obviously easier to resolve than their international equivalents, yet we do not respond by abandoning the quest for domestic justice.

Of course, pointing out that versions of problems that apply globally also apply nationally does not *resolve* the former set of problems – finding a resolution will require further philosophical labour. But what has been said so far should make us suspicious of theories that inflate problems that arise at the global level while remaining untroubled by analogous issues that arise domestically.

5.9 Conclusion

In this chapter, we have seen that a variety of nationalist arguments fail to undermine the case for global equality. Moreover, we have seen that a number of nationalist considerations actually bolster this case. If we care about ensuring that national communities can collectively determine their internal affairs, then we should support efforts to radically reduce global inequality. Moreover, we should take inspiration from the success of nation-building projects in expanding the scope of people's moral concern and seek to extend such projects outward, beyond the borders of the national realm, to encompass those distant strangers whom we have so often treated with unacceptable disregard.

---

63   Ibid.

6 IMMIGRATION

While this book was being written, Donald Trump took office as the 45th president of the United States. One of Trump's most headline-grabbing campaign pledges was his promise to build a wall along the US-Mexico border, a proposal which foreshadowed a more general crackdown on immigration initiated in the first months of his presidency. This crackdown has been controversial among Americans, and much of the resultant debate has focused on the question of whether tighter border controls serve the national interest. Some Americans resent the presence of immigrants in their country; others recognize the contribution that immigrants make to their economy and culture and worry that reduced immigration will make them worse-off. This way of framing the debate is not atypical. In popular discourse about immigration, the right of a political community to exercise discretionary control over its territorial borders is standardly taken for granted, and the contested issue is how best to exercise that right in order to enhance the community's prospects. Disagreement centres on what is good for the country, not on whether the good of the country is the only, or most relevant, consideration.

Although this approach is based on widely shared convictions, it is patently unacceptable from the standpoint of justice. More specifically, it is incompatible with the moral cosmopolitanism introduced in Chapter 4. Rehearsing the central tenet of that doctrine, Joseph Carens notes that it "is never enough to justify a set of social arrangements governing human beings to say that these arrangements are good for us, without regard for others".[1] Rather, we "have to appeal to principles and arguments that take everyone's interests into account or that explain why the social arrangements are reasonable and fair to everyone who is subject to them".[2] Accordingly, we cannot justify any given immigration regime simply by pointing out that it benefits members of the community imposing it; we must also be able to

---

1 Joseph Carens, *The Ethics of Immigration* (New York: Oxford University Press, 2013), p. 227.
2 Ibid.

demonstrate that the regime is reasonable from the perspective of outsiders. Our question, then, is what kind of immigration regime can satisfy this requirement. An answer to this question would enable us to determine, among other things, whether the Trump administration's crackdown is at worst *imprudent* – because arguably detrimental to the national interest – or also unjust.

With regard to the moral rights that states have in relation to prospective immigrants who wish to enter their territory, there are three possibilities. States may have an *unlimited* right to exclude, a *limited* right to exclude, or *no* right to exclude. If states have an unlimited right to exclude, then it is morally permissible for them to close their borders, excluding anyone who wishes to enter. If states have a limited right to exclude, then they are morally required to admit some but not all of those who seek admission. And if states have no right to exclude, then they are morally forbidden from excluding anyone. Few reasonable people claim that states have an unlimited right to exclude. It is widely accepted, for example, that states have a moral (as well as a legal) duty to admit that class of migrants recognized as refugees. Similarly, few reasonable people claim that states have no right to exclude. It is hard to imagine anyone arguing that states are morally required to admit known terrorists, for example, or individuals who pose a serious threat to public health. The relevant question, then, concerns the *extent* of the right to exclude. In this chapter, we shall examine considerations that have been thought to constrain the extent of that right as well as considerations that have been thought to expand it.

It is widely believed that although a state's right to exclude is not unlimited, it is nevertheless extensive. There is a duty to admit those fleeing political persecution in their country of origin, but beyond that, states are free to exclude at will. As we shall see, this widespread conviction is difficult to sustain.

6.1 Immigration and radical global inequality

The most significant considerations that appear to constrain a state's moral right to exclude are ones that we have already encountered. In Chapters 3 and 4, we saw that our world is staggeringly unequal. Whereas its more advantaged inhabitants reside in safe, prosperous democracies, which furnish many of their members with ample opportunities to cultivate meaningful and fulfilling lives, the worst-off languish in dysfunctional states plagued by severe, life-threatening poverty. Moreover, we saw that the position one occupies in this global hierarchy is typically an accident of birth, a product of brute luck. We concluded that the affluent have demanding duties to assist those who are disadvantaged by this radical inequality. But the maintenance of restrictive border controls can appear incompatible with the successful fulfilment of these duties. When US agents patrolling the Chihuahuan

Desert arrest families fleeing poverty and violence in Mexico and Central America, how, if at all, can the acts of the former be reconciled with the demands of global justice? When US politicians license border guards to exclude such migrants, are they not thereby neglecting their duties of assistance?

This concern cuts even deeper than may initially be apparent. When wealthy states coercively prevent desperately poor individuals from entering their territory, they do not simply fail to assist them; rather, they actively undermine the efforts of those who otherwise *would* provide assistance. There are businesses in Texan border towns like Hidalgo and McAllen that would willingly employ Mexican immigrants, and there are churches and other charitable bodies that would happily feed, clothe, and shelter them. By detaining such migrants, border guards in the Rio Grande Valley prevent those organizations from rendering assistance. This point is made by Chandran Kukathas, who writes:

> very good reasons must be offered to justify turning the disadvantaged away. It would be bad enough to meet such people with indifference and to deny them positive assistance. It would be even worse to deny them the opportunity to help themselves. To go to the length of denying one's fellow citizens the right to help those who are badly off, whether by employing them or by simply taking them in, seems even more difficult to justify – if, indeed, it is not entirely perverse.[3]

These considerations suggest that many of the immigration restrictions imposed by wealthy democratic states may be unjust in virtue of the role that they play in the preservation of radical global inequality. This view has been vividly expressed by Carens, who suggests that discretionary state control over immigration has produced, on a global scale, an institutional order that bears a troubling resemblance to medieval feudalism. He writes:

> In many ways, citizenship in Western democracies is the modern equivalent of feudal class privilege – an inherited status that greatly enhances one's life chances. To be born a citizen of a rich state in Europe or North America is like being born into the nobility (even though many of us belong to the lesser nobility). To be born a citizen of a poor country in Asia or Africa is like being born into the peasantry in the Middle Ages (even if there are a few rich peasants and some peasants manage to gain entry to the

---

3 Chandran Kukathas, "The Case for Open Immigration", in Andrew I. Cohen and Christopher Heath Wellman (eds.), *Contemporary Debates in Applied Ethics*, Second Edition (Malden, MA: Blackwell Publishing, 2005), p. 380.

nobility). Like feudal birthright privileges, contemporary social arrangements not only grant great advantages on the basis of birth but also entrench these advantages by legally restricting mobility, making it extremely difficult for those born into a socially disadvantaged position to overcome that disadvantage, no matter how hard they work.[4]

Carens concludes: "Like feudal practices, these contemporary social arrangements are hard to justify when one thinks about them closely".[5]

In criticizing restrictive immigration policies, Carens appeals to the value of equal opportunity. In Carens's view, an important objection to restrictive border measures is that they make equality of opportunity impossible.[6] Here, I want to focus on a narrower objection, one which Carens's view incorporates but goes beyond. According to this objection, immigration restrictions imposed by wealthy states contribute to the maintenance of severe global poverty. They do not merely obstruct the achievement of equality of opportunity (which might be bad enough in itself) but sustain the radical material inequality that exists between the exceptionally poor and the exceptionally rich. They do this by denying the world's poorest people a means of escaping their plight.

How could this be justified? Why should wealthy states enjoy the freedom to exclude the world's poor? Notice that international law does impose some constraints on the discretionary control that states can exercise over their borders: it compels them to admit refugees who arrive in their territory. But these constraints are fairly limited, for the law's understanding of a refugee is rather narrow. According to the 1951 Refugee Convention, to be recognized as a refugee one must be a target of persecution. The UN Refugee Agency (UNHCR) adopts a slightly broader understanding, recognizing as refugees those who are victims of *generalized* – and not only targeted – violence, such as that which occurs during civil wars. But this broader conception still excludes millions of individuals facing enormous threats to their most fundamental interests. It is natural to ask why, if the right of wealthy states to exclude outsiders is constrained by the interests of refugees, that right is not also constrained by the interests of the desperately poor.

In this connection, notice that the world's poor resemble refugees in a number of important respects. To begin with, both groups face threats to their basic interests, and it is hard to maintain that the threats faced by refugees are any more serious than those endured by the poor. As Thomas Pogge notes,

> the politically persecuted are not, in general, worse off than the desperately poor. Being imprisoned for one's beliefs is not, in

---

4 Carens, *Ethics of Immigration,* p. 226 (footnote omitted).
5 Ibid.
6 Ibid., pp. 227–228, 235–236.

general, worse than working 16-hour days while being permanently hungry. Being beaten to death for participating in a demonstration is not, in general, worse than dying of diarrhoea or simple starvation.[7]

Moreover, the threats endured by the poor, like those faced by refugees, are threats either that have been created by their government or that their government is unwilling or unable to address. And the poor, like refugees, could benefit enormously by being granted access to the developed world. Why, then, do we not insist that rich countries open their borders to the world's poor? Why compel states to admit those who suffer from political persecution or generalized violence but not those burdened by crushing poverty?

One possible response to this question begins by suggesting that states have a duty to admit refugees because this is the only way in which they can render assistance. Threatened individuals are recognized as refugees precisely when their grievances can be redressed only through relocation. By contrast, while wealthy states have a duty to contribute to the alleviation of world poverty, they can do this in a variety of different ways, and they are not required to pick any particular strategy from the available options. In other words, wealthy states have what is known as a *disjunctive* duty, a duty that they can discharge by acting in one of several specified ways. They *could* discharge their duty by opening their borders, but they could also discharge their duty by, say, redistributing resources or by promoting institutional reforms that can be expected to stimulate development in the Third World. Provided that they do at least one of these things, they meet their obligations to the world's poor. Therefore, they are not required to open their borders. This argument has been made by Christopher Heath Wellman, who writes:

> no matter how substantial their duties of distributive justice, wealthier countries need not open their borders. At most, affluent societies are duty bound to choose between allowing needy foreigners to enter their society or sending some of their wealth to those less fortunate.[8]

This objection can be taken further. It might be argued that opening borders is not merely one poverty-relief strategy among many but also a *suboptimal* strategy: wealthy states can discharge their duties to the world's poor more

---

[7] Thomas Pogge, "Migration and Poverty", in Veit Bader (ed.), *Citizenship and Exclusion* (Basingstoke: Macmillan, 1997), p. 15. Cf. Kukathas, "The Case for Open Migration", p. 386.

[8] Christopher Heath Wellman, "Immigration and Freedom of Association", *Ethics*, vol. 119, no. 1, 2008, pp. 109–141, at p. 127.

effectively in other ways. It is sometimes said that those who could actually take advantage of open borders would not be among the least advantaged. After all, in order to make the journey from the Third to the First World, one needs resources, resources which the worst-off simply do not have.[9] But other methods of poverty relief – such as foreign aid – can be carefully targeted at the neediest individuals.

A critic could add that although some poor individuals will be able to muster the resources necessary for travel, they will nevertheless find immigrating incredibly burdensome, and, for that reason, opening borders is not a morally acceptable way for wealthy countries to discharge their duties. As Carens concedes: "migration normally has significant costs for the migrants, and having a right to migrate for the sake of opportunity is not the same as having the opportunities one wants in the community into which one was born".[10] If a rich state does nothing to alleviate poverty other than open its borders, it is essentially saying that it will provide the benefits that it is duty-bound to provide only if the world's poor leave their homes and travel across the world to collect them; if the poor are unwilling or unable to do this, the benefits will be withheld. Making assistance conditional on the performance of such an onerous task does not seem reasonable.[11]

These are powerful arguments, but responses are available. To begin with, note that rich states that close their borders to the world's poor may not be able to get themselves off the hook simply by pursuing alternative strategies of poverty relief. Consider a would-be migrant attempting to flee poverty and violence in Honduras who is forcibly prevented from entering the US. Suppose that, in an attempt to justify their actions, US border guards point out that their country sends generous development aid to sub-Saharan Africa (and let us pretend, for the sake of argument, that this is true). How could this fact justify to the Honduran migrant the coercive exclusionary measures to which she is subject? *She* does not benefit from aid sent to Africa. Those funds do not provide *her* with an alternative means of survival. So how can she be expected to regard the US border regime as fair and reasonable? Perhaps development aid *is* a more effective tool for reducing poverty, but assisting some people effectively cannot justify coercively excluding third parties who do not receive that assistance.[12]

---

9 Pogge, "Migration and Poverty", p. 14; Michael Blake, "Discretionary Immigration", *Philosophical Topics*, vol. 30, no. 2, 2002, pp. 273–289, at pp. 281–282; David Miller, "Immigration: The Case for Limits", in Andrew I. Cohen and Christopher Heath Wellman (eds.), *Contemporary Debates in Applied Ethics*, Second Edition (Malden, MA: Blackwell Publishing, 2005), p. 368; Stephen Macedo, "The Moral Dilemma of U.S. Immigration Policy: Open Borders Versus Social Justice?", in Carol M. Swain (ed.), *Debating Immigration* (New York: Cambridge University Press, 2007), p. 79.

10 Carens, *Ethics of Immigration*, pp. 269–270.

11 Kieran Oberman, "Poverty and Immigration Policy", *American Political Science Review*, vol. 109, no. 2, 2015, pp. 239–251, at p. 248.

12 Michael Blake, "Immigration, Jurisdiction, and Exclusion", *Philosophy & Public Affairs*, vol. 41, no. 2, 2013, pp. 103–130, at p. 126.

Relatedly, although resource redistribution and institutional reform are important components of a long-term development strategy, it is important to note that such a strategy will take a considerable amount of time to reach fruition. To be sure, monetary donations can bring immediate and palpable benefits to the world's poorest – by funding a sight-restoring cataract operation, say, or the provision of bed nets that protect sleeping children from malarial mosquitos. But building the kinds of stable, well-functioning institutions that will enable deprived individuals to lead even minimally decent lives takes time. The basic point here is the same as the one made in the previous paragraph: we cannot justify coercively excluding a poor individual from the opportunities available in our country by pointing out that we are committed to poverty relief efforts whose benefits she might never see. This speaks to the point made above about the onerousness of immigrating. *Of course* immigrating is burdensome, but many people would rather bear that burden than waste away their lives waiting for long-term development strategies to bear fruit.

I have considered the claim that opening borders is a suboptimal tool for relieving severe poverty. A different claim is that opening borders is actually *counterproductive*. According to this objection, an open-borders policy undermines the development prospects of poor countries by engendering a phenomenon known as *brain drain*: the large-scale emigration of skilled workers from the Third to the First World. Understandably, when they are able to do so, talented individuals from developing countries often choose to pursue career opportunities in richer states rather than putting their skills to work in their country of origin. Consequently, poor countries lose those citizens most capable of remedying the problems that hinder development.

Brain drain is particularly visible in the medical sector of poor countries. As Lea Ypi reports:

> The number of Ethiopian, Kenyan, and Sierra Leonean doctors and nurses employed in Europe, North America or Australia is greater than in their home countries; South Africa – the state with the largest number of people infected by HIV – has lost a third of its medical staff, most of which has settled in Canada; in Ghana, by 2001, almost half of the University of Ghana Medical School had emigrated, leaving the country without academics to train future doctors and serious consequences for public health. Similar alarming data are reported on the Indian subcontinent and the Caribbean – again with serious loss for states with some of the worst healthcare indicators in the world.[13]

In addition to undermining the provision of important goods such as healthcare, brain drain is problematic because it involves the departure of

---

13 Lea Ypi, "Justice in Migration: A Closed Borders Utopia?", *Journal of Political Philosophy*, vol. 16, no. 4, 2008, pp. 391–418, at p. 402 (footnote omitted).

individuals who are more likely to advocate for the kinds of institutional reform needed to facilitate development. As Caleb Yong records:

> skilled workers are typically better equipped than low-skilled workers to articulate and press demands for reform in the face of inertia or resistance from existing elites. Moreover, advanced education is associated with greater support for democratization and political reform.[14]

Facts such are these are sometimes thought to yield the conclusion that, by welcoming skilled workers from developing countries, rich states actually wrong the world's poor by encouraging the departure of those who are best placed to improve their condition. On this view, global justice requires wealthy states to be *less* accommodating of would-be immigrants from the Third World, not more. Or rather, it requires them to be less accommodating of *certain kinds* of immigrants. In order to avoid perpetuating the debilitating effects of brain drain, rich countries should reduce their intake of *skilled* workers who have important roles to play in their home countries.

However, this matter is more complicated than it might initially appear. Although the emigration of skilled workers can have certain detrimental effects on sending states, it also brings a number of benefits. First, when educated individuals move abroad, they can act like representatives for their country of origin and stimulate the establishment of commercial ties between their old and new homes. They can function as intermediaries between sending and receiving states by encouraging citizens of the latter to invest in the former and by facilitating the establishment and maintenance of trade relations.[15] Second, skilled workers who move from poorer to richer countries often send a portion of their incomes (remittances) to the family members whom they have left behind. As Arash Abizadeh and his co-authors report, "household surveys suggest that about half of interstate migrants remit and the World Bank estimates that officially recorded remittances to developing countries in 2012 totaled $401 billion".[16] Third, after a period of time, emigrants often return to their homes, and when they do, they bring with them important skills and experiences acquired while living and working abroad. These skills enable them to facilitate economic and political development in their country of origin.[17]

---

14 Caleb Yong, "Justice in Labor Immigration Policy", *Social Theory and Practice*, vol. 42, no. 4, 2016, pp. 817–844, at p. 836 (footnote omitted).

15 Ibid., p. 836; Ypi, "Justice in Migration", p. 413.

16 Arash Abizadeh, Manish Pandey, and Sohrab Abizadeh, "Wage competition and the special-obligations challenge to more open borders", *Politics, Philosophy & Economics*, vol. 14, no. 3, 2015, pp. 255–269, at pp. 261–262 (references omitted).

17 Yong, "Justice in Labor Immigration Policy", p. 836.

Importantly, the empirical literature suggests that whether skilled labour emigration will be all-things-considered beneficial or detrimental to a country's development prospects is dependent on certain features of the country in question. The benefits that such emigration can bring are more likely to accrue to middle-income countries with larger populations, whereas the burdens are more likely to befall the least developed countries with smaller populations. This is partly because emigrants from the most dysfunctional states often have little incentive to return.[18]

These observations reveal that concerns about brain drain do not necessarily defeat the claim that wealthy states should take in migrants from poorer countries, even when the migrants in question are skilled workers. At the most, they suggest that wealthy states must exercise caution. While they should open their doors to skilled workers from larger, middle-income countries such as India, China, and Brazil, they have reason to exclude skilled workers from smaller and less developed countries. Yet it should immediately be observed that even this case for limited exclusion can be challenged. It is important to note that wealthy countries might be able to reduce the brain drain without even partially closing their borders. They could try to do this by contributing funds that poor countries can use to improve wages and working conditions, thereby reducing the incentives that their workers have to leave. They could also provide poor countries with funds to train a sufficient number of additional workers to ensure that the departures that do occur do not reduce the skilled workforce below adequate levels.[19]

I began by suggesting that the interests of the world's poor might constrain the moral right of wealthy states to control their borders. By maintaining restrictive border controls, wealthy states appear to disregard their duties to the world's poorest people. We have now considered several arguments that attempt to demonstrate that this appearance is illusory. We have seen that none of these arguments is successful. However, we have not yet vindicated the claim that wealthy states must open their borders to migrants from the Third World. Each of the counter-arguments that we have examined so far has appealed exclusively to the interests of the world's poor. These arguments attempt to show that opening borders is a suboptimal or even counterproductive way of alleviating global poverty. In other words, they try to show that, contrary to what one might think, open borders would actually be bad for the world's poor. A different argument that we have not yet addressed maintains that open borders should be opposed because they would be bad for the *domestic* poor. It is to this argument that we should now turn our attention.

---

18 Ibid., pp. 836–838.
19 Oberman, "Poverty and Immigration Policy", p. 249.

6.2 Immigration and the domestic poor

In the previous section, we encountered the claim that rich states are morally required to limit the entry of skilled workers from poor countries. However, in debates about immigration, one sometimes comes across advocates of the converse view, namely, that morality permits rich states to admit skilled workers but constrains their freedom to admit unskilled workers. According to the argument that we examined above, when rich states open their borders to skilled workers, they risk imposing undue burdens on the global poor by engendering brain drain. The argument that I want to consider here maintains that when rich states open their borders to *unskilled* workers, they impose undue burdens on the *domestic* poor (i.e., on their own poorer citizens).

This argument draws on empirical studies which suggest that the immigration of unskilled workers into developed countries such as the US lowers wages among the indigenous poor.[20] Native unskilled workers are forced to compete with immigrants for jobs, and a higher supply of labour relative to demand exerts downward pressure on wages. Employers benefit from cheaper labour, and wealthier individuals pay less for the services of cleaners, gardeners, and nannies, but the working poor see their condition deteriorate.[21] The perception that immigrants benefit the "elite" while "stealing" the jobs of working people is, of course, widespread in countries such as Britain and the US, and this perception has fuelled public anger toward current admission policies. Some commentators, impressed by available empirical evidence, believe that this anger is warranted and that a just immigration regime would limit the admission of unskilled workers in order to protect the domestic poor.

It should be borne in mind that this argument cannot be effectively countered by pointing to any positive *overall* impact that immigration may have on the economy. Immigration may be good for a particular country *taken as a whole* but this macro-perspective is not the perspective of justice. If unskilled domestic workers lose out from immigration, we must be able to justify our policies *to them*, and we cannot do this simply by pointing to benefits enjoyed by their more advantaged compatriots.[22] As Stephen Macedo writes, it "is not reasonable to expect our less well off fellow citizens to accede to a policy on the grounds that it makes those with the luck of superior endowment by nature and birth even better off".[23]

However, there may be *other* grounds on which it *is* reasonable to expect less advantaged citizens to bear certain burdens that immigration might create.

---

20 George J. Borjas, *Heaven's Door: Immigration Policy and the American Economy* (Princeton, NJ: Princeton University Press, 1999).
21 Macedo, "The Moral Dilemma of U.S. Immigration Policy", p. 67.
22 Kukathas, "The Case for Open Immigration", p. 381.
23 Macedo, "The Moral Dilemma of U.S. Immigration Policy", p. 81.

We cannot justify the imposition of these burdens by pointing to benefits reaped by those who are already better off, but the case for freer migration that I have been describing throughout this chapter makes no reference to those benefits. Rather, it highlights the significant advantages that freer migration would confer upon the denizens of the Third World. When it is *those* advantages that are placed in the scales and weighed against costs borne by native unskilled workers, a more plausible justification for an open admissions policy comes into view.

If we have to choose between giving a benefit to either the domestic poor or the global poor, the fact that the latter are *much* worse off tells in favour of giving the benefit to them. In his discussion of these matters, Yong notes that we can adjudicate between the interests of the domestic and global poor by appealing to a "comparative gravity" principle, according to which "reforms that target graver or more severe injustices should be given priority over reforms that target less grievous injustices".[24] As Yong goes on to explain, this "principle reflects the simple idea that the graver an injustice is, the stronger are the reasons for removing it".[25] Given that the injustices suffered by the world's poorest people are considerably graver than those experienced by the less advantaged members of rich societies, the comparative gravity principle recommends admitting the former even when this adversely affects the interests of the latter.

But perhaps this stark choice between benefitting either the domestic or global poor is not one that we actually have to face. After all, it is not as though we must turn our backs on native unskilled workers after opening our borders to disadvantaged outsiders. As several commentators have observed, the domestic poor can be *compensated* for any losses that they incur. If immigration makes the country as a whole better off, then the income gains it generates can be redistributed to those who would otherwise lose out. And if these income gains are inadequate to fund compensation at a sufficiently high level, the state can draw on revenue raised through general taxation. Moreover, the state could introduce more substantial unemployment insurance and roll out expanded job retraining schemes.[26]

The solution that I have just suggested is sometimes dismissed as inoperable. To see why, note that I have so far considered only one mechanism via which the immigration of unskilled workers might set back the interests of the indigenous poor: intensified competition in the labour market. But it is sometimes said that immigration harms the less advantaged in another way, namely, by undermining the social trust or solidarity that undergirds support for the welfare state.[27] As we saw in the previous chapter, some nationalist

---

24 Yong, "Justice in Labor Immigration Policy", p. 843.
25 Ibid.
26 Ibid., p. 829.
27 Macedo, "The Moral Dilemma of U.S. Immigration Policy", p. 68.

thinkers believe that individuals can be motivated to support redistributive policies only when the beneficiaries of such policies are members of the same cultural community. These thinkers maintain that the willingness of citizens to fund the institutions of the welfare state is contingent upon the perception that these institutions serve the interests of people with whom they share a common history and identity and to whom they can therefore relate. According to this view, immigration reduces public support for welfare programmes by diversifying the population and undermining the sense of cultural commonality among citizens. When immigration rates are high, support for the welfare state dwindles, as citizens no longer feel confident that the recipients of its benefits will be people adequately similar to themselves.[28]

We have already seen how to respond to this kind of argument. As I argued in Chapter 5, we should not think of currently prevalent attitudes as indicative of some deep and inalterable feature of human psychology that public policy must simply take for granted and strain to accommodate. Our current allegiances may not extend to those who are dissimilar to us in certain ways, but these allegiances were cultivated over time and are considerably more expansive than those they superseded; this fact should make us optimistic about the prospects for replacing them with yet more capacious alternatives. As Ryan Pevnick writes:

> There is no reason [to think] that shared identity is constrained to national communities; instead, groups of any size may come to experience the required identity. If so, the social trust view may provide reason to *create* the shared identity that best facilitates just redistributive institutions rather than – as typically claimed – justifying the maintenance of whatever identities *currently* facilitate redistribution.[29]

Instead of restricting immigration on the grounds that the entry of outsiders would undermine the sense of community that allows the preservation of the welfare state, we should strive to reconceptualize the boundaries of our community in a manner that renders it more inclusive.

In short, the interests of the domestic poor cannot be enlisted to justify restrictive immigration policies that exclude the world's poorest people. This finding bolsters the claim with which we began. The fact of radical global inequality constrains the moral right of wealthy states to exercise discretionary control over their borders. Because developing countries are so poor and

---

28 Stuart N. Soroka, Richard Johnston, and Keith Banting, "Ethnicity, Trust, and the Welfare State", in Philippe Van Parijs (ed.), *Cultural Diversity versus Economic Solidarity* (Brussels: De Boeck, 2004).

29 Ryan Pevnick, "Social Trust and the Ethics of Immigration Policy", *Journal of Political Philosophy*, vol. 17, no. 2, 2009, pp. 146–167, at p. 150 (original emphases).

developed countries so rich, the latter have a duty to admit members of the former in large numbers. This is perhaps the strongest reason for regarding the current immigration regimes of the advanced industrial societies as unjust. These regimes are unjust because they exclude desperately poor individuals who have a right to admission. The severity of this injustice can be brought into focus by recalling that, as we saw in Chapter 3, there are compelling reasons for thinking that the rich countries play a significant role in creating and maintaining severe global poverty. When these countries deny entry to the world's poor, they are turning their backs on the drowning passengers of a ship that they have helped to sink.

6.3 Freedom of movement

I have focused on radical inequality – the enormous gap between the exceptionally poor and the exceptionally rich – because it is the most powerful source of moral constraints on state admission policies. But it may not be the only source. If it were, there could be nothing unjust about border controls that restrict the entry of people who are not poor. But many political theorists claim that such border controls *can* be unjust. In this section, I consider one way in which this claim has been defended. In other words, I examine another potential source of constraints on a state's right to exclude. According to the argument to be considered here, the state's right to exclude is constrained by the human interest in freedom and, more specifically, by the human interest in freedom of movement. Whereas the upshot of the argument considered previously is that borders should be open to the world's poor, the upshot of the argument to be considered here is that borders should be open more generally.

This argument has been developed by Carens, who begins by drawing our attention to the extensive degree of free movement enjoyed *within* democratic states and to the importance that is typically attributed to such freedom.[30] To be sure, our internal mobility is constrained in certain ways – by traffic regulations, for example, and by the legal requirement to respect the private property of others – but we are not confined to particular geographic areas.[31] Democratic governments do not prevent their citizens from moving from one county, state, or province to another, and governments that do impose such restrictions are severely criticized for doing so.[32] Moreover, when the right to private property clashes with the right to free movement, it is not always the former that is deferred to (even outside of emergency situ-

---

30 Carens, *Ethics of Immigration*, pp. 238–239.

31 Joseph Carens, "Migration and Morality: A Liberal Egalitarian Perspective", in Brian Barry and Robert E. Goodin (eds.), *Free Movement: Ethical Issues in the Transnational Migration of People and Money* (Hemel Hempstead: Harvester Wheatsheaf, 1992), p. 27. Cf. Miller, "The Case for Limits", p. 365.

32 Carens, "Migration and Morality", p. 27.

ations). For example, right-to-roam legislation in Britain grants individuals the right to traverse uncultivated privately owned land. Indeed, freedom of movement within states is regarded as sufficiently important to be protected by a legal human right.[33] According to Article 13 of the Universal Declaration of Human Rights, "Everyone has the right to freedom of movement and residence within the borders of each state". Similarly, the International Covenant on Civil and Political Rights establishes that "Everyone lawfully within the territory of a State shall, within that territory, have the right to liberty of movement and freedom to choose his residence".

But if we attribute such importance to freedom of movement *within* states, it is natural to ask why we do not attribute comparable significance to freedom of movement *between* states. After all, the latter freedom appears to serve the same interests as the former. As Carens notes:

> Every reason why one might want to move within a state may also be a reason for moving between states. One might want a job; one might fall in love with someone from another country; one might belong to a religion that has few adherents in one's native state and many in another; one might wish to pursue cultural opportunities that are only available in another land.[34]

Carens infers from this that the "radical disjuncture that treats freedom of movement within the state as a human right while granting states discretionary control over freedom of movement across state borders makes no moral sense".[35]

Anyone who wants to defend this "radical disjuncture" will have to try to identify a relevant asymmetry between free movement within and among states. Carens argues that such an endeavour is bound to fail, but this can be challenged. Drawing on an argument advanced by David Miller, one might say that a key difference between the two types of freedom is that free movement within states is necessary to ensure that each individual has an adequate range of life options to choose from whereas free movement among states is not necessary to ensure this.[36] If this claim is correct, then ascribing less importance to the latter type of freedom might appear reasonable. Miller writes: "What a person can legitimately demand access to is an *adequate* range of options – a reasonable choice of occupation, religion, cultural activities, marriage partners, and so forth".[37] If an adequate range of options were unavailable in the absence of free movement between states, then free move-

---

33 Carens, *Ethics of Immigration*, p. 238.
34 Ibid., p. 239.
35 Ibid.
36 Miller, "The Case for Limits", p. 366.
37 Ibid.

ment between states would be something that people could legitimately demand. But Miller suggests that, for individuals living in liberal democracies, an adequate range of options can be accessed within the borders of their own state: immigration is unnecessary.[38]

This might be true. But in order to justify attributing differential levels of importance to freedom of movement within and between states, a further step has to be taken. It has to be shown that accessing the adequate range of options available within states requires internal freedom of movement. Miller suggests that freedom of movement between states is not necessary for an individual to enjoy an adequate range of options. But perhaps freedom of movement *within* states is not necessary either. In which case, the attribution of differential levels of importance to freedom of movement within and between states could not be justified by reference to the idea that individuals are entitled to an adequate range of options.

Carens denies that freedom of movement within states is necessary for individuals to enjoy an adequate range of options. To illustrate his grounds for this denial, he points out that "many states within the United States and several provinces in Canada have a larger population and a wider range of internal economic and social opportunities than many independent states".[39] (To give an example, Ontario has a population of roughly 13 million; Belgium has a population of roughly 11 million.) This suggests that people living in Canada or the US could access an adequate range of options even if confined to a relatively small part of their country's territory.

It follows from this that, unless some other relevant asymmetry can be identified, we are not justified in attributing differential levels of importance to free movement within and between states. If we think, for example, that Ontarians have a right to move freely around Canada despite enjoying access to an adequate range of options within Ontario, we cannot defend a refusal to recognize a right to move freely among countries by pointing out that such a right is not necessary to access an adequate range of options. A right to move freely around Canada is not necessary for this either, yet we would not think it acceptable to confine Ontarians to Ontario.

Carens considers a number of attempts to identify important distinctions between free movement within and between states and argues that each of these attempts fails. We might infer from this that we should increase the degree of importance that we attribute to freedom of movement between states. Alternatively, we might conclude that we should hold constant the degree of importance that we attribute to freedom of movement between states and *reduce* the amount of importance that we attribute to freedom of movement *within* states. If freedom of movement within states is not necessary to ensure access to an adequate range of options and if access to an adequate range of options is what really matters, then it might be said that

---

38 Ibid.
39 Carens, *Ethics of Immigration*, p. 244.

the importance of free movement within states has been exaggerated and that we should be willing to countenance, at the domestic level, the kinds of mobility regulation that we currently see internationally.

But for any friend of freedom, this will not be an attractive option. In the course of defending the importance of free movement, Carens invites us to consider a scenario in which governments restrain mobility within borders in the way that they currently restrain mobility across borders. Imagine that you live in New York but wish to move to Los Angeles. Imagine that, in order to do so,

> you have to notify the authorities that you want to move, but political officials in California (whom you have had no say in electing) are free to decide whether or not to let you in. They may make the decision based on announced policies but they are not required to do so. They do not have to take your interests into account in their policy and they generally don't. They don't have to justify the policy to any independent forum or prove that it meets any criteria. They apply their policy to your case in whatever way they see fit, and you have no recourse or basis of appeal if you think that the policy has been misapplied... [Y]ou may still be permitted to move but your rights [to move freely] have almost completely disappeared. Your freedom to move is entirely at the discretion of the authorities.[40]

This scenario differs drastically from the status quo. If you were actually a New Yorker wishing to move to Los Angeles, you would face very few constraints on your freedom to do so. As things stand,

> no official is entitled to prevent you from moving from New York to Los Angeles. You don't have to get the government's permission to make the move or to get on the highway or to buy gas or to set up residence in Los Angeles. Furthermore, you don't have to explain to any official why you have decided to move. You may (or may not) discuss your reasons for moving with your friends and relatives, and they may (or may not) think your reasons are good ones, but no official is entitled to a say in the matter.[41]

If you would oppose the introduction of the kinds of restrictions present in the hypothetical scenario that Carens describes, then the force of his challenge is clear. Why are we willing to endorse, at the international level, a regime of mobility regulation that we would never accept domestically?

---

40 Ibid., p. 252.
41 Ibid., pp. 246–247.

6.4 Immigration and cultural preservation

So far, I have discussed two main considerations that can limit a state's right to exclude: one which refers to the fact of radical inequality and one which invokes the value of liberty. I have also addressed the concern that respecting the interests of the domestic and global poor requires us to place restrictions on immigration. I now want to consider another argument in favour of restrictions, one which appeals to the importance of cultural preservation. We have already encountered the worry that immigration may reduce the sense of cultural commonality among a community's members and that this in turn may undercut support for the welfare state. But the dilution of a nation's culture may also be regrettable in itself, independently of any adverse effects it might have on redistributive institutions.

Immigrants bring with them their own languages, traditions, customs, values, and preferences, and we can expect their presence to alter the cultural identity of the societies that they enter. Although immigration can enrich a country by, say, diversifying the artistic, culinary, and intellectual dimensions of its cultural endowment, it can simultaneously deprive it of a distinctive character. Indeed, we may worry that the cultural transformations that immigration can precipitate are capable of engendering a sense of estrangement or alienation. Miller claims that people have an interest in trying "to maintain cultural continuity over time, so that they can see themselves as the bearers of an identifiable cultural tradition that stretches backward historically".[42] Miller notes two features of cultures that contribute to a community's temporally extended identity, each of which might be threatened by immigration: its language and its physical environment. He suggests that language is among a community's "most important distinguishing characteristics" and points to a "relationship between a nation's culture and its physical shape – its public and religious buildings, the way its towns and villages are laid out, the pattern of the landscape, and so forth".[43] Miller goes on to assert that "People feel at home in a place, in part, because they can see that their surroundings bear the imprint of past generations whose values were recognizably their own".[44] Miller concludes that because immigration can threaten the cultural continuity and distinctiveness upon which a sense of belonging is predicated, immigration should be restricted.

It is worth noting that even Carens – who, as we have seen, is a fierce critic of exclusionary policies – has claimed that some communities have a strong interest in restricting immigration in order to preserve their cultural distinctiveness. Carens suggests that this is especially true of relatively homogeneous societies, such as Japan. In an early article, he writes:

---

42 Miller, "The Case for Limits", p. 370.
43 Ibid.
44 Ibid.

> most people in Japan share a common culture, tradition and history to a much greater extent than people do in countries like Canada and the United States. It seems reasonable to suppose that many Japanese cherish their distinctive way of life, that they want to preserve it and pass it on to their children because they find that it gives meaning and depth to their lives... In these ways many Japanese have a vital interest in the preservation of a distinctive Japanese culture; they may regard it as crucial to their life projects.[45]

In response to these arguments, we should start by noting the practical limits of cultural preservationism. Proponents of cultural preservation cannot realistically hope to maintain their community's culture in the exact form that it currently assumes: cultures inevitably change over time. One reason for this is suggested by Samuel Scheffler, who points to the fact that a community's current members will gradually be replaced by subsequent generations.

> Suppose that our country were today to seal its borders and reduce to zero the number of immigrants that it accepted. The fact remains that, within a relatively short period of time – let us be very optimistic and say 150 years – every single one of the country's current residents will be dead. If the country survives, it will be populated entirely by people who are as yet unborn – immigrants from the future, if you like. Do we really suppose, or could we really wish, that, despite undergoing a complete population replacement, our country's national culture might remain *exactly the same* in 150 years as it is today? To think that this is either possible or desirable is to imagine nothing at all happening in or to the country in the intervening period: no new ideas, no new challenges, no new discoveries or inventions, no advances in science or medicine or technology, no new works of literature or art or music, no new heroes or villains, no changes in fashion or style or entertainment, no new achievements, no new successes, no new failures. It is, in short, to imagine that our successors might not actually lead human lives, that history might simply be frozen, that our country might go on functioning with a past but no future.[46]

If it is to survive, a community must acquire new members from *somewhere*, through either immigration or reproduction, so even a community

---

45 Carens, "Migration and Morality", p. 37.
46 Samuel Scheffler, "Immigration and the significance of culture", *Philosophy and Public Affairs*, vol. 35, no. 2, 2007, pp. 93–125, at p. 104.

that completely closed its doors to outsiders would nevertheless receive "immigrants from the future", in the form of its current members' progeny, and these immigrants will inevitably remould the community's cultural identity.

In reply, one might point out that, unlike immigrants from other countries, "immigrants from the future" arrive as blank slates, and their cultural orientation can be shaped in childhood by their compatriots. Children are likely to imbibe the culture of the community in which they grow up, and their parents can take active steps to instil favoured cultural commitments. Therefore, it might be argued that "immigrants from the future" are less likely to pose a threat to cultural integrity.

This response does not pose a strong challenge to Scheffler's core insight, which is actually obscured somewhat by the emphasis on population replacement. To see this, suppose that a country's population were not replaced. More specifically, consider a science-fiction scenario in which advances in medical technology allow humans to live indefinitely and in which humans have also ceased to reproduce. In such a scenario, the composition of the country's population remains constant, but there would *still* be cultural change; to think otherwise would *still* be to imagine "that history might simply be frozen, that our country might go on functioning with a past but no future". There would still be new ideas, challenges, discoveries, and so forth, and these would inevitably refashion the country's culture.

Still, the significance of this point should not be exaggerated. Although a community cannot completely prevent its culture from changing, immigration controls nevertheless enable it to influence the pace and direction of its evolution, and such controls might be advocated on those grounds.[47] We should therefore consider additional responses to the claim that immigration must be restricted in the name of cultural preservation.

A second response to the cultural preservation argument for immigration restrictions begins with the observation that, although there are certain exceptions, the majority of countries in the world are not culturally homogeneous. Rather, most states are composed of various different cultural groups. For multicultural states, restricting immigration in the name of cultural preservation is harder to justify than it is for culturally unified states. This is because the restrictions have to be justified not only to those who are being excluded but also to those members of the disfavoured culture *already present* within the state's borders, and this might be hard to do. Michael Blake writes: "To identify the purpose of the state with the preservation of a cultural group is inevitably to draw an invidious distinction against those citizens who do not happen to belong to that community".[48] The worry here is that when a

---

47 Miller, "The Case for Limits", pp. 369–370.
48 Michael Blake, "Immigration", in R. G. Frey and Christopher Heath Wellman (eds.), *A Companion to Applied Ethics* (Malden, MA: Blackwell Publishing, 2005), p. 232.

state refuses to admit certain individuals on the grounds that they belong to a particular culture, it thereby demeans or insults those among its citizens who share that culture: it singles them out as politically or socially inferior.[49] Blake illustrates this point using, as an example, the infamous "White Australia" policy, which sought to prevent the immigration of non-whites. Blake notes that an important objection to this policy is that it sent a message of social inferiority to non-white Australians, such as those belonging to Aboriginal groups.[50]

Still, White Australia is an extreme example, and there are perhaps culture-preserving restrictions that multicultural societies could adopt without drawing invidious distinctions among their members. We can distinguish between those policies that aim to promote a particular culture *at the expense of* others (as White Australia did) and those that aim to preserve a particular culture *alongside* others. A government that excludes certain individuals in order to purge their culture from its territory is clearly very different, morally speaking, from a government that excludes certain individuals in order to give a vulnerable competing culture room to breathe. We cannot rule out the permissibility of culture-preserving restrictions simply by pointing to their most pernicious instantiations.

A third response to the cultural preservation argument notes that we should not confuse the issue of *admission* with the issue of *integration*. While justice may require us to welcome immigrants into our country, it may also permit us to demand certain things of them. We may be permitted to institute rules that require immigrants to adopt certain aspects of our culture. For example, we may be permitted to require immigrants to learn the national language and to use it in certain contexts. The thought here is that we can open our doors to outsiders while still taking steps to reduce cultural change.

But even when immigration is incompatible with cultural preservation, it does not follow that immigration may permissibly be restricted. This is the final point I wish to make in response to the argument that we have been considering. Although preserving cultural distinctiveness may be important, it is not as important as all of the objectives with which it can clash. More specifically, it is not as important as enabling extremely disadvantaged individuals to escape from severe poverty. If a culture can be maintained only by abandoning the world's poor to their fate, then it is the culture, not the world's poor, that must be sacrificed.

In an ideal world, where there were not large inequalities among countries, culture-preserving restrictions would be easier to defend. Then again, in the absence of large international inequalities, it is unlikely that cultural distinctiveness would be threatened by immigration. If individuals did not

---

49   Ibid., p. 233. Cf. Blake, "Discretionary Immigration", pp. 282–286.
50   Blake, "Immigration", p. 233.

face poor life prospects as a result of being born on the wrong side of some line, they would lack the motivation to uproot themselves and move to a new, culturally alien country. Carens writes:

> Small numbers of people may be flexible or whimsical enough to move for trivial reasons to a place whose national culture is very different from their own, especially one in which the language of public life is not their own native tongue. Most people, however, need a fairly serious reason to undertake such a challenge... When the economic differences between states are not huge, relatively few people find such reasons to move.[51]

When immigration threatens cultural distinctiveness, it does so only because of persistent global inequality. Culture-threatening immigration, then, is the product of an injustice that the rich countries have negligently failed to address.

6.5 Moving beyond the status quo

We have seen that there are compelling reasons for wealthy states to radically revise their immigration policies and to adopt a more liberal approach to admissions. Current arrangements, which reflect the belief that states have an almost unlimited right to exclude, are unacceptable. Just how *limited* that right in fact is remains a matter of dispute. However, it is not difficult to imagine alternatives to existing arrangements that would clearly be superior from the perspective of justice. Carens describes a regime of mobility regulation that does not come close to completely depriving states of the right to exclude but that nevertheless imposes considerable limits on how that right may be exercised. Under this regime, state officials

> must show that denying you [a prospective immigrant] permission to move is necessary for the public policy goals that they are pursuing, that there is no other way to pursue the goal effectively that intrudes less on your freedom, and that the benefits gained by your exclusion outweigh the harm done to you by refusing you entry. [Furthermore] the authorities have to establish these claims in an independent forum in which you are entitled to present evidence and arguments challenging their claims and ... you have the right to appeal if the decision goes against you.[52]

---

51 Carens, *Ethics of Immigration*, p. 285.
52 Ibid., p. 251 (footnote omitted).

As Carens notes, under a regime of this kind,

> you are not simply free to move but you are not simply a passive subject, either. You are still treated as an agent whose will matters, you have a range of rights and your desire to move is a weighty consideration that must be taken into account in the final decision. In that respect your freedom still counts for a good deal ...[53]

This contrasts sharply with current arrangements, under which an individual's "freedom to move is entirely at the discretion of the authorities".[54] What these reflections reveal is that the freedom to move across borders could be significantly enhanced without being made as expansive as the freedom we currently enjoy to move within borders. Perhaps the regime Carens describes falls short from the perspective of justice. Perhaps, as Carens himself believes, justice demands something closer to open borders. What seems clear is that the excessively restrictive status quo cannot be tolerated.

---

53 Ibid.
54 Ibid., p. 252.

7 TRADE

The previous chapter was devoted to addressing ethical questions concerning the regulation of state borders. The current chapter continues that task by considering the issue of international trade. As we shall see, in important respects, the debate around trade resembles the debate around immigration. In both cases, a central question is whether states are ever morally required to open their borders or whether it can be morally permissible (or even obligatory) to impose certain restrictions on the flow of people, goods, or services from the outside. In both cases, there is (i) an open-borders argument that appeals to the interests of the world's poor, (ii) a closed-borders argument that appeals to the interests of the world's poor, and (iii) a closed-borders argument that appeals to the interests of unskilled workers in developed countries. Addressing these arguments will help us to morally assess the current system of world trade, which is governed by the World Trade Organization (WTO).

7.1 The world poverty argument for free trade

As we saw in the previous chapter, there is a powerful argument for the claim that rich countries should substantially open their borders to migrants from the Third World. Billions of people are born into countries crippled by severe poverty, and, by opening their borders, rich countries could enable many of these people to escape the crushing burdens that have been imposed upon them by an accident of birth. A similar argument can be made in the case of international trade. According to this argument, rich countries should open their borders to goods and services exported from the Third World, as doing so is important for enhancing the welfare and development prospects of poor countries. When the rich world restricts trade with poor countries, by imposing various kinds of protectionist measures such as tariffs and anti-dumping duties, it undermines the ability of people in those countries to climb their way out of poverty. Call this the *world poverty argument* for open borders.

Economic science identifies a variety of ways in which participating countries can gain from international trade. To begin with, trade enables countries to enhance the efficiency with which they can use their resources. One demonstration of this benefit comes in the form of Adam Smith's theory of "absolute advantage".[1] Suppose that Country A is better at producing wine than Country B but that Country B is better at producing cheese than Country A. The theory of absolute advantage recommends that A should export wine and import cheese and that B should export cheese and import wine. This division of labour allows each country to devote its factors of production (such as land, labour, and capital) to the productive processes in which they can be employed most efficiently.

Now suppose that A is better than B at producing both wine *and* cheese. The theory of "comparative advantage" – originally developed by David Ricardo – demonstrates that both countries can still benefit from trade under these circumstances.[2] While B lacks an absolute advantage in the production of either good, it may nevertheless possess a comparative advantage; that is, although it cannot produce either good as efficiently as A, it might be able to produce one good more efficiently than it can produce the other. Moreover, A's absolute advantage may be supplemented by a comparative advantage in the production of one of the two goods. Suppose that A is better at producing cheese than it is at producing wine but that B is better at producing wine than it is at producing cheese. The theory of comparative advantage tells us that A should export cheese while importing wine and B should export wine while importing cheese. Again, this allows each country to make the most efficient use of its resources. If A were to devote some of its resources to producing wine and B were to devote some of its resources to producing cheese, both countries would needlessly be diverting resources away from the line of production in which they can be used most efficiently.

Importantly, it is widely believed that trade can promote economic growth and that economic growth in turn can foster economic development.[3] One way in which trade can promote growth is by exposing firms to competition from their international counterparts and thereby encouraging them to become more efficient. In addition, by increasing the size of the market to which they have access, trade enables firms to achieve economies of scale.

It is believed that, under appropriate conditions, countries can achieve gains from trade simply by opening their own borders to imports (by

---

[1] Adam Smith, *An Inquiry into the Nature and Causes of the Wealth of Nations* (London: Strahan and Cadell, 1776).

[2] David Ricardo, *On the Principles of Political Economy and Taxation* (London: John Murray, 1817).

[3] Joseph E. Stiglitz and Andrew Charlton, *Fair Trade for All: How Trade can Promote Development* (Oxford: Oxford University Press, 2005), Ch. 2.

"liberalizing their markets") and irrespective of whether other countries open theirs. In other words, trade liberalization can sometimes be beneficial even when undertaken unilaterally.

Nevertheless, if trade barriers are maintained by other countries, the gains that can be achieved will be limited. When one's trading partners protect their markets, this drastically reduces the size of the market in which one can sell one's products, thereby diminishing the size of the benefits that trade can bring. Indeed, it is widely acknowledged that protectionist measures adopted in the rich world have dramatically undermined the ability of poor countries to improve their situation. As we saw in Chapter 3, rich countries have imposed exceptionally high tariffs on precisely those goods in which poor countries enjoy a comparative advantage (namely, labour-intensive goods such as textiles and apparel). In the absence of such barriers, poor countries could anticipate far larger gains from trade.

The preceding remarks are not intended to imply that trade automatically translates into economic growth nor that economic growth automatically translates into benefits for the poor. The economists who emphasize the importance of trade for development are often at pains to stress that, in order for trade to produce the desired outcomes, appropriate complementary policies will also have to be introduced.[4] Still, the claim that access to rich-world markets is important for development is widely endorsed and that is morally significant. Suppose that a wide range of experts believed that a particular drug could cure cancer. A doctor could not justify refusing to prescribe that drug to her patients simply by pointing out that some experts questioned the drug's effectiveness. Rather, there would be a strong presumption in favour of prescription, a presumption that could be overturned only by robust countervailing considerations. Similarly, since a wide range of experts believe that access to rich-world markets is important for development, there is a strong presumption in favour of rich countries removing protectionist measures. Whether there are countervailing considerations powerful enough to overturn that presumption is a question to which we should now turn our attention.

7.2 The sweatshop argument for trade restrictions

In the previous chapter, we saw that a concern about global poverty might leave us unsure about the kind of immigration policy that we ought to recommend. On the one hand, we might think that the rich countries should open their borders, for doing so will enable some of the world's poor to

---

4   Ibid.

escape their plight. On the other hand, we might worry that liberal border policies actually exacerbate the plight of the world's poor by facilitating the large-scale emigration of skilled workers from the Third to the First World. As we shall now see, attempting to formulate a trade policy that responds appropriately to the problem of global poverty can be similarly confounding. On the one hand, as was noted above, economics assures us that trade promotes growth and that growth in turn can promote development. On the other hand, the companies selling the goods that rich countries import often require their employees to work excessively long hours, for very low wages, in poor and sometimes dangerous conditions. Many consumers surely feel a pang of anxiety upon noticing that their new pair of jeans or trainers were manufactured in Bangladesh, Vietnam, or the Philippines. We might worry that, by purchasing goods that originated in "sweatshop" conditions, we are somehow wronging the impoverished workers who have toiled long hours to produce them.

This is a natural, even commendable, response. It is morally appropriate to experience unease when engaging in a practice that exposes our privileged position in the global hierarchy and that connects us directly to those on the bottom rungs. Moreover, such reactions cannot easily be dismissed as sentimental or misguided. The developing-country workers who labour to furnish our high-street stores with designer clothes and mobile phones may well have legitimate complaints that can plausibly be levelled against members of the rich world.

To begin with, these workers might object that firms and consumers in the rich world have *exploited* them. In other words, the complaint might be that rich countries engage in unfair advantage-taking. Developing-country workers are poorly treated, and the rich countries have benefitted from the cheap imports that their poor treatment makes possible. For this reason, the benefits received by those in rich countries might be regarded as ill-gotten gains, and the acceptance of such benefits might be viewed as disrespectful.[5]

Furthermore, developing-country workers might object that the rich countries are complicit in their poor treatment. When rich countries accept cheap goods from the developing world, they provide the companies that produce those goods with an incentive to continue doing what they are doing, namely, paying low wages and offering poor working conditions. It is the market demand created by rich-world consumers that ensures that sweatshops remain in business. When rich countries welcome the importation of cheap goods produced in sweatshop conditions, rather than insisting upon the implementation of higher standards as a condition of trade, they forego

---

5   Mathias Risse, 'Fairness in trade I: obligations from trading and the pauper-labor argument', *Politics, Philosophy & Economics*, vol. 6, no. 3, 2007, pp. 355–377, at pp. 361–363, p. 367.

an opportunity to improve the lot of developing-country workers and thereby become implicated in their poor treatment.[6]

What are the implications of these observations for trade policy? Should rich countries restrict the importation of goods that have been produced in sweatshop conditions? One important consideration that should make us pause before answering this question affirmatively is that such a policy might actually make things worse.[7] As we noted earlier, rich countries often *do* impose inordinately high tariffs on textiles and apparel, and, by doing so, they deny poor countries the opportunity to exploit their comparative advantage in labour-intensive manufacturing. If poor countries were coerced into adopting higher standards, their production costs would rise, and they would struggle to compete in the international market. Moreover, they would find it difficult to attract foreign investors, who "offshore" production precisely in order to benefit from lower labour standards abroad. We noted that market demand from rich countries provides firms with an incentive to continue offering low-wage work, but in the absence of such an incentive, they may simply offer no work at all.

It might be helpful at this point to introduce the distinction between *ideal* and *non-ideal theory*.[8] Ideal theory describes the just world that we should endeavour to create. By contrast, non-ideal theory provides guidance on how to make progress from the deeply unjust circumstances in which we currently find ourselves. Needless to say, the just world described by ideal theory does not feature sweatshops. But non-ideal theory can recommend tolerating sweatshops at present if doing so will provide an especially effective means of escape from our current predicament. Indeed, it is widely recognized that attempting to raise labour standards too rapidly might undermine progress toward a better world.

In his seminal text, *A Theory of Justice*, John Rawls noted that "when social circumstances do not allow the effective establishment of… basic rights… one can concede their limitation… [T]hese restrictions can be granted… to the extent that they are necessary to prepare the way for the time when they are no longer justified".[9] That some such restrictions may be justified in the conditions that currently prevail in parts of the developing world has been suggested by Mathias Risse. Writing in 2007, Risse remarked that "Indian workers are so well protected from exploitation by industrial bosses that they have no jobs at all".[10]

---

6   Ibid., pp. 361–363.
7   Ibid., pp. 363–365.
8   John Rawls, *A Theory of Justice*, Revised Edition (Cambridge, MA: Harvard University Press, 1999), pp. 7–8, 215–216, 308–309.
9   Ibid., p. 132.
10 Risse, 'Fairness in Trade', p. 364.

This is not an excuse for complacency in trade policy. As I mentioned earlier, trade does not automatically generate growth or alleviate poverty. In order for trade to promote development, poor-country governments will have to introduce supplementary measures. In some cases, it will be clear that such measures are not being implemented and that trade therefore will not yield widespread economic benefits for the general population. Moreover, in the most egregious cases, trade will even be contrary to the interests of those workers who produce the goods being exchanged. According to a recent report published by the International Labour Organization, at any given time in 2016 almost 25 million people were in forced labour.[11] The report notes that "Men, women, and children are forced to work in various settings across the globe, with examples of forced labour found in garment making in South Asian factories, digging for minerals in African mines … [and] working on farms in Latin America".[12] The report explains that "Coercion can take many forms, ranging from physical and sexual violence or threats against family members to more subtle means such as withholding of wages, retaining identity documents, threats of dismissal, and threats of denunciation to authorities".[13] The authors of the report stress that "In many cases, the products [these workers] made and the services they provided ended up in seemingly legitimate commercial channels. Forced labourers produced some of the food we eat and the clothes we wear".[14]

Workers in developing countries can have a legitimate complaint when those in the rich world enact policies that deny them the opportunity to engage in forms of employment that they have decided are in their best interests. But things look very different in the case of workers engaged in tasks that they have not chosen to undertake. It will be much harder to defend the claim that trade benefits the poor when it props up ruthless and contemptible "employers" who are essentially imprisoning their workers.

What these considerations suggest is that a just rich-world trade policy will be discriminating. In the previous chapter, we saw that an immigration policy that responds appropriately to the problem of global poverty must be sensitive to the "brain drain" phenomenon and therefore should perhaps distinguish between skilled workers from larger, middle-income countries (whose emigration can promote development) and skilled workers from smaller, less developed countries (whose emigration is likely to undermine development). Similarly, a trade policy that responds appropriately to the problem of global poverty should try to distinguish between goods produced by free labour in countries whose governments supplement trade with economic policies conducive to development, and goods

---

11 International Labour Organization, *Global Estimates of Modern Slavery: Forced Labour and Forced Marriage* (Geneva: International Labour Office, 2017), p. 22.

12 Ibid., p. 28.

13 Ibid.

14 Ibid., p. 22.

produced by forced labour in countries where essential economic reforms are unlikely to be forthcoming.

7.3 The domestic labour argument for trade restrictions

As we saw in the previous chapter, a common concern about immigration is that unskilled migrants increase the supply of unskilled labour and thereby exert downward pressure on wages. Sometimes, immigration is opposed on these grounds. It is argued that immigration harms the economic prospects of the native working class and that therefore it should be restricted. A similar concern arises in the case of trade. The concern is that the importation of cheap goods from abroad may undermine the economic vitality of local firms that produce those goods domestically. These firms may have to close down, make lay-offs, or lower wages. According to what we can call the *domestic labour argument*, rich countries are permitted (and perhaps even required) to restrict trade in order to protect members of the indigenous working class who would otherwise be harmed.

When it comes to identifying the kinds of restrictions that rich countries should impose, the domestic labour argument holds that rich countries should adopt restrictions that limit the importation of labour-intensive goods, for it is those goods that can be made by native low-skilled workers. In practice, this means restricting imports from the developing world. Indeed, it means restricting the importation of the very goods in which – because of their abundant supply of low-skilled workers – developing countries enjoy a comparative advantage.

The domestic labour argument contains a significant empirical premise. According to this premise, trade inflicts a number of socioeconomic harms on developed-country workers. It causes firms to collapse, jobs to be lost, and wages to shrink. Is this premise defensible? Although various associated phenomena – such as rising income inequality and the decline of manufacturing – are well documented, determining the degree to which these ills are caused by trade is not straightforward. One complicating factor is that increased trade has been accompanied by a variety of other developments that could also play a role in generating the problems that are often attributed to trade. Indeed, early attempts to explain the rising wage inequality that accompanied increased trade with the developing world downplayed the role of trade and granted explanatory primacy to changes in technology. However, more recent studies have cast some doubt on these earlier findings and apportioned a greater share of the blame to trade.[15]

---

15 Jessie Poon and David L. Rigby, *International Trade* (New York: Routledge, 2017), pp. 143–144. Cf. Kimberley Clausing, *Open: The Progressive Case for Free Trade, Immigration, and Global Capital* (Cambridge, MA: Harvard University Press, 2019), pp. 75–80, 88–90, 106–107, 111.

In an attempt to mitigate concerns about the adverse effects that trade might have on domestic workers, it is sometimes pointed out that although trade may destroy some jobs, it will also create new ones. Jobs may be lost in *import-sensitive* industries that are forced to compete with foreign firms for customers in the domestic market – workers in *these* industries may see their jobs disappear as the goods they produce are substituted by imports – but trade will enable *export-oriented* firms to reach larger markets, and as these firms expand to take advantage of increased demand, they will become capable of employing those workers whom trade has displaced.[16] Moreover, although trade may harm certain individuals in their capacity as displaced workers, it benefits those very same individuals in their capacity as consumers. It does this by granting access to cheaper goods.[17] In these ways, trade fixes the problems it creates.

This argument has its limits. Although displaced workers may well find new employment opportunities in expanding export industries and although they may also benefit from cheaper goods, there is evidence to suggest that the jobs trade creates often pay lower wages than the jobs trade destroys.[18] Therefore, although trade may to some degree *offset* the harms it inflicts, displaced workers may nevertheless see their living standards fall. Moreover, although some economists might take a cool view of trade-induced occupational reshuffling, we should not overlook the significant harm that can be done by even temporary periods of unemployment. Being forced from one's job can be stressful and stigmatizing; it deprives one of much-needed income; and it can significantly disrupt or derail one's life plans.[19] We should not pretend, then, that there is no cause for concern provided that displaced workers can find alternative employment in expanding export industries.

It is sometimes argued that developed countries should liberalize trade because, though doing so may lower the living standards of some of their inhabitants, trade is good for the country as a whole.[20] As we have already observed, trade can promote growth and enable the most efficient utilization of a country's resources. If trade maximizes a country's *aggregate* welfare, then, it might be said, trade should be pursued even if a minority loses out. This, it is sometimes argued, is preferable to depriving the majority of trade's benefits.

---

16 Douglas A. Irwin, *Against the Tide: An Intellectual History of Free Trade* (Princeton, NJ: Princeton University Press, 1996), pp. 54, 55, 58.

17 Fernando R. Tesón, 'Why Free Trade is Required by Justice', *Social Philosophy and Policy*, vol. 29, no. 1, 2012, pp. 126–153, at p. 132.

18 Cletus C. Coughlin, 'The Controversy over Free Trade: The Gap Between Economists and the General Public', *The Federal Reserve Bank of St. Louis*, January/February, 2002, pp. 1–22, at p. 16; Dani Rodrik, *The Globalization Paradox: Why Global Markets, States, and Democracy Can't Coexist* (Oxford: Oxford University Press, 2011), pp. 56, 87; Clausing, *Open*, p. 75.

19 James Christensen, *Trade Justice* (Oxford: Oxford University Press, 2017), p. 66.

20 Irwin, *Against the Tide*, p. 88.

We should record two problems with this argument. To begin with, it is important to notice that the gains that trade delivers to each of its developed country beneficiaries are often small whereas the costs that trade imposes are more substantial.[21] The reason why trade can nevertheless maximize aggregate welfare is that the small gains it creates are enjoyed by very large numbers of people. By contrast, the burdens that trade generates are distributed less widely. The problem here is that it is difficult to see why securing small benefits for the many should take priority over preventing large harms from burdening the few.

This first problem is exacerbated by a second: those who benefit from trade in developed countries tend to be skilled workers and owners of capital, who are relatively advantaged, whereas, as we have seen, those who lose out from trade are unskilled workers, who are relatively *dis*advantaged.[22] Favouring the provision of small benefits over the prevention of large harms looks especially misguided when the benefits will accrue to those who are already quite privileged while the harms will befall the less fortunate.[23] As we noted in our discussion of immigration, it does not seem reasonable to ask the domestic working class to make sacrifices to further improve the economic situation of their better-off compatriots.

However, as should be clear from what was said in section 7.1 and as was also emphasized in the previous chapter, the strongest case for fairly open borders does not appeal to the interests of advantaged members of developed countries. Rather, the strongest case for fairly open borders appeals to the interests of the world's poor, and it is far from clear that the legitimate grievances of domestic workers, serious as they are, carry enough weight to override those interests. As we noted in the previous chapter, we can adjudicate between the interests of the global and domestic poor by invoking a "comparative gravity" principle. As we saw, this principle recommends that we focus our attention on rectifying the most pressing injustices, and, as the global poor are much worse off than the domestic poor, an implication of taking this principle seriously is that we should prioritize the interests of the former. This means that if free trade will benefit the world's poor, then free trade should be adopted, *even if* this means that the domestic poor will be harmed. Notice that pursuing this line of argument does not require us to embrace the kind of aggregative reasoning that we rejected in the previous two paragraphs.[24] The claim being advanced is not that we should prioritize the interests of the global poor because this will maximize global aggregate welfare. Prioritizing the interests of the global poor *might* have this effect but

---

21 Aaron James, *Fairness in Practice: A Social Contract for a Global Economy* (New York: Oxford University Press, 2012), pp. 207–208; Christensen, *Trade Justice*, pp. 64–65; Clausing, *Open*, p. 108.
22 Clausing, *Open*, pp. 106–107.
23 Christensen, *Trade Justice*, p. 65.
24 James, *Fairness in Practice*, pp. 217–218.

that is not why it is recommended. Rather, it is recommended because meeting the needs of the global poor is more morally urgent. Indeed, there are circumstances in which we should prioritize meeting those needs even if, owing to some quirk of empirical realities, doing so would *reduce* aggregate global welfare.

Notwithstanding what has just been said, it is important to emphasize that we are not forced to choose between respecting the interests of the domestic poor and respecting those of the global poor. This is because displaced workers in rich countries can be *compensated* for the harms that they suffer.[25] A portion of the gains that trade creates can be used to fund trade-adjustment schemes, which offer unemployment benefits, retraining, out-of-area job search allowances, and reimbursement for moving expenses. Moreover, if displaced workers suffer a reduction in wages, their income can be supplemented by state payments.

7.4 A nationalist perspective

The theories of justice most likely to oppose trade policies that harm domestic workers are those with a nationalist orientation. As we saw in Chapter 5, nationalist thinkers like David Miller emphasize the importance of honouring special duties to one's compatriots. It is therefore interesting to note that Miller actually endorses the claim that rich countries should adopt a liberal policy toward developing world imports. He contends that constructing a fair economic order at the global level will involve "preventing the governments of rich countries from erecting tariff barriers as a way of protecting their own industries against competition from developing countries".[26] Strikingly, Miller makes this claim shortly after reminding his readers that there are limits to "how far citizens of rich states can be expected to sacrifice various domestic projects in order to discharge remedial responsibilities to foreigners".[27] Let us consider Miller's view in more detail.

Miller distinguishes between different types of duties that are owed to the world's poor. He contrasts what might be called "duties of assistance", which are grounded in "the bare fact of poverty itself", with duties to offer "fair terms of cooperation".[28] He suggests that only the latter count as duties of *justice* – duties that rich countries are "required to perform" – whereas the former are sometimes mere *humanitarian* duties, which are "less weighty".[29] Miller makes the controversial claim that although rich countries may have

---

25 Ibid., pp. 213–215; Christensen, *Trade Justice*, pp. 66–71; Clausing, *Open*, p. 112.
26 David Miller, *National Responsibility and Global Justice* (New York: Oxford University Press, 2007), p. 253.
27 Ibid., p. 248.
28 Ibid., p. 249.
29 Ibid., p. 248, pp. 251–259.

a "strong reason" to assist the world's poor, they are not required to do so when poverty is attributable, if only in part, to the incompetence, negligence, or malevolence of local elites.[30] But Miller maintains that the duty to provide fair terms of cooperation is different. Such terms can be "legitimately demanded" by all poor countries.[31] A situation in which the rules governing international interactions are not fair is described by Miller as one that involves "exploitation and other forms of injustice".[32]

Miller claims that it is the duty to offer fair terms of cooperation that imposes upon rich countries a duty to open their markets to the developing world. How can Miller defend this claim? Miller notes that open markets provide opportunities for development, but it is not obvious that terms of cooperation cannot be fair without providing such opportunities. (Presumably, terms of international military cooperation, for example, can be fair even if they do not promote development.) If the maintenance of trade restrictions is regarded as constituting a failure to offer fair terms of cooperation simply because it represents a foregone opportunity to assist the poor, then how is the duty to offer fair terms distinguished from the duty of assistance? And why is the status of the former duty as a duty *of justice* not affected by considerations of local responsibility?

The answer to these questions seems to lie in Miller's subscription to the view that trade is not merely important but *necessary* for development. (Miller suggests that integration into the world economy is a "precondition" for economic growth.[33]) If poor countries are incapable of developing in the absence of trading opportunities that are being withheld by rich countries, then it will be very hard for the latter to defend their actions by claiming that the former are responsible for their own plight. Miller's thought appears to be that terms of cooperation cannot be fair if they leave certain participants without reasonable opportunities for development and that trade restrictions imposed by rich countries are unfair for precisely that reason.

7.5 Special and differential treatment for developing countries

We have seen that the urgent needs of the global poor ground a strong case for the claim that rich countries should adopt a liberal policy toward developing world imports. We have seen that this case is not defeated by concerns about sweatshops or domestic workers but that accommodating those

---

30 Ibid., pp. 257–258.
31 Ibid., p. 253. I assume that, in Miller's terminology, what A can "legitimately demand" of B is what B is "required" to provide to A.
32 Ibid., p. 252.
33 Ibid., p. 253.

concerns will require a policy more nuanced than that implied by an unqualified endorsement of "free trade". Our focus so far has been on what the developing world can reasonably demand from the developed countries. Two additional questions ask what developed countries can reasonably ask of the developing world and what developed countries can reasonably ask of each other.

Of relevance here are two norms at the heart of the trade regime: the Most Favoured Nation (MFN) rule and the principle of reciprocity. According to the MFN rule, WTO member states must not treat any members less favourably than they treat any other. For example, if a tariff concession is offered to one state, it must be offered to all. According to the principle of reciprocity, states must endeavour to match the liberalization efforts of others; they must reciprocate the benefits that others have offered them. Rigid adherence to the MFN rule would mean that, if rich countries were to open their markets to the developing world, then they would be required to also open their markets to the other rich countries. And rigid adherence to the reciprocity principle would mean that, if rich countries were to open their markets to the developing world, the developing world would be required to open *its* markets to *them*.

However, the rules of the trade regime have (sensibly) not insisted on rigid adherence to these norms. Instead, they have recognized that the developing world is entitled to "special and differential treatment". Part IV of the General Agreement on Tariffs and Trade, which was added in 1965, proclaimed that the developing world was not bound by the reciprocity principle, and the Generalized System of Preferences, introduced in 1968, permitted developed countries to deviate from MFN by granting preferential market access to the developing world.

Nevertheless, rich countries often decline to avail themselves of the available opportunities and refuse to offer preferential treatment to their developing trading partners.[34] Meanwhile, they use the considerable bargaining power at their disposal to extract significant concessions from the poor.[35] Furthermore, other international institutions, such as the World Bank and International Monetary Fund, often force poor countries to lower their tariffs far below the levels that they have committed to in WTO negotiations.[36]

It is important to stress, then, that there are good reasons for holding that developing countries should be entitled to special and differential treatment and, more specifically, for denying that they can reasonably be expected to

---

34 Christopher Stevens, "Special and Differential Treatment", in Ivan Mbirimi, Bridget Chilala, and Roman Grynberg (eds.), *From Doha to Cancun: Delivering a Development Round* (London: Commonwealth Secretariat, 2003), p. 55.

35 Sarah Joseph, *Blame it on the WTO? A Human Rights Critique* (New York: Oxford University Press), p. 149.

36 Ibid.

rapidly open their markets to competition from the rich world. Consider three such reasons. First, import tariffs are an important source of revenue for poor countries. Joseph Stiglitz and Andrew Charlton note that whereas these tariffs account, roughly, for only one percent of revenues in rich countries, they account for roughly *thirty* percent of revenues in the least developed countries.[37] Moreover, Stiglitz and Charlton point to studies which suggest that trade taxes can be the best revenue-raising device that developing countries have at their disposal. This is because the collection costs associated with such taxes are often much lower than those of alternative forms of taxation.[38] Trade liberalization, then, can deprive governments in the developing world of an important means of raising revenue. Second, the harms suffered by displaced workers are often much greater in poorer countries. This is due to a variety of factors, including weaker social safety nets, limited opportunities for retraining, higher levels of unemployment, and lower levels of education.[39]

Third, some commentators have argued that if trade is to be an effective tool for development, poor countries must first establish the capacity to produce higher-quality goods. Because they possess abundant supplies of raw materials and cheap labour, the theory of comparative advantage recommends that poor countries should focus on the exportation of primary commodities and low-tech manufactures. But there are reasons to doubt the wisdom of this strategy. To begin with, the role that primary commodities play in production processes can be usurped by technology. For example, the apparel industry is often able to substitute cotton with cheaper synthetic fibres, and, as a result, the demand for cotton has shrunk.[40] Moreover, the advantages afforded by cheap labour can readily be undercut by competition from other countries. For example, manufacturing operations in Mexico were severely undermined by China's entry into the WTO, and China itself has subsequently been challenged by the arrival of Vietnam.[41] For these kinds of reasons, it is sometimes said that poor countries should not settle for the comparative advantage that they currently possess but should instead strive to cultivate a comparative advantage that is more likely to serve their long-term interests. In other words, they should adopt a *dynamic* conception of comparative advantage rather than thinking of comparative advantage in static terms.[42] Importantly, some economists believe that, in order to achieve this, poor countries will have to protect their "infant industries". If these

---

37 Stiglitz and Charlton, *Fair Trade for All*, p. 188. Cf. pp. 175–176.
38 Ibid., p. 28. Cf. p. 191.
39 Ibid., pp. 172, 175.
40 Poon and Rigby, *International Trade*, p. 109.
41 Joseph, *Blame it on the WTO?*, pp. 134–135.
42 Stiglitz and Charlton, *Fair Trade for All*, p. 30.

industries are exposed to global market forces prematurely, they will be crushed before they have the chance to become competitive.[43]

7.6 Fair trade as reciprocity

We have seen that there are good reasons to exempt poorer countries from the reciprocity principle and that it is morally problematic when members of the rich world pressure those countries into extensive and rapid market liberalization. But is the reciprocity principle a plausible principle to begin with? The reciprocity principle is often thought to specify a standard of fairness that should regulate trade among developed countries. But is the conception of fair trade embodied in the reciprocity principle an acceptable one?

Before we can answer this question, we shall need to acquire a clearer picture of what the reciprocity principle entails. The general idea behind the principle is that all parties should make roughly equivalent contributions to a shared endeavour. In the context of trade, the shared endeavour is the construction and maintenance of an international marketplace, which is achieved through the reduction and removal of various obstacles to trade. As we shall see, there are at least three distinct versions of the reciprocity principle. (Throughout this discussion, I will refer to the removal of tariffs, but it should be borne in mind that the principle also regulates the removal of other obstacles to trade.)

We can begin by considering *the standard reciprocity principle*. According to this version of the principle, each country should commit, in each round of trade negotiations, to a roughly equivalent set of concessions. For example, each country should cut the same number of tariffs, on the same products, and the cuts made should be of comparable size.[44] This version of the principle has intuitive appeal. As noted in the previous paragraph, adherence to a reciprocity principle is supposed to ensure that all parties make a roughly comparable contribution to a shared endeavour. The standard reciprocity principle appears to achieve that end by requiring all parties to make *exactly the same* contribution.

However, things are not so simple. Remember that the goal which member states are endeavouring to achieve is a free market. Now, in order to be able to establish whether the various countries have made comparable contributions to the achievement of that goal, we need to know not merely how many tariffs (and other obstacles) each country has *removed* but how many tariffs it erected in the first place.[45] Suppose that you and I share an office and that we both endeavour to keep the office clean and tidy. Now suppose that,

---

43 Joseph, *Blame it on the WTO?*, pp. 173–175.
44 Andrew G. Brown and Robert M. Stern, 'Concepts of Fairness in the Global Trading System', *Pacific Economic Review*, vol. 12, no. 3, 2007, pp. 293–318, at p. 300.
45 Christensen, *Trade Justice*, p. 101.

over time, the office becomes very cluttered and that this is largely my fault. It cannot plausibly be said that if we both do an equal amount of tidying we will thereby have contributed equally to the maintenance of a tidy office. If you and I do an equal amount of tidying but I have also created more mess, then I will have made a smaller contribution. Similarly, if, say, France and Germany each remove the same number of tariffs but France had more tariffs to begin with, then France will have made a smaller contribution. These reflections reveal that the standard reciprocity principle should be rejected. This principle should be rejected because adherence to it does not guarantee a reciprocal outcome.

A second version of the reciprocity principle avoids the shortcomings of the standard version that we have just considered. According to the *equal access reciprocity principle*, what matters is not the number and size of obstacles removed but the comparative openness of each country's markets: trade is fair when markets in each country are equally accessible.[46]

This version of the reciprocity principle comes in two varieties: *national* and *sectoral*.[47] According to the former, there must be equal access at the national level: the level of tariffs and other protectionist measures in one country must be no higher than the level of protectionist measures in other countries. On this view, the distribution of protectionist measures across different industries is unimportant. Australia may protect its agricultural industry to a greater extent than New Zealand, but if New Zealand protects its textile industry to a greater extent than Australia, then the demands of equal access reciprocity may nevertheless be satisfied.

By contrast, the *sectoral* version of the principle maintains that the distribution of market access must be the same in all countries. If New Zealand has few agricultural tariffs while Australia has many, then trade between these countries is regarded as unfair, irrespective of whether the level of protectionist measures employed by each country balances out at the national level.

Both versions of the equal access reciprocity principle are undermined by the same problem, namely, they produce unacceptable results. Consider the national version of the principle. Suppose that Australia and New Zealand impose the same number of tariffs but that Australia protects the markets of greatest value to New Zealand while New Zealand liberalizes the markets of greatest value to Australia. The national version of the equal access principle tells us that this situation is fair. But this judgement is clearly misguided. The national equal access principle is committed to this result because the overall number of tariffs imposed by each country is the same and this is taken to be the decisive consideration. No weight whatsoever is attributed to the fact

---

46 Kenneth W. Abbott, 'Defensive Unfairness: The Normative Structure of Section 301', in Jagdish Bhagwati and Robert E. Hudec (eds.), *Fair Trade and Harmonization: Volume 2 – Legal Analysis* (Cambridge, MA: MIT Press, 1996), p. 428.

47 Ibid., pp. 428–435.

that markets are valued differently by different countries. But this is surely an important consideration and one that should inform any attempt to assess the degree to which one country can be said to reciprocate the liberalizing efforts of another.[48] The example that I have given suggests that one shortcoming of the national equal access principle is that it produces "false positives": it tells us that situations are fair (in virtue of being adequately reciprocal) when in fact we have good reason to suspect that they are unfair (in virtue of being inadequately reciprocal).

Now consider the sectoral version of the equal access principle. Suppose that Country A has a comparative advantage in agriculture and therefore has a special interest in Country B ceasing to protect its agriculture market, while Country B has a comparative advantage in textiles and therefore has a special interest in Country A ceasing to protect its textiles market. Now suppose that both countries cease to protect their agriculture market while continuing to protect their textiles market to an equal extent. (For the sake of simplicity, ignore the various other industries that might exist in each country.) Because the distribution of market access in each country is the same (no agricultural protection, plus an equal degree of textile protection), the sectoral version of the principle tells us that this situation is fair. But this judgement, like those produced by the national version of the principle, fails to be informed by the fact that markets are valued differently by different countries. It completely overlooks the fact that Country B gives Country A everything it wants and that Country A fails to reciprocate.[49] The judgement therefore looks like another false positive.

7.7 Fair trade as equality

The various formulations of the reciprocity principle represent a conception of fair trade that is formally egalitarian in character. This conception is *formally* egalitarian in virtue of holding that trading partners should offer and receive equal (i.e., uniform) treatment. In the final section of this chapter, we should turn our attention to an alternative conception of fair trade that is *substantively* egalitarian in character.

We have seen that trade can promote growth and enable the most efficient utilization of a country's resources. In short, we have seen that trade enables countries to augment their incomes. According to a substantively egalitarian conception of fair trade developed by Aaron James, these national income gains should be distributed equally among all trading countries. In other words, all countries that participate in trade should benefit equally. If some participating countries benefit more than others, this is deemed to be unfair.[50]

---

48 Christensen, *Trade Justice*, p. 102.
49 Ibid., pp. 102–103.
50 James, *Fairness in Practice*, Ch. 6.

James allows some deviations from equality. To begin with, if inequality benefits poor countries, this is said to be acceptable. It is fair for poor countries to gain more than rich countries.[51] Indeed, James supports the kind of special and differential treatment for poor countries that was discussed in section 7.4. In addition, James allows inequalities of gain that arise because of certain national "endowments".[52] These include things like a country's climate, geography, and population size. Such features exist independently of trade and are likely to affect how much each country gains. James maintains that, when some countries do better than others as a result of their national endowments, such inequalities should be permitted.

So, James does not claim that the gains from trade must be distributed in a manner that is *strictly* equal. Rather, he claims that there is a *presumption* in favour of equal gain, which can sometimes be overturned. Why think that there is a presumption in favour of equal gain? At the heart of James's argument is the idea that the gains from trade are a product of social cooperation. All of the countries that participate in trade contribute to the creation of these gains.[53] They contribute by reducing barriers to trade and constructing an international marketplace, thereby enabling their trading partners to specialize according to comparative advantage. Because trading countries are "co-creators" of the gains from trade, each country has a presumptive claim to an equal share.

One objection to James's argument is that although all trading countries contribute to creating the gains from trade, some contribute more than others. An equal distribution looks natural if we assume that all countries contribute to the same degree, but if the contributions of each country vary, equality loses its intuitive appeal.

This point is illustrated by Mathias Risse and Gabriel Wollner, who ask us to consider trade between two fictitious countries, Skillistan and Resourcistan.[54] Skillistan "is poor in natural resources, but very rich in human resources: its people are skilled and creative" but "they need to import raw materials, e.g. rare earth elements, fully to unfold their abilities".[55] By contrast, Resourcistan is "enormously resource-rich".[56] Suppose that Skillistan imports the rare elements that it needs from Resourcistan, and its ingenious workers use these elements to create highly-sought-after high-tech gadgets. An implication of James's view is that Skillistan's profits should be shared equally with Resourcistan. Or rather, the large portion of Skillistan's

---

51 Ibid., p. 222.
52 Ibid.
53 Ibid., pp. 168–169, 177–178.
54 Mathias Risse and Gabriel Wollner, 'Critical notice of Aaron James, Fairness in Practice: A Social Contract for a Global Economy', *Canadian Journal of Philosophy*, vol. 43, no. 3, 2013, pp. 382–401, at pp. 394–395.
55 Ibid.
56 Ibid., p. 395.

profits that would not have been possible without trade should be shared equally. And this portion should be shared equally *because* it would not have been possible without trade. But this does not look like a plausible argument. As Risse and Wollner note, "This is as if one is making a cake but lacks the yeast: it would be odd if by giving some yeast somebody else would earn an entitlement to half the cake".[57]

This argument suggests an alternative account of how the gains from trade should be distributed. According to this account, "countries should benefit from trade in proportion to how much they contribute".[58] Countries that contribute more to the gains from trade should receive a larger share than those that contribute less. This contributory account abandons the egalitarianism with which we began.

But this account is also problematic. This is because how much a country contributes to the gains from trade may be influenced by its good or bad luck. For example, in the case described above, Resourcistan is able to contribute what it does in virtue of its abundant supply of natural resources. If some countries contribute less than Resourcistan simply because, through no fault of their own, they are not able to contribute more, it seems unfair for Resourcistan to walk away with a larger share of the gains.

Perhaps, then, we should aim for a distribution of the gains from trade that is free from what we earlier (in Chapter 4) called *morally arbitrary* inequality. We should ensure that no trading countries receive fewer gains than others through no fault of their own. The distribution of the gains from trade should be egalitarian in that sense.

But this is still not quite right. The problem with this view is that it attaches undue significance to gains reaped specifically through trade. We saw in Chapter 4 that a strong case can be made for global egalitarianism. However, global egalitarians do not believe that there should be an egalitarian distribution of *each and every* good that can be distributed. Rather, they believe that there should be an egalitarian distribution of (something like) opportunities for a flourishing life. From this perspective, whether or not there is an egalitarian distribution *of the gains from trade* is really neither here nor there. An egalitarian distribution of the gains from trade might contribute to the realization of global egalitarian goals and therefore be desirable. But it might also frustrate those goals.[59]

Suppose that, through sheer good fortune, a poor country does very well out of trade and receives a larger share of gains than its richer trading partners. Should a global egalitarian recommend redistributing these gains so that all countries – rich and poor alike – receive an equal share? Clearly not.

---

57 Ibid.
58 Ibid., p. 394.
59 Christensen, *Trade Justice*, pp. 141–142.

What global egalitarians should favour is a distribution of gains that promotes equal opportunity for flourishing. They should not worry about whether the distribution of gains itself conforms to an egalitarian pattern.[60]

7.8 Conclusion

We now have a clearer idea of what fair or just trade requires. Rich countries must offer their poorer trading partners special, more favourable, treatment. Moreover, rich countries cannot justify restricting trade with the poor by appealing to the interests of their domestic workers. This judgement can be defended even from a nationalist perspective. Rich countries will sometimes have reason to restrict the importation of goods produced under brutal conditions, but they must ensure that such restrictions will not actually make matters worse. The formal egalitarianism embodied in the various formulations of the reciprocity principle is unfounded, but a genuinely fair global economy will be egalitarian in a more substantive sense. This substantive egalitarianism need not require an equal distribution of the gains from trade, but rather a distribution of these gains that promotes the achievement of the more general egalitarian ends described in Chapter 4.

---

60 Ibid.

8 CLIMATE

Through agriculture and industry, the human species has repeatedly sought to transform its environment. We have mined and processed the earth's resources, cultivated the land, and constructed vast cities in once-desolate places. These efforts reflect a conscious endeavour to fashion a world more hospitable – more conducive to human habitation – than the one inherited by our ancestors. But scientists now believe that these efforts are also altering our planet in ways other than those we envisaged. Of course, it has never been a secret that human industry can have unintended consequences for our surroundings. Nineteenth-century Londoners could have been no less conscious of the fumes choking their streets than are the contemporary residents of Shanghai and Beijing. But there is now compelling evidence to suggest that the side effects of our industrial and agricultural practices are altogether more profound than was once widely recognized. Through their uncoordinated activities, human beings have been inadvertently and haphazardly interfering with the natural systems that regulate our planet's climate. As Stephen Gardiner has written, humans are unintentionally altering "the underlying dynamics of the planet's climate", thereby tampering with the processes that serve as "the basic life-support system both for themselves and all other forms of life on Earth".[1]

Alarming as this sounds, human-induced climate change was not immediately recognized as a cause for concern. On the contrary, the first person to publicly acknowledge the potential for such change was apparently unperturbed by its implications. Noting, in 1896, that accumulations of carbon dioxide (CO_2) in the earth's atmosphere could cause the planet's temperature to rise, the Swedish chemist Svante Arrhenius optimistically predicted that this would "allow all our descendants ... to live under a warmer sky and in a less harsh environment than we were granted".[2] In Arrhenius's view, climate

---

1 Stephen M. Gardiner, "Ethics and Global Climate Change", *Ethics*, vol. 114, no. 3, 2004, pp. 555–600, at p. 559.
2 Quoted in Steve Vanderheiden, *Atmospheric Justice: A Political Theory of Climate Change* (New York: Oxford University Press, 2008), p. 3.

change was a serendipitous occurrence, an unplanned development that was nevertheless to be welcomed.

Today's scientists are considerably less sanguine. As climate science has increased in sophistication, its outlook has become bleaker, and climatic change is now widely regarded as a serious threat to the future prospects of the earth's human and non-human inhabitants. This threat confronts present generations of our species with difficult practical challenges. How can dangerous climate change be avoided? How can political obstacles to action be overcome? It also confronts us with challenges that are ethical in character. How should the burdens associated with tackling climate change be allocated? What would constitute a fair distribution? And what are the moral costs of failing to take appropriately extensive action? In the first section of this chapter, I provide a brief overview of the relevant climate science. I then turn to the moral questions.

8.1 The nature of the problem

In 1988, the International Panel on Climate Change (IPCC) was established by the World Meteorological Organization and United Nations Environment Programme. It was tasked with collecting and evaluating "scientific, technological and socio-economic information in order to provide policymakers with a clear view of the current state of scientific knowledge relevant to climate change".[3] According to the IPCC's latest Assessment Report, which was published in 2014, the evidence for climate change is "unequivocal".[4] The research examined by the report's authors reveals that "[e]ach of the last three decades has been successively warmer at the Earth's surface than any preceding decade since 1850".[5] Moreover, in the Northern Hemisphere, "[t]he period from 1983 to 2012 was very likely the warmest 30-year period of the last 800 years".[6]

Why is climate change occurring? According to the IPCC, it is "extremely likely" that human activities "have been the dominant cause of the observed warming since the mid-20th century".[7] More specifically, it is widely believed that human beings are altering the climate by emitting huge quantities of "greenhouse gases" (GHGs). These gases include CO_2, methane, and nitrous oxide. They are produced by a variety of activities, including the burning of

---

3   International Panel on Climate Change, "IPCC Fact Sheet: What Literature does the IPCC Assess?", 30 August 2013, available at https://archive.ipcc.ch/news_and_events/docs/factsheets/FS_ipcc_assess.pdf.

4   R.K. Pachauri and L.A. Meyer (eds.), *Climate Change 2014: Synthesis Report. Contribution of Working Groups I, II and III to the Fifth Assessment Report of the Intergovernmental Panel on Climate Change* (Geneva: IPCC, 2014), p. 40.

5   Ibid.

6   Ibid.

7   Ibid., p. 47.

fossil fuels (coal, oil, and natural gas), deforestation, and the raising of cattle. These gases accumulate in the earth's atmosphere, where they form a "blanket" around the planet and prevent heat from escaping into space.

In order to properly understand the phenomenon with which we are concerned, it should be noted that there is an entirely natural "greenhouse effect" that occurs independently of human activities and that keeps the planet considerably warmer than it would otherwise be. But humans have dramatically enhanced this effect through the combustion of fossil fuels and other activities that significantly increase the concentration of GHGs in the atmosphere. According to the IPCC's latest Assessment Report, these concentrations "are at levels that are unprecedented in at least 800,000 years".[8] Elaborating, the report's authors note that concentrations of CO_2 have increased by 40% since 1750 and that concentrations of methane have increased by 150%.[9]

Our planet has natural mechanisms for "recycling" GHGs. The oceans and the biosphere (plants and soils) can and do absorb gases that collect in the atmosphere. But these mechanisms have been overwhelmed by the startling rate at which GHGs have been emitted. As Jerry Mahlman explains:

> When extra CO_2 first began to be added to the atmosphere through biomass and fossil fuel burning, the "unburdened reservoirs" of the upper levels of the oceans and the terrestrial biosphere were able to absorb a relatively large fraction of the "new" CO_2. However, over the 20th Century, more and more CO_2 has been deposited in these two "fast" reservoirs. As these fast reservoirs eventually become nearly saturated, their ability to absorb newly added CO_2 will become progressively less efficient.[10]

Mahlman concludes: "the earth's scientific 'deck' is stacked to make atmospheric CO_2 last in the future atmosphere considerably longer than it does today".[11]

The global warming produced by the enhanced greenhouse effect is having serious consequences for our planet. To begin with, the global mean sea level has risen and is predicted to continue rising.[12] This is partly because water

---

8 Ibid., p. 44.
9 Ibid.
10 Jerry D. Mahlman, "The Long Timescales of Human-Caused Climate Warming: Further Challenges for the Global Policy Process", in Walter Sinnott-Armstrong and Richard B. Howarth (eds.), *Perspectives on Climate Change: Science, Economics, Politics, Ethics* (Oxford: Elsevier, 2005), p. 17.
11 Ibid., p. 19.
12 Pachauri and Meyer, *Climate Change 2014*, pp. 42–44, 61–62.

expands as it warms and partly because ice sheets and glaciers located on land are melting and leaking into the oceans. As Henry Shue notes, a rising sea level could "have dramatic effects on New York, London, Shanghai, and other major cities, not to mention low-lying nations, such as Bangladesh and the Maldives".[13] Moreover, climate change is expected to increase risks from extreme weather events such as heat stress, storms, flooding, and landslides.[14] Such events will impose disproportionate costs on the world's poor. As the IPCC notes, "risks will be amplified for those lacking essential infrastructure and services or living in exposed areas".[15] Climate change is also expected to affect the distribution of "vectors" like mosquitoes and to thereby increase risks from serious diseases such as malaria and dengue fever.[16] In addition, climate change represents a serious threat to food security.[17] As Shue writes:

> [A]mong ecosystems, agricultural systems are especially touchy. Crops for humans need to be edible, which basically means they need to be just right. It cannot be too hot or too cold, too wet or too dry. If they are under-ripe, they cannot be eaten; if they are overripe, they cannot be eaten. If the rain comes too soon, they parch later; if the rain comes too late, they have already shrivelled or will rot. Farmers already gamble on the weather. Climate change is long-term weather change. Gambling on climate change is raising the odds greatly against the already wagering farmers, who keep us alive, when they are lucky.[18]

An especially alarming feature of climate change is that it appears to be creating the conditions for its own continuance. Climate scientists have identified a number of "positive feedback mechanisms", which are processes triggered by a rising temperature that in turn cause the temperature to rise further. One such mechanism involves the earth's surface reflectivity (or "albedo"). Ice and snow reflect the sun's rays back into space. They do this more effectively than vegetation and water and thereby play an important role in regulating the planet's temperature. When ice and snow melt, the earth absorbs more of the sun's energy. As a result, the planet grows still warmer, which leads to further melting of ice and snow, and the process continues.[19] Another potential positive feedback mechanism involves the

---

13   Henry Shue, *Climate Justice: Vulnerability and Protection* (Oxford: Oxford University Press, 2014), p. 288.
14   Pachauri and Meyer, *Climate Change 2014*, p. 69.
15   Ibid.
16   Ibid.
17   Ibid., pp. 67, 69.
18   Shue, *Climate Justice*, p. 268 (footnotes omitted).
19   Mahlman, "Long Timescales of Human-Caused Climate Warming", p. 12.

Arctic tundra. If the Arctic tundra were to thaw, it would release large quantities of methane. As methane is a potent GHG, this would stimulate further warming.

Disarming the threat of dangerous climate change will involve reducing our emissions of GHGs. What should be our target? According to one influential view, humanity should aim to ensure that the total amount of CO_2 emitted between the years 1750 and 2500 does not exceed one trillion tonnes.[20] But there are reasons to believe that this is an unduly permissive goal. The mean global surface temperature has already risen by about 1 °C above pre-industrial levels. Preventing the emission of the trillionth tonne is advocated as a way of avoiding a 2 °C rise above this baseline. But ensuring that emissions do not exceed a trillion tonnes will give us only a 50% chance of achieving this aim.[21] Moreover, the IPCC recently demonstrated that there are compelling reasons to ensure that the temperature peaks at a lower level: allowing the temperature to rise by 2 °C will expose us to dangers that could be avoided if the temperature were prevented from rising more than 1.5 °C.[22] Troublingly, if recent emission trends continue, humanity will fail to reach even the permissive target of 2 °C. We are currently expected to emit the trillionth tonne in 2035.[23] By the time the new generation of humans born this year reach college, humanity will have committed itself to dangerous climate change – unless it radically changes its ways.

8.2 The moral dimensions of our task: Avoiding the violation of human rights

In order to satisfy our needs and accomplish our goals, we human beings need access to energy, and, currently, the cheapest and most readily available sources of energy are fossil fuels. But, as our species now understands, using these fuels generates GHGs that threaten the environmental preconditions of a decent existence. If we are to live our lives in a manner that does not despoil our planetary home, we must find new ways of meeting our energy needs. We must end our reliance on fossil fuels and transition to a different kind of energy regime based on alternative forms of energy, such as solar energy, wind power, and hydroelectricity. Given the current dominance of fossil fuels in the marketplace, enacting this transition will most probably require some form of state intervention (such as a carbon tax or the

---

20 Myles Allen et al., "Warming Caused by Cumulative Carbon Emissions Towards the Trillionth Tonne", *Nature*, vol. 458, 2009, pp. 1163–1166.
21 Ibid.
22 Myles Allen et al., *Special Report: Global Warming of 1.5 °C* (Geneva: IPCC, 2018).
23 http://trillionthtonne.org/

establishment of a scheme in which emission permits must be purchased) to raise the price of fossil fuels, along with efforts to stimulate research and investment into alternative sources of energy. Moreover, governments will have to end their current practice of subsidizing the fossil fuel industry.

Radically reducing our combustion of fossil fuels – and thereby our emissions of GHGs – is a practical challenge. But it is important not to overlook the fact that this challenge comprises significant moral dimensions. Two moral aspects of our task are particularly noteworthy. First, a failure to address climate change adequately will amount to the infliction of unjust harm. If we fail to prevent the emission of the trillionth tonne of CO_2 and thereby allow mean global temperature rises to exceed 2 °C, there is good reason to believe that we will be violating human rights. Second, it matters morally *how* we address climate change. Reducing carbon emissions will create a variety of burdens, and the manner in which those burdens are shared can be just or unjust. This section and the next will consider these two moral dimensions of climate change in turn.

The primary victims of climate change will be future generations. Individuals not yet alive will suffer the consequences of ecological processes set in motion before they were born. The mere fact that we, present generations, have the ability to rescue future persons from a miserable fate, and to do so at comparatively little cost to ourselves, is itself a compelling reason to act to avert climate change. As we saw in Chapter 3, where we considered Peter Singer's drowning child analogy, we have demanding duties to assist those in distress. As Shue writes:

> The accumulation of carbon dioxide in the Earth's atmosphere will continue to increase unless those of us in the here and now cut back our emissions of it. There is no one else to do it: it is our fate to be alive when the problem of climate change has first been understood.[24]

From this perspective, tackling climate change can be seen as a form of "Good Samaritanism".[25]

But this way of framing the issue does not get the nature of our duties quite right. Although it is true that there is no one else to address climate change – either it will be solved by us or it will be solved by no one – this problem has not simply materialized out of the blue. Climate change has been caused by present generations and by our ancestors. This means that, to re-use terminology introduced in Chapter 3, our duties to future persons are not merely *positive* duties of assistance but *negative* duties to refrain from inflicting undue harms. As Shue observes, "unlike the Good Samaritan, we

---

24 Shue, *Climate Justice*, p. 289.
25 Ibid.

are not confronting an opportunity to help with a problem that is not of our own making … [W]e are not merely declining to be benevolent or charitable".²⁶ Elaborating, Shue writes:

> To persist in the activities that make climate change worse, and thereby make living conditions for future generations worse, is not merely to decline to provide protection. It is to inflict danger, and to inflict it on people who are vulnerable to us and to whom we are invulnerable. The relationship is entirely asymmetric: they are at our mercy, but we are out of their reach.²⁷

How should we conceive of the harms that climate change threatens to inflict? According to Simon Caney, if we do not act to minimize climate change by radically reducing our emissions of GHGs, the burdens that we impose on future generations will constitute violations of their human rights.²⁸ More specifically, by emitting the trillionth tonne, we will violate future persons' rights to life, health, and subsistence. Each of these rights can be interpreted more or less expansively, but Caney persuasively demonstrates that, even when they are interpreted minimally, climate change will engender their violation.

Consider, first, the right to life. An expansive interpretation of this right might entitle individuals to all kinds of protections against the various dangers that can threaten their lives. By contrast, a minimal interpretation holds simply that individuals may not be deprived of their lives in an arbitrary manner. This conception of the right to life is doubly limited. First, it is a *negative* right, in the sense that it imposes only a duty of restraint – a duty to refrain from killing – rather than any duties of protection or rescue.²⁹ Second, it is a duty to refrain from killing *arbitrarily*. Framed in this way, the right to life does not rule out forms of killing that can reasonably be regarded as non-arbitrary.³⁰ (Under certain conditions, self-defensive killings might be non-arbitrary in the relevant sense. No doubt, some would surely also claim that the death penalty is non-arbitrary when administered for the worst crimes, but we need not enter into that controversy here.)

This interpretation of the right to life – which appears in the International Covenant on Civil and Political Rights – is exceedingly limited, and yet, as Caney demonstrates, it would be violated by a failure to drastically curtail

---

26 Ibid., pp. 290–291.
27 Ibid., p. 270 (footnote omitted).
28 Simon Caney, "Climate Change, Human Rights, and Moral Thresholds", in Stephen Humphreys (ed.), *Human Rights and Climate Change* (Cambridge: Cambridge University Press, 2009).
29 Ibid., p. 76.
30 Ibid.

the emission of GHGs.³¹ As noted above, climate change will expose future persons to a variety of severe weather events, including violent storms, floods, and landslides, all of which threaten the lives of those they affect. It is difficult to deny that individuals killed by such phenomena will have been killed arbitrarily. The expected victims lack any morally relevant characteristics that could plausibly be thought to make the taking of their lives non-arbitrary. They will not have *deserved* their deaths as a punishment for some crime, nor will they have made themselves *liable* to acts of self-defence by threatening the vital interests of others. (The distinction between deserving of and liability for will be explained in the next chapter.) Rather, they will have been recklessly exposed to extreme dangers by earlier generations, including our own, with whom they could not interact in any way. The point is well made by Shue, who notes that the above considerations

> put the kind of wrong done by the avoidable precipitation of severe climate change ... in the general moral category of the infliction of damage or the risk of damage on the innocent and the defenceless. This is far worse than simply neglecting to protect rights, as wrong as that is, and is more like recklessly dropping bombs without knowing or caring whom they might hit.³²

Relatedly, Shue notes that climate change will also impose harms on "other species, most with no capacity for morally responsible action but full of capacity for suffering and frustration".³³

Consider, next, the right to health. Like the right to life, this right can be interpreted either expansively or minimally.³⁴ An expansive interpretation of the right to health appears in the International Covenant on Economic, Social and Cultural Rights, according to which each person has a right "to the enjoyment of the highest attainable standard of physical and mental health". Interpreted more minimally, the right to health can be seen as a right not to have one's health seriously threatened by others.³⁵ The latter interpretation is weaker than the former in two respects. First, it is a negative right. It does not demand that anyone *promote* the health of the right-holder (let alone ensure that it is maximized) but simply requires that everyone refrain from engaging in acts that would threaten to *reduce* the health of the right-holder in certain ways.³⁶ Second, the minimal version of the right to health

---

31 Ibid., pp. 77–78.
32 Shue, *Climate Justice*, p. 273.
33 Ibid.
34 Caney, "Climate Change, Human Rights, and Moral Thresholds", pp. 78–79.
35 Ibid., p. 79.
36 Ibid.

does not rule out *all* forms of health-threatening activity. Provided that the activities in question do not generate *serious* threats to a person's health, they can be pursued without violating the right to health.

Now, although climate change might undermine the ability of persons to enjoy "the highest attainable standard of physical and mental health", it might be denied that that is a compelling reason to tackle climate change, for a critic might argue that the existence of a right to enjoy the highest attainable standard of health is implausible. After all, ensuring that such a standard is achieved would seem to require diverting resources away from all other important projects, and it is natural to doubt whether such diversion can be justified.[37] But for present purposes, the important point to note is that climate change threatens the right to health even when that right is interpreted minimally. As we saw above, by engaging in activities that produce climate change, we are thereby exposing numerous individuals to enhanced risks from a variety of diseases such as malaria and dengue fever. By doing so, we are creating a serious threat to their health. Thus, even if we set aside the expansive (and more controversial) interpretation of the right to health and focus exclusively on the minimal version, we still arrive at the conclusion that the right to health is violated by climate change.[38]

Consider, finally, the right to subsistence. The International Covenant on Economic, Cultural, and Social Rights interprets this right expansively when it asserts that every person has a right "to an adequate standard of living for himself and his family, including adequate food". This wording appears to imply that when an individual is unable to secure an adequate standard of living, she can demand assistance from others.[39] This formulation can be contrasted with a more minimal version of the right, which holds only that each person has a right not to be deprived of the means of subsistence by others.[40] The expansive version of the right is entirely plausible, but its invocation is not necessary to demonstrate that climate change threatens the right to subsistence. As recorded in the previous section, climate change poses a serious threat to food security. Changes to the weather and climate disrupt agriculture and thereby undermine the ability of communities to feed themselves. This is especially true of poor communities in the Third World. We can therefore see that contributing to climate change violates the right to subsistence, even when that right is interpreted minimally.[41]

---

37 Ibid., pp. 78–79.
38 Ibid., pp. 79–80.
39 Ibid., pp. 80–81.
40 Ibid.
41 Ibid., pp. 81–82.

8.3 The moral dimensions of our task: Sharing the burden

We have now encountered the most important sense in which climate change is a moral issue. If we continue to emit GHGs and thereby produce dangerous climate change, there is good reason to think that we will be violating some of the most fundamental human rights of future persons. We should now turn to a second sense in which climate change is a moral issue. In order to bring this issue into focus, we can begin by noting that tackling climate change will involve a variety of distinct tasks. First, tackling climate change will entail efforts to reduce the size of the problem that we face. In other words, it will entail pursuing a strategy of *mitigation*.[42] Humanity's first priority is to prevent the global temperature from rising to dangerous levels. In order to do this, we will have to dramatically reduce our emissions of GHGs. This can be done in a variety of ways, but in order to ensure a reduction of the required magnitude, we will ultimately have to revolutionize our methods of attaining energy. What Shue calls "our technologically primitive energy regime based on setting fire to fossil fuels"[43] will have to give way to a new system built around alternative sources. Promoting this revolution will require considerable investment. In addition to reducing emissions of GHGs, mitigation involves the creation and maintenance of "carbon sinks" (such as forests), which can absorb GHGs and thereby prevent them from accumulating in the atmosphere.

Second, responding to climate change will involve ensuring that the world's population is adequately protected against those climatic dangers that we are no longer able to prevent from arising. Our planet has already warmed, and a certain degree of further warming is now unavoidable. It is therefore important to implement measures that will enable us to cope with this warming. In other words, responding to climate change will entail pursuing a strategy of *adaptation*.[44] This strategy might involve building sea walls to protect coastal communities from sea level rises; inoculating vulnerable populations against infectious diseases; augmenting drainage systems to cope with increased precipitation; implementing sophisticated early warning systems to protect people from storm surges; subsidizing the moving expenses of those who are forced to vacate dangerous areas; and sending food parcels to regions stricken with famine.[45]

Strategies of mitigation and adaptation are costly to implement. The second important moral issue raised by climate change concerns the manner in which these costs are allocated. How can the burdens associated with

---

42 Simon Caney, "Climate Change and the Duties of the Advantaged", *Critical Review of International Social and Political Philosophy*, vol. 13, no. 1, 2010, pp. 203–228, at p. 204.
43 Shue, *Climate Justice*, p. 263.
44 Caney, "Climate Change and the Duties of the Advantaged", p. 204.
45 Ibid.

tackling climate change be fairly shared? What would constitute an equitable distribution? We can make a start on trying to answer this question by considering two different moral principles: the *polluter pays principle* (PPP) and the *ability to pay principle* (APP). Before we describe these principles, it is worth noting that they can be applied to a variety of different entities. For example, they may be used to allocate costs to individual men and women, to states, to corporations, to international organizations, and so forth.[46]

According to the PPP, the costs associated with tackling climate change should be borne by those who caused the problem. Moreover, the size of the costs that one is expected to bear should reflect the extent of one's complicity. In other words, the more damage one inflicts, the more one should be required to pay.[47] This means that the costs of mitigation and adaptation should be paid by those who have emitted large quantities of GHGs, and the heaviest burdens should be shouldered by those who have emitted the most.

The APP comes in two different versions. Underpinning both versions is the thought that the costs associated with tackling climate change should be shouldered by those who are most capable, and the extent of one's responsibilities should reflect one's capacity to bear them.[48] The first version of the APP maintains that the responsibility for addressing climate change should be borne by the wealthy, and the most demanding responsibilities should be borne by the wealthiest.[49] If a particular agent, such as a state, is wealthier than another, then that agent's share of the burden should be proportionately greater. According to the second version of the APP, climate change should be addressed by those who can take effective action while making the smallest sacrifice.[50] If, say, tackling climate change is less demanding for state A than for state B – if A can act as effectively as B while incurring a smaller cost – then A should be expected to do more. This is true even if A and B are equally wealthy and even if B is wealthier.

The central difference between the PPP and the APP can be captured by saying that the former is a *backward-looking* principle whereas the latter is a *forward-looking* principle.[51] The PPP identifies who should pay by asking what has happened in the past. Who has emitted what? By contrast, the APP identifies who should pay by considering the different capacities of various agents to make a positive difference in the future. Who is best placed to implement a solution?

---

46 Ibid., p. 219.

47 Peter Singer, *One World: The Ethics of Globalization* (New Haven, CT: Yale University Press, 2002), pp. 32, 33–34.

48 Edward Page, "Climatic Justice and the Fair Distribution of Atmospheric Burdens: A Conjunctive Account", *The Monist*, vol. 94, no. 3, pp. 412–432, at p. 418.

49 Ibid.

50 Ibid.

51 Caney, "Climate Change and the Duties of the Advantaged", pp. 205, 213.

Each of these principles is intuitively plausible, but in some cases they pull in different directions. This point can be illustrated by comparing the wealth and CO_2 emissions of Australia and Germany. Between 1900 and 2004, Australia emitted 11,929 million tonnes of CO_2, and in 2006 its gross domestic product (GDP) per capita was $35,547; in the same period, Germany emitted 73,626 million tonnes of CO_2, and in 2006 its GDP per capita was $32,322.[52] Given that Germany has emitted a much larger amount of CO_2, the PPP suggests that Germany should do more to address climate change (assuming that Germany would still be the bigger polluter once GHGs other than CO_2 are taken into consideration). But because Australia's GDP per capita is higher, the APP suggests that Australia should do more to address climate change (or at least this is what is suggested by the first of the two versions of the APP distinguished above).

Because the PPP and the APP sometimes provide divergent answers to the question of how climate-related responsibilities should be distributed, we shall have to adjudicate between them if we are to work out what should be done. Which of the two principles should we prefer? Let us consider their relative strengths and weaknesses.

8.3.1 The polluter pays principle

At first blush, the PPP is an appealing principle. In many cases where we have to select someone to pay the cost of fixing a particular problem, the person who caused the problem will be an obvious candidate. This is for multiple reasons. First, having a rule that requires people to fix the problems that they created gives each person a strong incentive to refrain from creating problems in the first place. Thus, a principle like the PPP is an appropriate rule to implement if we wish to minimize the creation of problems (which we obviously do). Of course, the PPP cannot serve this incentive-creating function when it is applied *retroactively* – i.e., when the principle is introduced to allocate the costs of repairing a problem that already exists. It serves this function only when applied *prospectively* – i.e., when it is used to allocate the costs of repairing *future* problems. A second virtue of principles like the PPP is that they seem intuitively fair. Since the costs of fixing any given problem will inevitably fall on *someone*, it seems only right that they be made to fall on those who have caused the problem rather than on some innocent third party.

However, this last observation exposes the PPP to a seemingly powerful objection. We have drawn a moral distinction between problem-makers, on the one hand, and third parties, on the other, by appealing to the innocence of the latter, thereby implicitly suggesting that the former are *not* innocent but rather *culpable* or *blameworthy*. But from the fact that an individual

---

52 Page, "Climatic Justice and the Fair Distribution of Atmospheric Burdens", p. 419.

causes a problem, we cannot infer that she is culpable. Some problems may arise from morally innocent activity. Moreover, we have good reason to doubt the culpability of certain polluters. This reason for doubt is the fact that many emitters of GHGs were excusably ignorant of the consequences of their activities.[53] As noted at the beginning of the chapter, the climate-altering potential of fossil fuel combustion was first recognized, by Svante Arrhenius, well over a century ago. However, it is only in recent decades that a fully adequate understanding of climate change has been achieved and widely disseminated. As was also noted at the beginning of the chapter, it was not until 1988 that the IPCC was established, and it was a further two years before the IPCC released its first report. It can therefore plausibly be argued that prior to 1990, emitters of GHGs could not reasonably be expected to have foreseen the harmful consequences of their actions. Yet, in allocating adaptation and mitigation costs to *all* polluters, regardless of when their polluting activity took place, the PPP is insensitive to this fact. A fairer approach, it might be argued, would distinguish between *culpable polluters* (those who could have been reasonably expected to foresee the harmful consequences of their actions) and *innocent polluters* (those who could not have been reasonably expected to foresee the harmful consequences of their actions). The PPP could then be applied to culpable polluters but not to innocent polluters. Call this the *innocent polluter argument*.

Is this argument persuasive? Should the PPP be applied only to culpable polluters, or is it plausible to think that it should also be applied to innocent polluters? In defence of the claim that the PPP should be applied to at least *some* innocent polluters, it has been pointed out that, in certain cases, innocent polluters have not merely caused environmental damage but also *benefitted* from causing such damage. By emitting large quantities of GHGs, some states, firms, and individuals have been able to acquire economic advantages that would otherwise have been unobtainable. According to Caney, this fact is morally relevant.[54] If the harmful activities that an innocent polluter has (blamelessly) engaged in have not only inflicted damage but also gifted the innocent polluter with resources that could be used to *rectify* those damages, then perhaps it is reasonable to expect the innocent polluter to pay (at least if the costs incurred are proportionate to the benefits reaped). Call this the *polluter-beneficiary argument*.

The polluter-beneficiary argument for applying the PPP to some innocent polluters is problematic. To see why, consider the following scenario. Suppose that Anne engages in one seemingly innocent activity (Activity A) and derives benefits from doing so, while Ben engages in some other seemingly innocent activity (Activity B) and likewise derives benefits from doing so. Suppose, further, that the benefits reaped by Anne and Ben from their

---

53 Caney, "Climate Change and the Duties of the Advantaged", p. 208; Page, "Climatic Justice and the Fair Distribution of Atmospheric Burdens", pp. 416–417.

54 Caney, "Climate Change and the Duties of the Advantaged", pp. 209–210.

respective projects are identical. It is subsequently discovered that Activity A produces harmful consequences, which Anne could not reasonably have been expected to foresee, while Activity B produces no harmful consequences. An upshot of the polluter-beneficiary argument is that Anne should be required to relinquish her benefits in order to fix the damages caused by her innocent activity. But surely this treats Anne unfairly. From a moral perspective, Anne and Ben have acted identically. They have each engaged in activities that they reasonably believed were morally innocent. From Anne's point of view, the fact that Activity A turned out to be harmful is simple bad luck. So why is Anne being penalized? Why not distribute the costs of fixing Activity A's harmful side effects equally between Anne and Ben rather than letting these costs fall exclusively on Anne? If we assume that there are no further relevant differences between Anne and Ben, this looks like a fairer policy.

Note that the polluter-beneficiary argument is likely motivated, in part, by the thought that its recommendations leave Anne no worse off than she would have been had she never engaged in Activity A. This thought is prompted by reflection on the fact that Anne is required to relinquish only those gains that Activity A made possible. But this motivating supposition is groundless. This is because Anne's engagement in Activity A likely entailed non-negligible *opportunity costs*. By engaging in Activity A, Anne forewent opportunities to engage in various other activities (Activities B, C, D, and so forth), all of which could have yielded significant returns. Depriving Anne of the benefits that Activity A made possible likely *does* make her worse off than she would have been had she never engaged in Activity A, for if she had not engaged in Activity A, then she likely would have undertaken some other beneficial endeavour. The time that Anne devoted to Activity A is time that she will not get back. The recommendations of the polluter-beneficiary argument can thus make innocent polluters considerably worse off than they could otherwise have been, and, as we have seen, this disadvantage is imposed in response to the fact that innocent polluters suffer from simple bad luck.

While the polluter-beneficiary argument fails, there is another, stronger, reason for thinking that the PPP should often be applied even to innocent polluters. Notice that many polluters who may have been reasonably ignorant about climate change prior to 1990, and who therefore may be classed as innocent polluters up until that date, have continued to pollute heavily *subsequent* to 1990. In other words, these polluters have continued to emit large quantities of GHGs even after ignorance about climate change could no longer be regarded as reasonable. Yesterday's innocent polluters are today's culpable polluters. Yet if a polluter has continued to emit GHGs post-1990, when he could reasonably be expected to foresee the harmful consequences of doing so, then we are justified in thinking that his reasonable ignorance was not the primary explanation of his polluting activities *pre*-1990. More specifically, we are justified in believing that he would have engaged in these activities even if he had *not* been reasonably ignorant of their harmful consequences. Given this justified belief, the fact that the polluter in question *was* reasonably ignorant prior to 1990 does not seem to constitute a compelling reason to restrict application of the PPP. We should expect the polluter to pay for his pre-1990 emissions regardless of the fact that he was reasonably ignorant of their likely consequences.[55]

The foregoing reflections reveal that concerns about reasonable ignorance are not as threatening to the PPP as initial appearances might suggest. The PPP can be applied to both culpable *and* innocent polluters, at least when the latter have continued to emit large quantities of GHGs after the point at which they could no longer plausibly claim to be reasonably ignorant. Nevertheless, the PPP faces a further potential challenge. This challenge, like the innocent polluter argument, begins with the thought that the PPP fails to draw relevant distinctions between different kinds of polluters. More specifically, it begins by highlighting the fact that the PPP does not distinguish between wealthy polluters, on the one hand, and poor polluters, on the other. Although many of the largest contributors to climate change are exceptionally rich states, such as the US, some considerably poorer countries also emit large quantities of GHGs. Most notably, China now emits more GHGs per year than does any other country. An implication of this is that the PPP would require China to make very large contributions to tackling climate change. But since China is a developing country, and many of its citizens continue to live in abject poverty, it is natural to question whether it is reasonable to treat China in the same way as other, wealthier, polluters. Given that discharging burdensome climate-related responsibilities is likely to undermine China's economic development and thus its ability to meet the most basic needs of its poorest citizens, the imposition of such responsibilities looks patently unjust.[56] This observation reveals that the two moral dimensions of climate change – (i) avoiding the imposition of unjust harm and (ii) allocating climate-related responsibilities in an equitable manner – are not entirely distinct. Certain allocations of responsibilities are unfair precisely because they impose unjust harms on the poor.[57]

Now, in order to ensure that it does not licence policies that would saddle the poor with crushing burdens, the PPP could be modified to apply only to those countries that cross a suitably defined development threshold. This modification allows the PPP to escape one objection but exposes it to another. If the PPP holds only wealthy polluters responsible for fixing the problems they have created, while exempting poorer polluters, certain climatic responsibilities will remain unallocated: the costs associated with remedying climate harms produced by poorer countries will not be paid. The

---

55 Ibid., pp. 208, 209.
56 Ibid., pp. 212, 213.
57 Shue, *Climate Justice*, p. 337.

PPP thus falls short of completing its task, which is to explain how the costs of tackling climate change should be distributed.

Let us consider one final shortcoming of the PPP. This shortcoming becomes apparent once we recognize that many polluters are long dead. Some of the CO_2 that is saturating the biosphere and oceans and accumulating in the atmosphere was released by individuals from previous generations who are no longer alive. The PPP tells us that the costs associated with tackling climate change must be borne by those who have caused climate change and that the costs one bears should be proportionate to one's contribution to the problem, but, clearly, costs cannot be paid by those who are no longer around. This observation reveals that there is a further set of costs – those associated with fixing problems created by polluters who have subsequently died – that the PPP fails to allocate.[58] Once again, we have reason to think that the PPP will inevitably fall short of completing its task.

Having noted several challenges to the PPP, let us now consider its main rival: the APP.

8.3.2 The ability to pay principle

Recall that, according to the APP, the costs of addressing climate change should be borne by those who are most able to bear them. This is the core idea underlying the principle's different instantiations. As mentioned above, the APP is a forward-looking principle. In determining who should bear which costs, it pays no attention to what has happened in the past. More specifically, in deciding who should pay to tackle climate change, the principle makes no reference to facts about who has caused climate change.

One important advantage of the APP is that it is likely to ensure that all costs are allocated. As we saw, the main weakness of the PPP is that it leaves some costs unassigned. This is because it allocates costs for remedying climate harms to the polluters who caused them, but (i) some polluters are dead and (ii) poor polluters have to be exempted. The APP avoids this problem. While the PPP limits our attention to those who have caused particular climate harms, the APP allows us to cast a wider net. From the perspective of the APP, if there are people who are capable of bearing a cost, there are people to whom that cost can be allocated. And, given that there are many people in the world who are vastly wealthy, it is unlikely that we will struggle to find people by whom the relevant costs can be borne.

The APP avoids the main deficiency of the PPP by severing the link between two kinds of responsibility: (i) responsibility for creating a problem and (ii) responsibility for fixing that problem. The APP holds that one can be responsible for fixing a problem irrespective of whether one is also responsible for creating it. In fact, the APP says that in identifying who should do

---

58 Caney, "Climate Change and the Duties of the Advantaged", pp. 210–211.

what to fix climate change, we should pay no attention whatsoever to who contributed what to creating climate change. Those who contributed little to its creation can be expected to contribute significantly to its resolution (if and because they have the ability to do so), and those who contributed significantly to its creation can be expected to contribute little to its resolution (if and because they are less able to do so). This implication of the APP renders the principle vulnerable to criticism. Should one's responsibility for fixing a problem not be proportionate to one's responsibility for creating it? Why should capable individuals be required to make sacrifices in order to fix problems that they have not contributed to creating, when those sacrifices could be made instead by individuals who *have* contributed? If certain polluters are incapable of fixing the damage that they have caused (e.g., because they are dead), then we will obviously have to look elsewhere in order to assign responsibility, and considerations relating to ability might appropriately guide our search. Similarly, if certain polluters will suffer massive harms if they are expected to fix the damages that they have caused (e.g., because they are poor), then again we will have good reason to assign responsibility elsewhere, and considerations relating to ability might again be relevant. But it seems unfair to simply set aside, from the outset, the question of who caused which damages and to focus exclusively on the question of ability.

We have seen that there are significant problems with both the PPP and the APP. The former leaves certain costs unallocated, whereas the latter looks unfair. However, it is important to note that these problems arise only when each principle is employed in isolation. So far, we have assumed that if either principle is used, it will serve as our exclusive guide to how the costs of climate change should be allocated. But this assumption is unwarranted. Rather than adopting either principle in isolation, we could combine the two principles.[59] Importantly, this would enable us to avoid the various problems associated with each. To start with, if the PPP were not employed in isolation, its inability to allocate every last cost would not be a fatal deficiency. As we saw, the PPP cannot assign some costs since some polluters are dead, and, in order to be defensible, the PPP would have to be qualified so as not to assign costs to the poor. Until now, we have inferred from this that certain costs will simply not be paid. But if the PPP is supplemented with the APP, the leftover costs could be assigned instead to those who are most able to pay them. Moreover, if the APP is employed only in this limited manner, it avoids the criticism of unfairness. When the APP is used simply as a mechanism for allocating those costs that are left unassigned by the PPP, it cannot be said that we are unfairly setting aside considerations of complicity. We assign costs to those most able to bear them only when it is not possible to assign them to the relevant polluters (because they are dead) or because it

---

59 Caney, "Climate Change and the Duties of the Advantaged", p. 213; Page, "Climatic Justice and the Fair Distribution of Atmospheric Burdens", pp. 425–430.

would be unreasonable to assign them to the relevant polluters (because they are poor).

We have been trying to establish how the costs of combating climate change can be distributed in an equitable manner. In our search for principles to govern this distribution, we have seen that two promising candidates encounter significant problems when used in isolation but also that these problems can be circumvented when the two principles are employed in combination. In short, we have seen how the difficulties associated with the second moral dimension of climate change can be resolved.

8.4 Why not make future generations pay?

I have suggested that a significant share of the burden of addressing climate change should be borne by present generations of polluters. I have also suggested that if present generations do not take adequate action to mitigate the effects of climate change, and to introduce adaptations that will enhance our ability to cope with the climatic changes that are now inevitable, the human beings who currently inhabit the planet will violate the rights of future persons.

These views are sometimes challenged. One occasionally encounters the claim that current generations should not shoulder the burdens of dealing with climate change but should instead allow those burdens to be borne by our descendants. Perhaps surprisingly, this claim is made not only by the pathologically selfish but also by those who profess to care about equity. It is sometimes argued that allowing the costs of climate change to fall on future generations is in fact the fairest course of action.

How has this claim been defended? One line of defence appeals to considerations of ability: as was noted in the previous section, some people are better placed to tackle climate change than others. In some cases, this differential ability is attributable to differential wealth. Some people are richer than others, and since the task of addressing climate change is costly, this task often can be undertaken more effectively, and with greater ease, by those who are better off. Now, one argument made by those who think that climate change should be dealt with by future generations begins with the premise that our descendants will be considerably wealthier than we are. It is then pointed out that if future generations will be richer, they will have more resources with which to address climate change. From this, it is sometimes inferred that addressing climate change will be less burdensome for future generations than it is for us and that present generations therefore are justified in shifting a large degree of responsibility to future persons.

An argument of this kind is made by the economist William Nordhaus, who writes:

> Industrial countries have witnessed more or less continual growth in living standard for more than a century... Most global change models project continued rapid growth of living standards in the future... Society might [therefore] well feel that it is appropriate for later, richer generations to pay a larger fraction of greenhouse gas (GHG) control costs, just as high-income people pay a larger fraction of their income in income taxes.[60]

The policy Nordhaus recommends is known as *growth discounting* because it "discounts" future burdens (i.e., it regards these burdens as less significant) and does so on the grounds that these burdens will be borne by individuals who, as a result of economic growth, will be better off than individuals alive today.

What can be said in response to the advocates of growth discounting? A first reply appeals to considerations that were first canvassed in our discussion of the APP. As was noted above, focusing exclusively on ability, and completely ignoring the question of who was responsible for causing climate change in the first place, simply looks unfair. Suppose that my colleague, Polly, is caught speeding and is subsequently forced to pay a fine. If I am wealthier than Polly, then paying the fine might be less burdensome for me than it would be for her. But, under normal circumstances, it would nevertheless be unreasonable for Polly to expect me to pay the fine on her behalf. Similarly, dealing with climate change might be less burdensome for future generations than it is for us. But given that current generations have done more than any other to cause climate change, it seems unreasonable for those generations to expect the lion's share of the costs to be borne by future persons who have not done *anything* to contribute to climate change and could not have done anything to prevent it.

Second, we should not think of future generations as a homogeneous entity. The individuals who comprise future generations, like the individuals who comprise current generations, will each face very different circumstances, and the ability to adapt to climate change will not be equally distributed among them. More specifically, the prospects of adaptation among the poor will be bleaker than those among the rich. Third, we should avoid the chauvinistic temptation to focus primarily or exclusively on the adaptability of future generations *of our own species*. The climatic changes that human beings are creating pose serious threats to all of the species that inhabit the earth, not only to our own, and any advantages enjoyed by future humans need not yield benefits for future animals. Maybe future generations will have the capacity and inclination to protect the animals with whom they will share a perhaps ravaged planet, or maybe they will prove to be just as

---

60 William D. Nordhaus, "Discounting in economics and climate change: an editorial comment", *Climatic Change*, vol. 37, no. 2, 1997, pp. 315–328, at p. 317.

negligent as our own. The previous two points are both made by Shue, who writes: "It might be that wealthy people could, at great expense, adapt rapidly enough after changes in climate had occurred, but poor people and many species of plants and animals could not".[61]

Fourth, we should not simply assume that greater wealth will enable future generations to purchase solutions to the problems that they will have to confront if aggressive mitigation strategies are not implemented in the present. Solutions to these problems may not be available to them, at any price. This is because there are limits to the degree to which human beings (and all other species) can adapt, regardless of how much they are able and willing to spend. As Caney notes, "there are limits to the extent to which the destruction of *natural resources* can be addressed by the substitution of capital and *human resources*".[62] The point is well made by Shue:

> Any plant or animal [including humans] can handle gradual increases or decreases across a certain range at up to a certain rate in critical parameters such as temperature, moisture, nutrition, sunlight, top wind speed, length of growing season, and so on. But at some point for each parameter for each species, a limit is reached. And of course many species are interdependent: if a plant becomes extinct, an animal for which it was food may become extinct, and a predator for which that animal was prey may, as well. The extent of adaptation is astounding; and the resilience of individuals and species can be remarkable. Nevertheless, adaptation has severe – in fact, fatal – limits for each species on the rate at which adjustments can occur.[63]

In short, shifting climate-related responsibilities onto our descendants cannot be justified by arguments built around the premise that future persons will be more advantaged than present generations. However, advocates of such a policy sometimes invoke an argument that does not employ this premise. It is sometimes argued that shifting responsibilities onto our descendants is justified regardless of whether or not subsequent generations will be better off. Policies of mitigation and adaptation introduced today will create benefits for future generations that would otherwise have been unavailable. However, if these policies are undertaken, benefits that could otherwise have been enjoyed by the present generations that implement them will have to be foregone. According to some economists, we should attach more value to benefits that can be enjoyed in the present than to benefits that could be

---

61 Shue, *Climate Justice*, p. 101.

62 Simon Caney, "Climate Change, Intergenerational Equity and The Social Discount Rate", *Politics, Philosophy & Economics*, vol. 13, no. 4, 2014, pp. 320–342, at p. 330 (emphases added); cf. Caney, "Climate Change and the Duties of the Advantaged", p. 220.

63 Shue, *Climate Justice*, p. 229.

made available in the future. From this, it is sometimes inferred that we should not attempt to tackle climate change today, for doing so will sacrifice more valuable present-day benefits for the sake of less valuable future benefits. This approach is known as *pure time discounting* because it "discounts" future benefits (regards them as less significant) and does so on the grounds that they are further away in time.

What can be said in defence of this approach? According to one commonly made argument, pure time discounting reflects human psychology. If we look at people's actual preferences, we will see that they typically do attach greater value to present benefits than to those that are further away in time. As one economist suggests, human beings have a "preference [for] immediate over postponed consumption".[64] To illustrate, suppose that my colleague asks me to cover her teaching for the week. If, in return, she offers to unburden me of an equivalent amount of administrative duties and to do so before the end of the month, this might look like a reasonable proposal. By contrast, if my colleague offers to do an equivalent amount of my administrative duties but in ten years' time, the proposal will look considerably less attractive. This might be because I regard present benefits as more valuable than future benefits, even when the benefits in question are identical.

The next move in the argument for pure time discounting is to suggest that our account of climate justice ought to correspond to the way in which people actually think about the future. Given the nature of our inborn preferences, we ought to delay action on climate change. This will involve giving up certain benefits that would otherwise have been available in the future, but in return we will be free to enjoy the more valuable benefits that are available today and that would otherwise have had to be surrendered.

It is not hard to see where the reasoning behind pure time discounting goes awry when applied to the case of our climatic responsibilities. Suppose that each of us really does have an inborn preference for present over future benefits. This preference relates to the way in which we each value the various benefits that might be available to us at different stages of our own lives. But policies of mitigation and adaptation do not postpone our enjoyment of benefits that would otherwise have been available to us today. Rather, such policies transfer these benefits to subsequent generations. To put the point the other way around, postponing mitigation and adaptation does not enable us to access now benefits that we otherwise would have received at a later date. Rather, such postponement gifts us advantages that have been taken from our descendants.[65] It is one thing for me to attach less value to benefits that I could enjoy in the future to those that I could enjoy today and to substitute the latter for the former. It is something else entirely for me to attach

---

64 Samuel Fankhauser, "The Social Costs of Greenhouse Gas Emissions: An Expected Value Approach", *The Energy Journal*, vol. 15, no. 2, 1994, pp. 157–184, at p. 172.

65 Thomas C. Schelling, "Intergenerational Discounting", *Energy Policy*, vol. 23, no. 4/5, 1995, pp. 395–401, at p. 396.

less value to the benefits that *other people* could enjoy in the future and to substitute *my* benefits for *theirs*.[66] We cannot justify discounting across generations by pointing out that we typically discount within our own lives.[67] Our personal consumption preferences have no implications whatsoever for how we ought to value the consumption opportunities available to future persons.

Other arguments might be offered in defence of pure time discounting and these would have to be assessed on their own merits, but it is important to note that there is a powerful argument against pure time discounting. During our discussion of global inequality in Chapter 4, we encountered the idea that there are certain aspects of persons that are "morally arbitrary". These are characteristics such as social class and country of birth for which individuals cannot be held morally responsible and that fail to track any considerations that could appropriately be used to determine one's entitlements. As we saw in Chapter 4, it is unfair to allow such morally arbitrary characteristics to affect people's life prospects. Now, for present purposes, it is important to observe that the date on which one is born is also a morally arbitrary characteristic. We are not responsible for when we are born, and the good or bad luck of arriving in this world at one period of history rather than another cannot plausibly be regarded as a consideration that ought to determine one's entitlements. It is thus unfair to implement policies that allow persons' life prospects to be determined by their date of birth. Yet this is precisely what is recommended by advocates of pure time discounting. The point is well made by Caney, who writes:

> [W]e have no reason to attribute fundamental moral importance to someone's location in time... [S]omeone's temporal location seems on a par with their racial identity or gender or ethnicity; and in the same way that it is wrong to penalize or discriminate against someone because of their race or gender so it is also wrong to discriminate against someone because of their date of birth. It is not the right kind of property to confer on people extra or reduced moral status.[68]

We have been considering the claim that present generations should delay action on climate change and thereby shift climatic responsibilities onto the shoulders of our descendants. We have seen that reasons adduced for doing so are not compelling and that there are also powerful arguments against this course of action. These observations embolden us to stand by the

---

66 Darrel Moellendorf, *The Moral Challenge of Dangerous Climate Change: Values, Poverty, and Policy* (Cambridge: Cambridge University Press, 2014), p. 112.

67 Ibid., p. 95.

68 Caney, "Climate Change, Intergenerational Equity and The Social Discount Rate", pp. 323–324.

conclusions that we reached in previous sections. Strategies of mitigation and adaptation should be pursued immediately. If they are not, our generation will violate the human rights of future persons. However, there is one further challenge that must be addressed before these conclusions can be vindicated.

8.5 The problem of uncertainty

The future of our planet is uncertain. This is partly because we do not know how influential members of our species will act.[69] (Will future leaders of powerful countries like the US take bold steps to curb emissions? Or will they act with the same breath-taking recklessness exhibited by their forebears?) But the future would remain uncertain even if this information were available to us. We know that the various paths that humanity could pursue are likely to lead to particular outcomes, some worse than others, but the probability of these outcomes occurring cannot be calculated. (When the term is used in a technical sense, this is precisely what it means to say that something is uncertain: that the probability of its occurrence resists calculation.) But if we do not know for certain which precise outcomes correspond to which courses of action, does this not undermine the case for mitigation and adaptation? Why not continue with business-as-usual?

Shue points out that climate change has three important characteristics that make the fact of uncertainty largely irrelevant to what we ought to do.[70] First, the harms that climate change could produce are very large.[71] As we have seen, climate change seriously threatens very basic interests in health, subsistence, and life itself. Second, although it is not possible to specify the probability of these harms, there is a significant likelihood that they will occur. The causal process that would lead to their occurrence is well understood. Scientists have identified the mechanism that would produce such harms, and, crucially, the conditions that allow this mechanism to function are taking shape.[72] We understand that the burning of fossil fuels produces CO_2, that CO_2 accumulates in the atmosphere and causes the planet to warm, and that rising temperatures produce various phenomena detrimental to the wellbeing of the planet's inhabitants. Moreover, we know that fossil fuels are being burned at an extraordinarily high rate, that copious amounts of CO_2 have been released, and that the planet is indeed warming. We can therefore see a clear route from where we are now to a future scenario in which the earth offers a considerably less habitable environment.

---

69 Moellendorf, *Moral Challenge of Dangerous Climate Change*, pp. 64–65.
70 Shue, *Climate Justice*, pp. 265–276.
71 Ibid., pp. 268–269, 269–274.
72 Ibid., pp. 268, 269.

Third, the costs of addressing climate change are not unduly large, at least if they are shared equitably.[73] Given the severity of the harms that unchecked climate change could produce, the costs of mitigation and adaptation are able to satisfy a proportionality requirement: these costs are not excessive in relation to the harms that we are trying to avoid.[74] Moreover, for rich countries, the opportunity costs of tackling climate change are not extreme; curbing emissions does not require us to sacrifice anything that is especially important. Shue makes the point bluntly: "Much of our current GHG emissions ... result from thoughtlessness, laziness, and wastefulness; and much serves purposes that are opulent, frivolous, or pointless".[75]

In the absence of one or more of these three characteristics, uncertainty could make the pursuit of mitigation and adaptation unwise. If the anticipated harms of climate change were relatively trivial, or the costs of preventing them very high, then the fact that their occurrence is also uncertain might tip the balance in favour of inaction. But since all three characteristics are present – the anticipated harms are large and likely and can be prevented at tolerable cost – the fact that the occurrence of these harms is uncertain does not seem pertinent. The possible gains of inaction are too small; the likely costs much too high.

---

73 Ibid., pp. 268, 269, 273–274, 274–276.
74 Ibid., p. 274.
75 Ibid., p. 273.

9 WAR

Throughout this book, we have encountered a variety of ways in which members of one political community can adversely affect the life prospects of those in another (e.g., by excluding would-be immigrants, restricting trade, and emitting greenhouse gases). In this chapter, we turn to one of the most conspicuous and dramatic ways in which harms can be inflicted across national borders, namely, through acts of war. We shall consider under what conditions, if any, war can satisfy the requirements of justice.

One might be doubtful that war can ever satisfy those requirements. For we think of justice as a noble and virtuous ideal, the mark of a civilized society, whereas war seems primitive and brutish, a vulgar remnant of a less enlightened age. One might suppose that, if we are to be progressives, we must side with the anti-war activists who take to the streets whenever military action is proposed. When faced with a choice between acting violently or peacefully, one might be inclined to think that we must always favour the latter, for peace is surely the more natural companion to justice.

But just institutions are often threatened and sometimes destroyed. When this happens, we rightly wish to ensure that justice is preserved or restored, and one cannot simply assume that, in such a scenario, recourse to war is never morally acceptable. As we have seen, justice endows each individual with a variety of entitlements that we call human rights. Many of these entitlements are what we might refer to as *first-order* rights: that is, rights to enjoy certain goods and to be free from certain burdens. But justice also confers various *second-order* rights, which grant us permission to ensure that other people respect our first-order rights. As was noted in Chapter 2, for example, there is a human right to self-defence. This is a second-order right.

A complete theory of justice will identify both first- and second-order rights. In other words, it will tell us what a just state of affairs looks like, but it will also identify the range of actions in which an individual or community may engage in order to ensure that a just state of affairs is established, maintained, or restored. Many philosophers believe that war is among those actions.

To be sure, most people are appalled by violence, at least when the violence in question is *actual* (as opposed to the simulated violence we encounter in novels and films) and *non-consensual* (in contrast to the violence involved in, say, a boxing match). Moreover, the killing and maiming involved in warfare are particularly extreme forms of violence, and for that reason, we are naturally especially reluctant to accept that it could be morally permissible. But a moment's reflection reveals that we are sometimes willing to countenance violence, even when it is actual, non-consensual, and extreme. Suppose that you are attacked on the street. The attack is completely unprovoked, and your assailant has initiated the attack simply because he hates you for no good reason. Suppose, further, that your life is endangered and that you lack a viable means of escape. You can defend yourself effectively only by acting in a manner that will impose severe, and perhaps lethal, injury upon your assailant. (Suppose, also, that you can do this without harming any innocent bystanders.) In such a situation, it would be unreasonable to claim that you are morally required to refrain from defending yourself. Most people would no doubt say that you are morally permitted to kill your attacker. But if we concede that the infliction of non-consensual extreme violence is sometimes permissible, we should at least be willing to consider the possibility that war might sometimes be permissible.

If war is sometimes permissible, it is permissible only under exceptional circumstances. The "just war" tradition – which originates with the Christian theologian Augustine of Hippo and is today the most widely adopted approach to the ethics of war – identifies a variety of strict conditions that must be satisfied in order for a war to be just. These conditions are typically *not* satisfied, and there is therefore good reason to think that the majority of wars that states actually wage are spectacular violations of people's rights. Accepting that war is sometimes just does not prevent us from criticizing most wars – and the politicians who initiate them – in the strongest possible terms. (As we shall see later in the chapter, it can also be appropriate to criticize the soldiers who participate in a war.) Far from silencing dissent, the just war theory enables us to see exactly why many wars are so seriously unjust and thereby provides the intellectual resources with which to mount the fiercest opposition.

In the next two sections, I discuss some of the key conditions that just war theorists have claimed must be satisfied in order for a war to be just. In the third section, I consider the relationship between the rules that govern the resort to war and those that govern conduct within war.

It is worth noting that this chapter could have taken a variety of different forms. It could, for example, have exhaustively examined each of the principles that just war theory comprises. Alternatively, it could have detailed the main differences among different "camps" within the just war tradition (and, more specifically, between so-called "traditionalists" and so-called "revisionists"). I have not pursued either of these options. My sense is that, for this book, which is likely to be read by some people who will never encounter another academic treatment of the just war theory, these approaches would be suboptimal. Instead, I have endeavoured to present a relatively simple and streamlined statement of some complementary ideas that I take to be especially important. The ideas I foreground are those of Jeff McMahan, an Oxford philosopher who is perhaps the most influential just war theorist of our generation.

Before proceeding, I should address one potential source of confusion. Reluctance to accept that war can sometimes be just might be attributable to the fact that the term "war" is ambiguous. As McMahan notes, the term commonly "refers to the aggregate fighting of a number of belligerent parties".[1] When we talk about World War II, for example, we are referring to the fighting of Germany, Britain, Japan, and a variety of other countries. But, as McMahan points out, we can also use the term in a different way, namely, to refer to the fighting of each individual country. For example, "we can … say of each belligerent in World War II that it fought a war. Britain fought a war against Germany and Germany fought a war against Britain (among others). Each of those wars was a part of World War II".[2] Although it would be odd to say that World War II taken as a whole was just, given that it included wars waged by the Axis Powers in pursuit of patently unjust aims, it is much more plausible to suggest that some of the wars that World War II comprised, such as the wars waged by Britain and the US, were just. It is thus the latter sense of the term "war" that I shall be employing for most of this chapter.

9.1 *Jus ad bellum*: Regulating the resort to war

Just war theorists distinguish between two sets of conditions, each of which must be satisfied if war is to be justified. The first set (referred to as *jus ad bellum*) regulates the resort to war, whereas the second set (referred to as *jus in bello*) regulates conduct within war. In this section, I consider the constituent conditions of *jus ad bellum*; in the next, I consider those of *jus in bello*. The conditions of *jus ad bellum* are as follows.

Jus ad bellum:

1. There must be a *just cause* for war. Those wishing to initiate a war must have an acceptable reason for doing so.

---

1 Jeff McMahan, *Killing in War* (New York: Oxford University Press, 2009), p. 5.
2 Ibid.

2. War must be a *proportionate* method for achieving the just cause. The harms that war can be expected to inflict must not be excessive in relation to the goods that it is expected to produce.

3. The war must have a *reasonable chance of success*.

4. War must be a *last resort*.

5. The war must be waged with the *right intention*. More specifically, it must be waged with the intention of achieving the just cause and not for some other end.

6. The war must be authorized by a *legitimate authority*.

I shall not discuss each of these conditions in detail, but I shall comment briefly on *just cause, proportionality*, and *last resort*. (*Reasonable chance of success* and *right intention* will be addressed in the next chapter.) The just cause condition holds that those wishing to initiate a war must have an acceptable reason for doing so. There must be an aim or goal that can justify the resort to war. In popular discourse, claiming that there is a just cause for war is often a way of expressing one's belief that going to war is justified *all things considered*. However, as the list above makes clear, in the just war tradition a just cause is only one of several conditions that must be satisfied in order for the resort to war to be justified. A just cause is *necessary* – war cannot be just without one – but it is not sufficient; it must be supplemented by the other conditions enumerated above. As Helen Frowe writes, "Just cause should … be understood as the foundation of a case for war – the trigger that begins the debate about whether the war could be morally permissible".[3]

Simple intuition suggests that certain aims constitute just causes whereas others do not. We noted earlier that, in small-scale, interpersonal cases, it can be reasonable to countenance violent acts when such acts are self-defensive. Intuitively, the same appears to be true in larger, international, cases. It is natural to assume that if one country is subject to aggression by another (and it has not done anything to make such aggression appropriate), it has a right to defend itself. (Poland possessed a just cause for war when it was invaded by Nazi Germany in 1939.) By contrast, expansion of territory looks like a clear example of an unjust cause. (Germany's cause was unjust when it waged war against Poland.)

But many cases are less clear-cut, and therefore it would be helpful to have some criteria with which to distinguish between those causes that are just and those that are not. In searching for such criteria, McMahan points out that we must be attentive to the kind of enterprise that war is. War is a

---

3 Helen Frowe, *The Ethics of War and Peace: An Introduction*, Second Edition (New York: Routledge, 2016), p. 53.

practice characterized by extreme violence. When war is waged, people are killed and maimed, often in large numbers. In order for there to be a just cause for war, then, there must be a goal the pursuit of which can license killing and maiming.[4] Killing and maiming are, of course, presumptively wrongful, but, as we have already noted, there are circumstances in which we judge them to be permissible. Are these intuitive judgements supported by good reasons?

To introduce a helpful term, we can say that individuals sometimes behave in a way that renders them *liable* to be harmed. The notion of liability is often cashed out in terms of rights forfeiture. By behaving in a particular manner, we can forfeit (or lose) our right not to be harmed in certain ways. Suppose, again, that you are the victim of an attack. Your assailant clearly means to cause you significant wrongful harm, and you can defend yourself only by breaking his arm. In this situation, we can say that your assailant has forfeited his right not to have his arm broken by you in self-defence. (Alternatively, we might say that the attacker never possessed a right not to have his arm broken under such circumstances. By wrongfully attacking you, he steps outside of the domain in which he is afforded protection by his right not to have his arm broken.)

Why think that certain kinds of behaviour can render us liable to harm? Suppose that, in the case I just described, the aim of your assailant is to break your arm. If his attack is successful, your arm will be broken. By contrast, if you succeed in defending yourself, *his* arm will be broken. Why is it better, from a moral perspective, that the attacker's arm be broken? One plausible answer to this question points to the fact that it is the attacker who is responsible for creating a situation in which someone will suffer a broken arm. His actions make it inevitable that either you or he will bear a harm. Given that the attacker is responsible in this way, it seems only fair that the harm be borne by him. Breaking the attacker's arm, rather than allowing him to break yours, ensures that harms are distributed justly.[5]

Notice that being liable to harm is not the same as *deserving* harm. Liability and desert are distinct concepts. To say that someone is deserving of harm is to say that the infliction of harm upon that person is an end in itself; we have a reason to harm him regardless of whether doing so will serve any further purpose. By contrast, if someone is liable to be harmed, the infliction of harm upon that person is a means or side effect of pursuing some independent end (namely, the prevention or correction of some other harm).[6] In other words, liability is instrumental whereas desert is non-instrumental.[7] As McMahan

---

4 Jeff McMahan, "Just Cause for War", *Ethics and International Affairs*, vol. 19, no. 3, 2005, pp. 1–21, at p. 11.
5 Jeff McMahan, "The Limits of Self-Defense", in Christian Coons and Michael Weber (eds.), *The Ethics of Self-Defense* (New York: Oxford University Press, 2016), p. 192.
6 Ibid.
7 Ibid.

notes, it is possible "that harm inflicted on the basis of liability is always regrettable and bad in itself, whereas deserved harm is generally regarded as good in itself, even though it is bad for the person who deserves it".[8]

The foregoing observations suggest a criterion for identifying just causes for war. Individuals sometimes commit (or threaten to commit) wrongs that render them potentially liable to certain harms (namely, those harms that are necessary to prevent or correct the wrongs that they (have threatened to) commit). There is a just cause for war when the wrongs in question are serious enough to render the perpetrators liable to be killed or maimed.[9] If those who are to be warred upon have not committed any wrongs or if the wrongs they have committed are insufficiently serious to render them liable to be killed or maimed, then there is no just cause.

As McMahan notes, this criterion "does not automatically generate a list of just causes, but it does provide some much-needed guidance in identifying what may be a just cause for war".[10] Elaborating, he writes:

> We can ... consult our beliefs – which are quite robust and stable – about which kinds of wrong are sufficiently serious that the killing or maiming of the perpetrator could be justified if it were necessary to prevent or correct the wrong. Most people agree, for example, that one person may permissibly kill another if that is necessary to prevent the other person from wrongfully killing, torturing, mutilating, raping, kidnapping, enslaving or, perhaps, imprisoning her ... If each of these types of wrong is such that its prevention – or, when possible, its correction – can justify killing, then its prevention or correction can also be a just cause for war.[11]

These reflections suggest a number of aims that could plausibly be regarded as just causes for war. These include self-defence against wrongful aggression, the defence of others against wrongful aggression, the prevention of genocide, and the termination of severe oppression.

Having considered the first principle of *jus ad bellum*, let us now move on to consider the second. According to the *proportionality* condition, the harms that war can be expected to inflict must not be excessive in relation to the goods that it is expected to produce. Before initiating a war, one must weigh up the anticipated good and bad effects of doing so and may proceed only if the latter do not greatly exceed the former. Even when there is a just cause for war, pursuing it would be impermissible if the expected good effects will predictably be dwarfed by the bad effects. To illustrate: the Soviet invasion of

---

8   Ibid., p. 193.
9   McMahan, "Just Cause for War", p. 11.
10 Ibid.
11 Ibid., pp. 11–12.

Czechoslovakia in 1968 provided NATO with a just cause for war, but because pursuing that cause would have risked precipitating the use of nuclear weapons, doing so would have violated the proportionality condition.[12]

Several further points should be noted about this condition. First, it should not be confused with the distinct idea of "proportionality in reprisal".[13] According to the latter, the harms that war can be expected to inflict upon one's adversary must not be excessive in relation to the harms that one's adversary has itself already inflicted. We might be drawn to understand proportionality in this way if we thought that the point of war was to punish wrongdoing; proportionality in reprisal would then ensure that the "punishment fits the crime". But on the account of just cause sketched above, the point of a just war is not to punish wrongdoing but to prevent or correct it. If this is the role that a just war serves, then it is inappropriate to interpret the proportionality condition as proportionality in reprisal. The harms that war can be expected to produce might be excessive in relation to the harms that one's adversary has inflicted in the past, but not in relation to the good that war can be expected to achieve (because, for example, the war might prevent one's adversary from committing further harms in the future). Alternatively, the harms that war can be expected to produce might *not* be excessive in relation to the harms that one's adversary has inflicted, but nevertheless be excessive in relation to the good that the war can be expected to achieve (because, for example, the war might be unlikely to achieve *any* relevant good: it might be unlikely to prevent any future wrongs from occurring or to correct those that have already been committed). Properly understood, then, proportionality requires us to compare the expected good effects of going to war with the expected bad effects of doing so, not the harms that war will inflict with the harms that have already been imposed by one's adversary.

The second point to note is that, at least on one interpretation, a war can satisfy the proportionality requirement even if it is expected to end more lives than it is expected to save. This is because just war theory does not attach equal weight to the interests of all affected parties. More specifically, it attaches greater weight to the interests of the innocent than to the interests of the non-innocent. Consequently, a war that kills more people than it saves can be proportionate if the individuals saved are innocent whereas those killed are not.[14] (Who counts as innocent in the relevant sense is a question to which I shall return.)

---

12 Thomas Hurka, "Proportionality in the Morality of War", *Philosophy and Public Affairs*, vol. 33, no. 1, 2005, pp. 34–66, at pp. 35–36.

13 Jeff McMahan, "Proportionality and Time", *Ethics*, vol. 125, no. 3, 2015, pp. 696–719, at pp. 696–697.

14 Jeff McMahan and Robert McKim, "The Just War and the Gulf War", *Canadian Journal of Philosophy*, vol. 23, no. 4, 1993, pp. 501–541, at p. 513.

Third, the bad consequences that must be weighed up in the proportionality calculation include harms inflicted by one's adversary.[15] Earlier, I distinguished between war as an enterprise undertaken by a single country and war as the aggregate fighting of several different countries, and I said that for most of the chapter I would be referring exclusively to the former. But for the purposes of proportionality, the latter notion of war becomes relevant. If the bad effects of resorting to war will greatly exceed the good effects, then resorting to war is impermissible, even if the disproportionality is attributable to the actions of one's adversary.

Fourth, proportionality can be understood as incorporating the *reasonable chance of success* condition mentioned above. If a war does not have a reasonable chance of achieving the just cause, then the war will be disproportionate because it will not be expected to produce good effects capable of adequately offsetting its bad effects.[16]

Let us now consider the *last resort* condition. According to one formulation of this requirement, one may permissibly initiate a war only if there is no alternative means of achieving the just cause. If the just cause could be achieved through diplomacy, say, then resorting to war would be unjust. This formulation of the last resort requirement would be plausible if we assumed that the bad effects of war will invariably be worse than the bad effects associated with alternative means of achieving the just cause. It would also be plausible if we assumed that the good effects of pursuing an alternative will always be superior to the good effects of resorting to war. But neither of these assumptions is defensible.[17] It is true that waging war will *often* have more harmful effects than more peaceful alternatives, but war is not more harmful *by definition*. The crude use of economic sanctions, for example, can impose large deprivations on civilian populations, and there are no grounds for assuming that the harms associated with sanctions will never exceed those that would be produced by war. When a peaceful strategy – such as the levying of sanctions – will impose upon the innocent greater harms than those that would be imposed by a violent strategy, then it is *peace* that should be the last resort.[18]

Similarly, there are no grounds for assuming that the good effects of war will inevitably be inferior to the good effects that can be produced by available alternatives. It is important to note that while there may often be two (or more) viable strategies for achieving a just cause – war and diplomacy, say – the two strategies will often differ both in their *probability* of achieving

---

15 Ibid., p. 510.
16 Hurka, "Proportionality in the Morality of War", p. 37.
17 McMahan and McKim, "The Just War and the Gulf War", p. 524.
18 Kasper Lippert-Rasmussen, "Global Justice and Redistributive Wars", *Law, Ethics, and Philosophy*, vol. 1, 2013, pp. 65–86, at p. 74.

the just cause and in the *degree* to which they can achieve the just cause.[19] If, for example, a diplomatic approach has a low probability of averting an imminent massacre whereas war has a high probability of doing so, it is hardly plausible to suggest that considerations of justice mandate the diplomatic route. And if war could liberate an entire population from severe oppression whereas diplomacy would liberate only half of the population, the fact that there is an alternative to war that can achieve the just cause to some degree is hardly sufficient to render war unjust.

In light of these problems, we should abandon the account of last resort that we have been considering. But we should not dispense with last resort altogether, for a superior formulation is available. Interpreted in a more satisfactory manner, last resort functions as an expanded version of the proportionality condition. It requires us to first weigh up the good and bad effects of war (the original proportionality calculation discussed above), then to weigh up the good and bad effects of available alternatives to war, and finally to compare the net expected value of resorting to war with the net expected value of pursuing the various alternatives. If the net expected value of war exceeds that of the alternatives, then it is permissible; if it does not, then it is prohibited.[20]

A refined last resort condition of this kind was invoked by the more sophisticated critics of the war waged against Iraq in 2003. These critics pointed out that there was an alternative means of addressing the threat posed by Saddam Hussein – a strategy involving a combination of "smart" sanctions, UN weapons inspections, and overflights to enforce no-fly zones above parts of the country – and they noted that although this approach undoubtedly had its downsides, its consequences would be less pernicious than those of war.[21] Their claim was not merely that the US and its allies had an alternative to waging war against Iraq – meaning that war could not be regarded as a last resort in a crude, literal sense – but also that the net expected value of pursuing the alternative was higher than the net expected value of pursuing war – meaning that war would fail to satisfy the refined version of the last resort condition described above.

As I mentioned previously, there are further *ad bellum* conditions that I shall not address here. It should also be noted that I have provided but a cursory sketch of those conditions that I have discussed, each of which yields further complexities that cannot be explored here. I hope that what I have said is sufficient to render plausible the notion that resorting to war can

---

19 McMahan and McKim, "The Just War and the Gulf War", p. 524; Jeff McMahan, "Just War", in Robert E. Goodin, Philip Pettit, and Thomas Pogge (eds.), *A Companion to Contemporary Political Philosophy, Volume 2*, Second Edition (Malden, MA: Blackwell Publishing, 2012), p. 673.

20 McMahan and McKim, "The Just War and the Gulf War", p. 525; Hurka, "Proportionality in the Morality of War", pp. 37–38.

21 Michael Walzer, *Arguing about War* (New Haven, CT: Yale University Press, 2004), pp. 153–155.

sometimes be permissible but also that doing so is sharply constrained by moral considerations.

9.2 *Jus in bello*: Regulating conduct within war

Even if *resorting* to war on a particular occasion is just, the war may nevertheless be unjust overall by virtue of being fought in a manner that is morally unacceptable. In order to be just all-things-considered, a war must satisfy not only the conditions of *jus ad bellum* but also those of *jus in bello*, which regulate the conduct of war. The conditions of *jus in bello* are as follows.

Jus in bello:

1. Those planning and prosecuting military operations must *discriminate*, or distinguish, between legitimate and illegitimate targets, directing military force only at the former.
2. Military operations must produce goods that are *proportionate* to their expected harms.
3. An attack may be carried out only when *necessary* for the achievement of a military goal.

Traditionally interpreted, the first *in bello* condition mandates that military attacks be directed exclusively at *combatants* and never at *non-combatants*. (It is sometimes called "the principle of non-combatant immunity".) Determining who should count as a combatant is not straightforward. An explication of the distinction will have to make reference to the various ways in which individuals occupying different roles can contribute to the threat and infliction of harm during wartime, but not all forms of contribution are relevant, and there will inevitably be difficult cases.[22] A soldier is clearly a combatant, but what about army doctors or munitions factory workers? Soldiers count as combatants by virtue of the threat they pose to their adversaries, but, in their different ways, doctors and munitions factory workers both contribute to that threat. Should those occupying these latter roles therefore also be classified as combatants?

Thomas Nagel suggests that in determining where to draw the line, we must pay attention to the way in which a particular activity contributes to the threat that soldiers pose.[23] Does it contribute to that threat by (i) serving the needs that soldiers have in their capacity *as soldiers* or, alternatively, by (ii) serving the needs that soldiers have simply in their capacity as human

---

22 Thomas Nagel, "War and Massacre", *Philosophy & Public Affairs*, vol. 1, no. 2, 1972, pp. 123–144, at p. 140.
23 Ibid.

beings?[24] Nagel suggests that only those who contribute in the first way should be regarded as combatants. He writes:

> The threat presented by an army and its members does not consist merely in the fact that they are men, but in the fact that they are armed and are using their arms in the pursuit of certain objectives. Contributions to their arms and logistics are contributions to this threat; contributions to their mere existence as men are not. It is therefore wrong to direct an attack against those who merely serve the combatants' needs as human beings ...[25]

If Nagel is right, then munitions factory workers should be regarded as combatants (and therefore as legitimate targets) but army doctors should be regarded as non-combatants (and therefore as illegitimate targets). For, "medical attention is a species of attention to completely general human needs, not specifically the needs of a combat soldier, and our conflict with the soldier is not with his existence as a human being".[26]

Some individuals occupy roles that serve only those needs that soldiers share with the rest of us, the needs they would continue to have even if they left the military. Among these are the need for food, shelter, and medical care. Individuals who occupy these roles (such as farmers, cooks, and doctors) do not count as combatants. By contrast, other individuals occupy roles that serve the needs that soldiers have only because they are soldiers (e.g., the need for weapons). Individuals who occupy *these* roles (such as munitions factory workers) *can* be classed as combatants.

It is important to note that the discrimination condition does not condemn *every* military operation that causes non-combatant deaths. Rather, it distinguishes between *targeted* and *collateral* killings of non-combatants and condemns only the former. In drawing this distinction, the discrimination condition is often thought to appeal to an influential principle that was originally promulgated by Catholic theologians, namely, the "doctrine of double effect". This doctrine claims that when an action will have both good and bad consequences, performing the action can be morally permissible if one intends only the good consequences. The action is prohibited if the bad consequences are part of the goal that one is trying to achieve or part of the means that one uses to achieve it. But the action is permitted if the bad consequences are merely a foreseen but unintended side effect.

---

24 Cf. Michael Walzer, *Just and Unjust Wars: A Moral Argument with Historical Illustrations* (New York: Basic Books, 1977), pp. 145–146; Elizabeth Anscombe, "Mr. Truman's Degree," in *Ethics, Religion, and Politics: Collected Philosophical Papers, vol. 3* (Minneapolis, MN: University of Minnesota Press, 1981), p. 67.
25 Ibid.
26 Ibid., p. 141.

Consider two cases. In the first, a pilot drops a bomb on a residential area in an attempt to terrorize the enemy into surrendering. In the second case, a pilot drops a bomb on a munitions factory in an attempt to destroy that factory while foreseeing that some non-combatants living in the vicinity will be killed. Suppose that the same number of non-combatants is killed in each case. According to the doctrine of double effect, the second pilot's action is potentially justifiable whereas the first pilot's is not. This is because the first pilot, unlike the second, kills non-combatants as *a means to his end*; he uses his victims as tools or instruments to achieve his goal. Notice that the second pilot need not have any cause for disappointment if she miraculously manages to destroy the munitions factory without killing any non-combatants in the process, for killing non-combatants plays no part in her plan. By contrast, if the first pilot fails to kill any non-combatants, he will have failed in his task.

The discrimination condition is frequently violated. It is violated not only by despotic regimes that one would expect to flout the rules of war but also by political leaders who like to think of themselves as representatives of civilized countries. For example, it was violated by the Allies during World War II, most notoriously in Hiroshima and Nagasaki, but also by British and US firebombing raids on Tokyo, Dresden, and a large number of other Japanese and German cities. This means that although Britain and the US undoubtedly had just cause for waging war against the Axis Powers, their wars were unjust in important respects, as they were conducted in a manner that involved the mass murder of innocent civilians. The US Department of Energy has estimated that when American pilots dropped the atomic bomb on Hiroshima, 70,000 people died instantly and a further 30,000 died over the next few months.[27] Five years later, 200,000 deaths could be attributed to the American attack.[28] McMahan notes that this makes the bombing of Hiroshima "the most destructive single terrorist act" ever committed.[29]

The discrimination condition was also violated by the US Air Force's intensive bombing raids during the Vietnam War. (In a taped conversation about civilian casualties in 1972, Richard Nixon told his National Security Advisor, Henry Kissinger: "The only place where you and I disagree … is with regard to the bombing…. You're so goddamned concerned about the civilians and I don't give a damn. I don't care".[30]) And the discrimination condition was violated during the Gulf War by US attacks on Iraqi sewerage systems and water treatment facilities, attacks which "left urban populations without drinkable water and flooded both streets and rivers with raw sewage, thereby creating conditions for the epidemics of disease that ensued".[31] As

---

27 Figures cited in McMahan, *Killing in War*, pp. 128–129.
28 Ibid., p. 129.
29 Ibid.
30 Quoted in Richard W. Miller, *Globalizing Justice: The Ethics of Poverty and Power* (Oxford: Oxford University Press, 2010), p. 187.
31 McMahan and McKim, "The Just War and the Gulf War", pp. 538–539.

McMahan and McKim note, these attacks, which killed civilians indirectly by destroying civilian infrastructure, constituted "a sanitized mode of terror bombing".[32]

Of course, even when a military attack satisfies the discrimination condition, we cannot infer from that fact alone that it is justified. In order to be permissible, a discriminate attack will also have to be proportionate and necessary. As the *in bello* proportionality condition closely resembles its *ad bellum* counterpart, and as the necessity condition closely resembles the *ad bellum* last resort condition, I shall assume that their meaning is adequately clear and not devote space to discussing them.

9.3 The relationship between *jus ad bellum* and *jus in bello*

According to traditional just war theory, *jus ad bellum* and *jus in bello* are logically independent. This means not only that a war can be fought unjustly even if its initiation were just but also, more surprisingly, that a war can be fought justly even if its initiation were unjust. A consequence of this traditional view is that, from a moral perspective, all combatants involved in a conflict are symmetrically situated. No moral distinctions are drawn between those who fight in a justly initiated war (just combatants) and those who fight in an unjustly initiated war (unjust combatants). All combatants enjoy the same rights and all are bound by the same restraints; they are permitted to kill their adversaries on the battlefield (excluding those who have surrendered or been incapacitated), and they are prohibited from intentionally killing non-combatants and from inflicting upon non-combatants unintended harms that are disproportionate. This means that combatants do no wrong simply by fighting, even if the war in which they fight were initiated unjustly. Although we should condemn political leaders who initiate unjust wars, we should not condemn combatants simply for participating in those wars. Provided that a combatant adheres to the rules of *jus in bello*, he or she satisfies the requirements of justice, irrespective of whether the war in which he or she fights is itself just. This idea, known as "the moral equality of combatants", is recognized by international law. It appears in the Geneva Conventions, which note that the rules of *jus in bello* apply "without any adverse distinction based on the nature or origin of the armed conflict or on the causes espoused by or attributed to the Parties to the conflict".[33]

---

32 Ibid., p. 539.

33 International Committee of the Red Cross, "Preamble," *Protocol Additional to the Geneva Conventions of 12 August 1949, and Relating to the Protection of Victims of International Armed Conflicts (Protocol I), 8 June 1977*, hosted at the International Committee of the Red Cross, available at https://ihl-databases.icrc.org/applic/ihl/ihl.nsf/7c4d08d9b287a42141 256739003e636b/f6c8b9fee14a77fdc125641e0052b079?.

In recent years, this traditional understanding of the relationship between *jus ad bellum* and *jus in bello* has come under fire. "Revisionist" critics, such as McMahan, have argued that the rules governing the resort to war cannot be logically independent of the rules governing conduct within war. If a war is initiated unjustly (e.g., without a just cause), then it cannot be fought in conformity with the rules of *jus in bello*. An implication of this view is that the doctrine of the moral equality of combatants is false. Combatants fighting an unjust war cannot be the moral equals of those fighting a just war, because whereas the latter are capable of satisfying the requirements of *jus in bello*, the former are incapable. And if unjust combatants cannot fight in a manner that satisfies the requirements of *jus in bello*, this means that when they do fight, they act wrongfully. By participating in an unjust war, unjust combatants implicate themselves in the injustice initiated by their leaders.

Let us consider the revisionist critique in more detail. More specifically, let us consider how it applies to the *in bello* discrimination requirement. Recall that, traditionally conceived, this requirement permits combatants to attack other combatants but prohibits them from intentionally attacking civilians. When the discrimination requirement is understood in this way, there is no reason to think that unjust combatants should be any less capable of meeting it than just combatants. After all, participation in an unjust war does not deprive one of the ability to distinguish between combatants and civilians. But revisionist just war theorists have argued that the traditional understanding of the discrimination requirement should be rejected. To see why, we can start by asking why we should think that although they are prohibited from attacking civilians, all combatants – just and unjust alike – are permitted to attack each other. The standard answer to this question is that civilians are innocent whereas all combatants shed their innocence the moment they take up arms. Combatants on all sides of a conflict threaten others and thereby render themselves liable to attack. As Walzer writes: "our right not to be attacked … is lost by those who bear arms … because they pose a danger to other people". A combatant may "be personally attacked only because he already is a fighter. He has been made into a dangerous man".[34]

Notice that the definition of innocence relied upon here deviates from ordinary language. Usually, we use the word "innocent" to refer to those who are not responsible for, or guilty of, a wrong. But this is not the sense of innocence invoked in the standard explanation of the traditional discrimination requirement. As Nagel explains: "the operative notion of innocence is not *moral* innocence, and it is not opposed to moral guilt… [Rather] 'innocent' means 'currently harmless', and it is opposed not to 'guilty' but to 'doing harm'".[35] The innocent are those who are not "nocentes" – a Latin

---

34 Walzer, *Just and Unjust Wars*, p. 145.
35 Nagel, "War and Massacre", p. 139 (emphasis added).

term referring to those who threaten or injure.[36] The traditional account of just war theory holds that combatants are non-innocent not because they are responsible for or guilty of any wrong but simply because they pose a threat. This is why they lose their right not to be attacked.

But is it really plausible to think that people lose their right not to be attacked simply by posing a threat to others, irrespective of the reasons they have for posing that threat? Revisionist critics point out that, outside the context of war, we would never accept this idea.[37] Suppose a serial killer is about to claim his latest victim when a police officer intervenes. The police officer points her gun at the killer and announces that she will shoot him unless he releases his victim. The police officer is threatening the killer with potentially lethal violence, but we do not think that, by doing so, she thereby forfeits her right not be attacked. Whereas the police officer may use violence to defend the victim from the killer, the killer may not use violence to defend himself against the police officer. When the killer attacked his victim, he did so wrongfully and thereby made himself liable to defensive action. Because he is liable to such action, the police officer does not wrong him by taking it. The killer and the police officer are both acting in a threatening manner, but it seems clear that they do not have the same moral status.[38]

This is uncontroversial. But then why think that there is moral equality between just and unjust combatants? Those who fight without a just cause employ lethal violence in the pursuit of unjust ends. It is natural to suppose that, in doing so, they make themselves liable to defensive attack. But if they are liable to defensive attack, the just combatants who launch such an attack do no wrong. So why think that, by taking up arms to resist the wrongful pursuits of their adversaries, just combatants thereby forfeit their rights?

The revisionist objection is nicely illustrated by Seth Lazar:

> Allied soldiers landing on the shores of Normandy during World War II were fighting against genocide and imperialist expansion; their adversaries were defending those iniquitous ends. Why should the Allies lose their rights, only by doing what they are clearly morally permitted, perhaps even required, to do?[39]

Revisionists deny that we can lose any of our rights simply by posing a threat to others. Whether or not we lose any of our rights – whether or not we become liable to attack – depends upon the moral status of the threat for which we are responsible. If we are responsible for a threat that is *unjust*,

---

36 McMahan, *Killing in War*, p. 11.
37 Ibid., pp. 13–14.
38 Ibid., p. 14.
39 Seth Lazar, "Evaluating the Revisionist Critique of Just War Theory", *Daedalus*, vol. 146, no. 1, 2017, pp. 113–124, at p. 117 (reference omitted).

then we render ourselves liable; but if we are responsible for a threat that is *just*, then we do not. This means that while just combatants may permissibly attack unjust combatants, the converse if false: unjust combatants may *not* permissibly attack just combatants. Just combatants are not liable; they have not done anything that could cause them to lose their rights against attack.[40]

Because revisionists deny that just combatants are liable, they reject the traditional interpretation of the discrimination requirement, which holds that all combatants may permissibly be attacked. But they do not reject the discrimination requirement altogether. Rather, they endorse an alternative, more general, formulation of that requirement, which holds that combatants must distinguish between legitimate and illegitimate targets and target only the latter.[41]

We are now in a position to see why revisionists claim that unjust combatants cannot satisfy the discrimination requirement. As we have seen, this requirement demands that combatants distinguish between legitimate and illegitimate targets. But if just combatants have not done anything to forfeit their rights, then this means that *un*just combatants will not be able to fight in a way that distinguishes between legitimate and illegitimate targets because, typically, they will *not have any* legitimate targets.[42] Even if unjust combatants limit their attacks to the just combatants against whom they are fighting and do not target civilians, they will be attacking individuals who each have a right not to be attacked.[43]

A qualification needs to be made here. Although revisionists claim that just combatants do not lose any rights simply by taking up arms, they recognize that just combatants can lose their rights in a different way, namely, by violating the rules of *jus in bello*. When just combatants violate these rules, they make themselves liable to defensive attack.[44] To illustrate: McMahan suggests that, because they posed an unjust threat, the US airmen who bombed Hiroshima were liable to defensive force. If the Japanese could have shot them down before they released their payload, they would have been permitted to do so.[45] So there are *some* cases in which unjust combatants can fight permissibly. But so long as just combatants act in conformity with the rules of *jus in bello*, unjust combatants will lack legitimate targets and therefore will be unable to satisfy the discrimination requirement.

---

40 McMahan, *Killing in War*, p. 14.
41 Ibid., pp. 11–12.
42 Jeff McMahan, "The Ethics of Killing in War", *Ethics*, vol. 114, no. 4, 2004, pp. 693–733, at p. 718.
43 McMahan, *Killing in War*, p. 16.
44 Ibid., pp. 16–17.
45 Ibid., p. 16.

9.4 The blameworthiness of unjust combatants

McMahan acknowledges that there will often be certain mitigating conditions that reduce the degree to which unjust combatants are *culpable* or *blameworthy*. They may, for example, be acting under duress: they may have been coerced into fighting and deprived of a viable alternative. Many of those who fight in unjust wars have been conscripted into the military. Those who refuse to participate may be fined, imprisoned, or even executed.[46] Even those who choose to enlist in the army may be in some sense coerced: they may be compelled by the nature of their economic and social circumstances. In economically stratified societies, disadvantaged individuals faced with a paucity of career options may feel that signing up to the military is the best way to secure a steady income and, perhaps more importantly, the respect and esteem of their friends, family, and compatriots. These economic and social pressures exist even in wealthy societies but are especially acute in the world's poorest regions.[47]

Another mitigating condition that can reduce the culpability of unjust combatants is ignorance. Those who fight may do so without knowledge of relevant facts or pertinent moral considerations. Governments often withhold information about the wars that they are waging and sometimes they tell outright lies.[48] Moreover, the deliberative capacities of soldiers are often intentionally blunted by the military institutions they serve. As McMahan writes:

> In most military organizations, the ability of soldiers to engage in autonomous reflection and deliberation about the content of their orders is ... deliberately and systematically sabotaged. They are subjected to intensive conditioning and indoctrination, to endless drills, and to processes intended to efface their individuality and subvert their autonomy. The suppression of individual identity is achieved in part through shaving of the heads of males and making all soldiers wear the same uniform. They are all to look and act in exactly the same ways. Their wills are broken through intimidation, bullying, and humiliation by their instructors, through demands for repeated public displays of deference and submissiveness, and so on. The aim is to convert them into largely unreflective instruments of the wills of their superiors.[49]

But McMahan argues that the presence of such mitigating circumstances means only that unjust combatants have an *excuse* for participating in an unjust war: it does not mean that they act permissibly. Moreover, McMahan

---
46 Ibid., p. 117.
47 Ibid.
48 Ibid., p. 119.
49 Ibid.

contends that unjust combatants are often merely *partially* excused. The absence of relevant knowledge and the presence of duress *reduce* their culpability but do not eliminate it altogether.

Consider, first, why duress will often ground only a partial excuse. Those who refuse to fight will be punished, but, in liberal democracies at least, the penalties for refusal are not especially severe.[50] Moreover, the penalties imposed will often be less severe than the hardships that combatants would otherwise face in war. McMahan makes this point in relation to American men who resisted conscription during the Vietnam War. He writes:

> the alternative for American conscripts was to live, for at least as long as they would have had to spend in prison, in appalling physical conditions at high risk of being killed or maimed. Thus, in objective terms, the threatened harm from exposure to the conditions of war in Vietnam exceeded the threatened harm from imprisonment for a comparable period".[51]

Being imprisoned for resisting conscription was bad, but accepting conscription and engaging in combat were *worse*.

Now consider why ignorance of relevant considerations will often fail to be fully excusing. We noted that soldiers are intensively conditioned and indoctrinated and that these processes subvert their capacity for moral reasoning. Because of this, they may find it more difficult to evaluate the moral status of the wars in which they are ordered to fight. But these are familiar facts about military life. When men and women choose to sign up to the armed forces, they *know* that they will be indoctrinated; by signing up they are voluntarily surrendering their moral autonomy.[52] In an early article, McMahan suggested that "following one's superiors into an unjust war is roughly analogous to committing a crime while drunk".[53] Both the soldier and the drunken offender may claim in their defence that their judgement had been impaired, but they remain culpable to a considerable degree by virtue of the fact that they allowed their deliberative capacities to be dulled in the first place.[54]

There are several further reasons for doubting that duress or ignorance could fully excuse unjust combatants. First, when a combatant chooses whether or not to participate in a war, the moral stakes are extraordinarily high. A combatant contemplating this choice is deciding whether or not to participate in an enterprise that involves intentionally killing people. Given

---

50 Ibid., pp. 132–133.
51 Jeff McMahan, "Pacifism and Moral Theory", *Diametros*, vol. 23, 2010, pp. 44–68, at p. 51.
52 McMahan, *Killing in War*, pp. 152, 183.
53 Jeff McMahan, "Innocence, Self-Defense and Killing in War", *Journal of Political Philosophy*, vol. 2, no. 3, 1994, pp. 193–221, at p. 207.
54 Ibid.

the gravity of the situation, combatants have a demanding moral duty to deliberate exceptionally carefully. They must identify and consider relevant moral and empirical facts and endeavour to overcome the various obstacles that impede their ability to formulate considered judgements about the justness of the war. Moreover, if they conclude that the war is in fact unjust, they have a demanding moral duty to resist those who try to force them to fight.[55] As McMahan writes:

> While it is true that soldiers are typically manipulated, indoctrinated, and lied to in order to get them both to join and to fight, it is also true that war is a monstrous evil when it is unjust and that it is consequently not unreasonable to expect a person to exercise considerable care in deliberating about whether or not to participate in it. The fact that the human race has always taken its wars rather casually merely reveals how readily we follow the multitude to do evil ...[56]

In addition to the moral gravity of war, there are several further general facts about war that soldiers can be expected to be cognisant of and that should further impress upon them the importance of eschewing mindless obedience to authority. Perhaps most significantly, they can be expected to recognize that the probability of their war being just is at best 50/50. This follows from the widely accepted view that, in war, only one side can be in the right. In every conflict, at least one side is fighting a war that is unjust. As McMahan asks: "if both sides are in the right, how could either be justified in fighting the other?"[57] A moment's further reflection should reveal that the probability of fighting in a just war is actually considerably lower than 50/50. This is because although a war can be just on only one side, it can be unjust on both: in many conflicts, *neither* party has right on its side.[58]

We have been exploring the revisionist claim that many soldiers – those who participate in wars that are unjust – act wrongfully merely by fighting, and we have identified a variety of reasons for believing that a large proportion of these soldiers are at best partially excused for their actions: they remain culpable to a considerable degree. The point of philosophical inquiry into these matters is not to establish that unjust combatants ought to be punished. On the contrary, there are good reasons not to standardly regard these combatants as war criminals. But revisionist just war theorists believe that such inquiry does serve a practical end – and a vitally important one at

---

55 McMahan, "Innocence, Self-Defense and Killing in War", p. 214; McMahan, *Killing in War*, pp. 132–133, 150–152, 185; McMahan, "Pacifism and Moral Theory", pp. 54–55.
56 McMahan, "Innocence, Self-Defense and Killing in War", p. 214.
57 McMahan, *Killing in War*, p. 143.
58 Ibid., pp. 143, 185.

that. By promulgating the view that it is permissible to fight regardless of a war's moral status, we facilitate injustice. When we tell the young, impressionable individuals who comprise our armed forces that they can do no wrong merely by fighting, we invite them to forego moral reflection. Yet if we are to prevent our governments from waging wars that are unjust, then moral reflection – especially among those tasked with fighting – is essential. As McMahan writes:

> Unjust wars can occur only if enough people are willing to fight in them... It would, of course, be absurdly utopian to expect that people would refuse to fight in unjust wars ... if they came to believe that participation in an unjust war is wrong. But it would also be naïve to doubt that the widespread acceptance of the moral equality of combatants has facilitated the ability of governments to fight unjust wars. Wars are now and have always been initiated in the context of the general and largely unquestioned belief that the moral equality of combatants is true. If that background assumption were to change – if people generally believed that participation in an unjust or morally unjustified war is wrong – that could make a significant practical difference to the practice of war... Many people, including active-duty soldiers, would be more reluctant to fight in wars they believed to be unjust. Eventually there would have to be institutional accommodations to people's changed moral beliefs... In that altered institutional environment, governments could expect to encounter increased risks of resistance to their efforts to initiate unjust wars. And the prospects of resistance, particularly from within the military, and the consequent risks of humiliation and failure, could deter at least some attempts to initiate unjust wars ...[59]

9.5 Conclusion

We have identified a number of demanding conditions that must be satisfied in order for a war to be initiated and fought in conformity with the requirements of justice. Moreover, we have seen that the principles regulating conduct within war are not logically independent of those regulating the resort to war. A war that lacks a just cause cannot be fought justly and this fact has drastic implications for combatants. By signing up to fight, soldiers risk not only life and limb but also their moral integrity. If the wars in which they fight are unjust, the killings that soldiers carry out will often be murders, even if they direct their attacks exclusively at enemy combatants. The moral stakes could scarcely be higher.

---

59 Ibid., pp. 6–7.

10 INTERVENTION

As I write this book, civil war rages in Syria. The conflict, which began with the violent repression of peaceful protesters in 2011, pits the despotic regime of Bashar al-Assad against a variety of rebel groups (such as the Syrian Democratic Forces) and also against terrorist organizations like Daesh. Since the war began, foreign parties have intervened militarily on multiple occasions. For example, Britain, France, and the US have conducted airstrikes against oil installations controlled by Daesh and also against government weapons facilities. The case for some of these interventions has been couched in terms of self-defence, as politicians in the West have emphasized the importance of protecting their citizens from terrorist threats developing abroad. But intervention has also been defended on *humanitarian* grounds. Some commentators have argued that military action should be taken in order to protect the basic rights of the Syrian people.

The case for such humanitarian intervention is powerful. To be sure, many of us harbour pacific intuitions and are reluctant to endorse violence of any kind. Violence is an awful thing, and many observers will have found the macho rhetoric that has accompanied recent US interventions difficult to swallow. But in the kinds of conditions witnessed during the Syrian crisis, keeping one's own hands clean can mean standing idly by while evil people subject the innocent to abominable abuse. In the territories that it has managed to conquer, Daesh has built cities akin to prisons: vicious, totalitarian ghettos where "crimes" such as blasphemy and homosexuality are punished by beheading, adultery by stoning, and the consumption of alcohol by eighty lashes.[1] For its part, the Assad regime has tortured, mutilated, and killed thousands of prisoners.[2] It also stands accused

---

1   Jeff McMahan, "Syria is a modern-day holocaust. We must act", *The Washington Post*, 30 November 2015, available at https://www.washingtonpost.com/news/in-theory/wp/2015/11/30/syria-is-a-modern-day-holocaust-we-must-act/?utm_term=.1e2ff34a56a7
2   Ian Black, "Syrian regime document trove shows evidence of 'industrial scale' killing of detainees", *The Guardian*, 21 January 2014, available at https://www.theguardian.com/world/2014/jan/20/evidence-industrial-scale-killing-syria-war-crimes

of attacking civilians with chemical weapons[3] and of deliberately destroying a United Nations aid convoy.[4]

Under conditions such as these, outside parties have a just cause to intervene. As we saw in the previous chapter, the goals that constitute a just cause for war are "the prevention or correction of wrongs that are serious enough to make the perpetrators liable to be killed or maimed". Furthermore, we noted that the list of wrongs that are sufficiently serious in this sense includes wrongful killing, torture, imprisonment, and enslavement. When a group of individuals commits (or threatens to commit) such wrongs, its members render themselves liable to acts of warfare that are necessary to curtail their wrongful activities. Given the severity of the wrongs that they are perpetrating (and are committed to continue perpetrating), it is hard to avoid the conclusion that Assad's troops and Daesh fighters are liable to be killed.

This does not mean that intervention is justified all-things-considered. As we saw in the previous chapter, just cause is only one of several conditions that must be satisfied in order for a war to be just. Moreover, the case of specifically humanitarian war raises distinctive issues that were not addressed in our previous discussion. In this chapter, I will identify and assess the most powerful arguments that can be made against humanitarian intervention. Few of these arguments claim that humanitarian intervention can *never* be justified. Rather, they provide reasons for thinking that it can be justified only in exceptional circumstances. I will consider whether these challenges can be answered.

Before proceeding, we should get clear about the nature of the practice that we are discussing. Humanitarian intervention is not a simple idea. Its definition comprises no fewer than six elements. It can be defined as (1) military action (2) in a foreign state, which is (3) intended to protect a group of individuals within that state (4) whose most basic rights are threatened (5) by another group within that state and which is (6) undertaken without the permission of the foreign state's government.

Although there is some disagreement about which historical cases should be classed as instances of humanitarian intervention, commonly cited examples include the following: the 1971 Indian intervention in East Pakistan, which responded to the mass killing and mass rape of Bengali civilians by the Pakistani military; Vietnam's 1978 intervention in Cambodia, which ousted the genocidal Khmer Rouge from power; Tanzania's 1978 intervention in Uganda, which ended the murderous rule of Idi Amin; the 1999 Australian-led intervention in East Timor, which was initiated in response to attacks on

---

3 Kareem Shaheen, "Dozens killed in suspected chemical attack on Syrian rebel enclave", *The Guardian*, 8 April 2018, available at https://www.theguardian.com/world/2018/apr/08/syrian-government-accused-of-chemical-attacks-on-civilians-in-eastern-ghouta

4 Nick Cumming-Bruce and Anne Barnard, "U.N. Investigators Say Syria Bombed Convoy and Did So Deliberately", *New York Times*, 1 March 2017, available at https://www.nytimes.com/2017/03/01/world/middleeast/united-nations-war-crimes-syria.html

Timorese civilians after the vote for independence from Indonesia; the NATO intervention in Bosnia and Herzegovina, which included the enforcement of a UN-established no-fly zone and a large-scale bombing campaign against Serb targets following the Srebrenica massacre; and the NATO intervention in Kosovo, which sought to end the killing of Kosovar Albanians by Milošević's security forces.

10.1 State sovereignty and communal self-determination

When a government is brutally persecuting its own people (or allowing, or failing to prevent, such persecution), the case for humanitarian intervention is intuitively powerful. But how might that case be resisted? One common argument against humanitarian intervention is built around an analogy between states and persons. According to this argument, states, like individual men and women, are agents whose freedom and autonomy must be respected. Just as individuals should be free to form and pursue their own goals, provided that they do not violate the rights of others, so states should be free to form and pursue *their* own goals, provided that they do not transgress the rights of other states. In other words, states have a right to *sovereignty*, which is the international equivalent of the right to liberty enjoyed by individuals. This right confers upon states ultimate decision-making authority within the territory that they control and imposes upon outsiders a duty of non-interference. This line of argument is associated with the 17th century German philosopher Christian Wolff, who wrote: "Just as by force of natural liberty it must be allowed to everyman that he abide by his own judgement in acting ... as long as he does nothing which is contrary to your right, so likewise by force of the natural liberty of nations it must be allowed to any one of them to abide by its own judgement in the exercise of sovereignty".[5] On this view, the problem with humanitarian intervention is that it violates state sovereignty. Interventionist policies are objectionable because they undermine the freedom of states to organize their own affairs, and thereby fail to respect their autonomous agency. We can call this the *state sovereignty argument*.

In order to evaluate this argument, we should return to the basic cosmopolitan outlook that I introduced in Chapter 4. Recall that underlying this view is the idea that human beings are ultimate units of moral concern. According to cosmopolitans, human beings have independent value; they matter in and of themselves. By contrast, collective entities (such as states) are regarded as possessing merely *derivative* value; they matter only to the degree that they further the interests of humans (and other ultimate units of

---

5   Christian Wolff, *Jus gentium methodo scientifica pertractatum* (1749), trans. Joseph H. Drake (Oxford: Clarendon Press, 1934), para. 255.

moral concern, such as sentient non-human animals). This is a judgement in which many have great confidence. Each of us thinks that it is important, in itself, that our life goes well, and it is a short step from this conviction to the judgement that it is important, in itself, that the lives of others also go well. This is why we think that humans should enjoy freedom and autonomy. Without these things, the quality of our lives would be radically diminished. By contrast, it is difficult to see why it could be important, in itself, for institutions like states to enjoy the freedom and autonomy necessary for them to flourish. Such institutions do not appear to possess the fundamental moral importance that we attribute to persons. This means that, contrary to what is claimed by proponents of the state sovereignty argument, states and persons are importantly *dis*analogous. Consequently, we cannot simply assume that states are entitled to the kind of freedom that we deem important for humans.

Now, it is sometimes said that the autonomy of states should be respected not because state autonomy is valuable in itself but rather because state autonomy protects the integrity of the human communities over which states preside. Put differently, the claim is that state autonomy enables human communities to achieve the valuable goal of self-determination. According to what we can call the *self-determination argument*, humanitarian intervention is objectionable because it places this goal out of reach. When foreigners intervene in the affairs of others, they undermine the capacity of local communities to determine their own destinies.

A notable virtue of this argument is that the value of communal self-determination can be explained by reference to the interests of individuals and therefore can be defended in cosmopolitan terms. This point is made by Michael Walzer, who argues that "the idea of communal integrity derives its moral and political force from the rights of contemporary men and women to live as members of a historic community and to express their inherited culture through political forms worked out among themselves".[6]

The value that communal self-determination possesses for individual men and women is further explained by Jeff McMahan, who writes: "Just as individuals are loath to relinquish control of major decisions in their lives … so individuals in groups feel a fundamental need for the group itself to exercise control of its own destiny".[7] Elaborating, McMahan suggests that "the desire for communal autonomy is an extension of the need of individuals to control their own lives".[8] McMahan concludes: "The deep-seated desire of persons, both individually and as members of communities, to control their

---

6   Michael Walzer, "The Moral Standing of States: A Response to Four Critics", *Philosophy & Public Affairs*, vol. 9, no. 3, 1980, pp. 209–229, at p. 211.

7   Jeff McMahan, "The Ethics of International Intervention", in Kenneth Kipnis and Diana T. Meyers (eds.), *Political Realism and International Morality: Ethics in the Nuclear Age* (Boulder, CO: Westview Press, 1988), p. 83.

8   Ibid.

own affairs is … a fact of fundamental importance that must be reflected in our [account of] morality".[9]

These reflections demonstrate that a plausible relationship can be established between communal self-determination, on the one hand, and the interests of individuals, on the other. But can we establish a relationship between communal self-determination and the autonomy of *states*? Is it true that respect for communal self-determination rules out humanitarian intervention against states? Walzer suggests that the government, and the state apparatus it commands, is the people's instrument[10], and we can agree that this is its proper role. When operating in an appropriate manner, states serve as effective institutions through which self-determining communities organize their collective affairs. If military intervention were carried out against a state that does a good job of representing its people, the self-determining capacities of the people would certainly be compromised. However, we all know that states often fail to operate appropriately. Many governments employ state machinery in a fashion that treats the people they rule not as citizens to be served but as resources to be plundered and as potential threats to be brutally suppressed. In such cases, it is not plausible to claim that military intervention against the government would undermine the capacity of the people to be self-determining.

In response to this challenge, Walzer argues that foreign observers are not well placed to make judgements about the relationship between a government and its people. He asserts that foreigners "don't know enough about its history, and they have no direct experience, and can form no concrete judgments, of the conflicts and harmonies, the historical choices and cultural affinities, the loyalties and resentments, that underlie it".[11] Walzer claims that, given their ignorance, it is incumbent upon outsiders to act on the presumption "that there exists a certain 'fit' between the community and its government and that the state is 'legitimate'".[12] Outsiders must presume that the government "is not a gang of rulers acting in its own interest" and that the community is "governed in accordance with its own traditions".[13] Walzer maintains that this "presumption is simply the respect that foreigners owe to a historic community and to its internal life".[14]

Walzer concedes that this presumption can sometimes be overturned, but he maintains that this will happen only in exceptional circumstances. He insists that the presumption may not be suspended and that outsiders may not intervene "unless the absence of 'fit' between the government and

---

9   Ibid.
10 Walzer, "Moral Standing of States", p. 211.
11 Ibid., p. 212.
12 Ibid.
13 Ibid.
14 Ibid.

community is radically apparent".[15] And he claims that the absence of fit is "radically apparent" only in those exceptional circumstances in which governments inflict "extreme" oppression.[16] On Walzer's definition, the list of extremely oppressive practices is very short. It includes massacre, enslavement, and mass population expulsions.[17] When the government maintains practices that constitute what Walzer calls "ordinary" oppression[18] (i.e., any form of oppression that does not belong in the "extreme" category), we cannot conclude that such a nation is not "governed in accordance with its own traditions". Intervention, therefore, is unacceptable.

Perhaps unsurprisingly, this claim has struck many of Walzer's readers as incredible. It does not seem plausible to claim that the unrepresentativeness of a government can be established only when it engages in the most extreme forms of oppression. When the authorities are kidnapping, imprisoning, torturing, and executing political dissidents, it seems perfectly appropriate to infer that the government is not an agent of the people but a gang of self-serving thugs. As David Luban remarks, in "ordinary" oppressive regimes, it is more than apparent that the "government fits the people the way the sole of a boot fits a human face".[19]

Return to Walzer's claim that outsiders lack the requisite knowledge to make judgements about the relationship between the government and the people. A number of critics have pointed out that this claim lacks merit. Luban asks: "why presume we are ignorant? We aren't, usually. There are, after all, experts, experienced travelers, expatriates, scholars, and spies; libraries have been written about the most remote cultures".[20] In fact, as McMahan points out, there "are many cases in which external observers can know *more* about what is happening within a country than its inhabitants".[21] This is because oppressive governments often constrain freedom of speech, censor the internet, and promulgate misinformation through state-run news agencies.

When outsiders have extensive information about the internal affairs of a particular state and when that information reveals that the government is acting with outright contempt for its people, it is hard to see why intervention should be regarded as necessarily contrary to the achievement of communal self-determination. In such cases, curbing the autonomy of the government can promote the autonomy of the people. Of course, in some cases, the government may adequately represent the interests of one

---

15 Ibid., p. 214.
16 Ibid., pp. 217–218.
17 Ibid.
18 Ibid., p. 218.
19 David Luban, "The Romance of the Nation State", *Philosophy & Public Affairs*, vol. 9, no. 4, 1980, pp. 392–397, at p. 396.
20 Ibid., p. 395.
21 McMahan, "Ethics of International Intervention", p. 91.

community within its borders while neglecting or subverting the interests of another. Under such circumstances, intervention against the government could frustrate the first community's attempts at self-determination while aiding the latter's.[22] Conversely, suppose that an outside power in a position to intervene refuses to do so. This refusal to act would be conducive to the self-determination of the community with which the government is aligned, but it would disregard the interests of the community that the government fails to represent.[23] In such cases, one cannot argue against intervention by appealing to the value of self-determination, for that value will be compromised (and promoted) whether or not intervention is undertaken.

Furthermore, it should be stressed that the right to self-determination does not entitle a community to do whatever it pleases. The right of a particular community to pursue its ends is constrained by the rights that *other* communities have to pursue *their* ends.[24] We acknowledged this point in Chapter 5, in relation to national communities, when we noted Miller's observation that the principle of self-determination has a "reiterative" character: it grants rights to *all* communities. This point is emphasized by McMahan, who remarks: "the right to self-determination does not encompass a component right to persecute, expel, or massacre innocent members of another group. Such acts are not protected by any right".[25] Thus, intervention could frustrate a community's attempts at self-determination without violating its *right* to self-determination. This would be the case if the community in question were pursuing its ends in a manner that involved the persecution of others. Moreover, if intervention enhances the ability of the persecuted group to exercise its own right to self-determination, then concern for the protection of rights to self-determination gives us a reason to endorse intervention.

So far, the discussion has relied on an intuitive understanding of what self-determination involves. We should now take a closer look at this idea, for some aspects of the debate about humanitarian intervention reflect disagreement about how it should be defined. As we have seen, Walzer's arguments appeal to the idea of a "fit" between a government and a people, and it seems that, in Walzer's view, a community can be regarded as self-determining provided that it is governed in accordance with its own history and traditions. This is what has been called a "minimalist" account of self-determination.[26] But self-determination can (and perhaps should) be understood differently.

---

22 Ibid., p. 84; Jeff McMahan, "Humanitarian Intervention, Consent, and Proportionality", in N. Ann Davis, Richard Keshen, and Jeff McMahan (eds.), *Ethics and Humanity: Themes from the Philosophy of Jonathan Glover* (New York: Oxford University Press, 2010), pp. 47–48.

23 McMahan, "Ethics of International Intervention", p. 84.

24 McMahan, "Humanitarian Intervention, Consent, and Proportionality", pp. 47–48.

25 Ibid., p. 47.

26 Charles Beitz, "The Moral Standing of States Revisited", *Ethics and International Affairs*, vol. 23, no. 4, 2009, pp. 325–347, on p. 337.

Consider two alternative conceptions. At the opposite end of the spectrum from Walzer's, we find a "maximalist", or democratic, account.[27] According to this view, a community can be genuinely self-determining only if it is governed democratically. This means that the individuals who comprise the community must be free to participate in political institutions that allow them to collectively control political outcomes. In the absence of such institutions, the community cannot be said to exercise self-determination. Between these two extremes is an intermediary conception. According to this account, self-determination does not require democracy, but it does require institutional mechanisms through which citizens can voice their opinions and express political grievances. Moreover, legislators must be required to publicly demonstrate that the laws and policies that they enact conform to a widely shared conception of the common good.[28]

We can say that the second and third conceptions described above both insist that, in order for a community to be regarded as self-determining, there must be a sense in which the community's members can be said to actively participate in *self-government*. By contrast, the first, "minimalist", conception lacks this requirement. Which account should we prefer? In order to answer this question, we must consult the reasons that we have for caring about self-determination in the first place.[29] Consider two such reasons. First, self-determination serves an instrumental function. As Charles Beitz observes: "self-determining political communities are more likely than any political form practically available to protect people's basic interests as the people, themselves, understand them".[30] Call this the *instrumental* value of self-determination. The second reason is one that we have encountered already, during our discussion of national culture in Chapter 5. As we noted there, communal membership can become an important part of our identity. The communities in which we live play a role in shaping our preferences, attitudes, and values and help us to formulate a plan for life.[31] Beitz points out that interference in a "culture's internal life risks threatening the stability of the sense of membership and disrupting the pursuit of ends in which individuals have invested themselves".[32] These considerations draw our attention to what we might call the *identarian* value of self-determination.

If these are our reasons for caring about self-determination, which of the three conceptions of self-determination that I described above should we endorse? Remember that the options are (i) the "maximalist", democratic,

---

27 Ibid., pp. 336–337.
28 Ibid., pp. 337–338.
29 Ibid., p. 338.
30 Ibid.
31 Ibid.
32 Ibid., p. 339.

interpretation; (ii) the "minimalist" interpretation favoured by Walzer, which equates self-determination with governance according to tradition; and (iii) an intermediate conception that is not democratic but that nevertheless emphasizes the importance of a form of self-government.

Beitz argues that we must reject the maximalist, democratic, conception on the grounds that it fails to take seriously the *identarian* value of self-determination.[33] Not all communities are democratic, yet their members might nevertheless identify with the political institutions by which they are governed. Of course, this is not to say that communities organized democratically will *not* be self-determining; they often will be. But from the fact that a community is not organized democratically, we cannot infer that it also fails to be self-determining. Beitz also holds that we must reject the minimalist conception favoured by Walzer. We must reject this account because it sanctions political arrangements that fail to instantiate the *instrumental* value of self-determination.[34] Authoritarian regimes that offer no opportunities for citizens to voice opinions or express grievances may nevertheless govern in accordance with the community's history and traditions and are therefore compatible with self-determination minimally conceived. Yet such governments cannot be relied upon to protect people's basic interests.

This leaves us with the intermediate conception. In order to count as self-determining, a community need not be organized democratically, but it does need to provide its members with meaningful opportunities for self-governance. When these opportunities are absent, as they are in authoritarian regimes, the community cannot be regarded as self-determining. What this analysis suggests is that intervention against authoritarian regimes cannot be criticized on the grounds that it undermines the community's capacity for self-determination, for the community in question cannot plausibly be thought to possess that capacity in the first place.

10.2 Humanitarian intervention and the principles of just war

In the previous chapter, we identified a number of conditions that, according to just war theory, must be satisfied in order for the resort to war to be justified. In this section, I consider the distinctive issues that some of these principles raise in the context of specifically humanitarian war. I shall address *just cause*, *proportionality*, *right intention*, and *reasonable chance of success*.

---

33 Ibid. Cf. McMahan, "Ethics of International Intervention", pp. 82–83.
34 Beitz, "Moral Standing of States Revisited", pp. 339–340; Cf. McMahan, "Ethics of International Intervention", p. 82.

10.2.1 Just cause and crimes against humanity

As we saw in the previous section, there is disagreement about the kinds of injustice that are serious enough to warrant humanitarian intervention. Recall that, according to Walzer, intervention is justified only in cases of "extreme" oppression. This point is sometimes framed in terms of the just cause principle introduced in Chapter 9. For example, Nicholas Wheeler suggests that there is a just cause for intervention only in those circumstances that constitute a "supreme humanitarian emergency".[35] Elaborating, Wheeler suggests that "it is important to distinguish between what we might call the ordinary routine abuse of human rights that tragically occurs on a daily basis and those extraordinary acts of killing and brutality that belong to the category of 'crimes against humanity'".[36] Similarly, James Pattison writes:

> we should generally endorse a just cause criterion similar to that outlined by the ICISS [International Commission on Intervention and State Sovereignty]. This asserts that, for humanitarian intervention to be warranted, there must be serious and irreparable harm occurring to human beings or imminently likely to occur. In particular, there must be circumstances of actual or apprehended (a) 'large-scale loss of life', with or without genocidal intent ... or (b) 'large-scale ethnic cleansing', whether carried out by killing, forced expulsion, or acts of terror or rape.[37]

That there is just cause for intervention in cases of catastrophic moral breakdown is not seriously contested (which is not to say that intervention will necessarily be justified all-things-considered; remember that just cause is merely one of several conditions that must be satisfied in order for war to be permissible). But why think that "the routine abuse of human rights" cannot also constitute a just cause? In the previous section, we examined Walzer's reasons for holding that routine (or "ordinary") oppression cannot justify intervention, and we saw that those reasons do not stack up. Let us now consider a different reason. Pattison draws our attention to the obvious but important fact that military intervention, even when undertaken with benign intentions, is likely to harm some individuals whom are not liable to be harmed.[38] When armed forces conduct air strikes or engage in urban warfare, it is almost inevitable that some innocent bystanders – including the intervention's intended beneficiaries – will be killed or maimed. Given that

---

35 Nicholas J. Wheeler, *Saving Strangers: Humanitarian Intervention in International Society* (New York: Oxford University Press, 2000), p. 34.
36 Ibid.
37 James Pattison, *Humanitarian Intervention & the Responsibility to Protect: Who Should Intervene?* (Oxford: Oxford University Press, 2010), pp. 23-24 (reference omitted).
38 Ibid., p. 22.

it can be expected to have these awful side effects, intervention must have a very important goal. Without such a goal, it will not be able to achieve results that are of sufficient value to outweigh its anticipated harms.[39] War is a blunt instrument, and the worry is that if war is waged in an attempt to extinguish routine abuses of human rights, it will do more harm than good. By contrast, when war is waged to prevent crimes such as genocide – crimes which "shock the moral conscience of mankind" – we can often be reasonably confident that its bad effects will be outweighed by the good that it achieves.

Important as these considerations are, we should resist the claim that only extreme oppression can constitute a just cause for intervention. What is revealed by the points reviewed in the previous paragraph is not that ending "ordinary" oppression can never be a just cause for intervention but rather that intervention with that goal will often be *disproportionate*. Drawing this distinction has important practical implications. If we hold that ending ordinary oppression is not a just cause, then intervention with that goal will *never* be permissible. In other words, ordinary oppression will not give us any reason to even contemplate intervening. By contrast, if we hold that ending ordinary oppression can be a just cause but that pursuing it will often be disproportionate, ordinary oppression *can* give us a reason for such contemplation. To recycle a remark of Helen Frowe's quoted in the previous chapter, ordinary oppression can act as a trigger that kick-starts a debate about whether war could be permissible all-things-considered. This is important, because while intervention aimed at ending ordinary oppression may *often* do more harm than good, we can imagine situations in which it might, in fact, be proportionate. This point is actually conceded by Pattison, who writes:

> practical concerns [regarding the harmful side-effects of intervention] provide the strongest case for generally maintaining that the bar for humanitarian intervention should be set high. There may, however, be particular instances when intervention in response to a less serious crisis is likely to cause little harm. There would be little reason to reject such a case as morally problematic …[40]

We should accept, then, that the prevention of ordinary oppression *is* a just cause for intervention while acknowledging that interventions with this goal will often – though not always – be ruled out on grounds of proportionality. This comports with the account of just cause endorsed in the previous chapter. There is just cause when those warred against are responsible for wrongs that are sufficiently serious to render them liable to be killed or maimed. The wrongs involved in ordinary oppression are wrongs of this kind.

---

39 Ibid., pp. 22–23.
40 Ibid., p. 24.

10.2.2 Proportionality and the international order

We have just noted that humanitarian intervention will be impermissible when its anticipated costs are expected to outweigh its anticipated benefits (i.e., when it is expected to be disproportionate). We noted that an obvious and serious harm associated with intervention is the collateral killing of innocent bystanders. Let us now consider another potential harm that should perhaps be weighed in the proportionality calculation. According to critics, a significant harm inflicted by intervention is the subversion of the international order. There are, in fact, two distinct concerns here, and we shall turn to the second shortly. The first is that the practice of humanitarian intervention threatens to erode the international system of state sovereignty.[41] The international system is built around the principle that, within their territorial boundaries, states should enjoy ultimate and comprehensive authority. Moreover, as we acknowledged in the previous section, the autonomy bestowed by the doctrine of state sovereignty can facilitate communal self-determination, at least when the state upon which sovereignty is bestowed is representative of its people. Of course, humanitarian intervention, when undertaken responsibly, is aimed at states that are *not* representative of their people, but some worry that the practice of intervention will undermine state sovereignty more generally.

Suppose that humanitarian intervention really does pose a serious threat to the system of state sovereignty. This would be a cause for concern if we had strong reasons for preserving that system, but perhaps we should be willing to let it go. Although it is true that the autonomy conferred by sovereignty can promote communal self-determination, we should not lose sight of the important point that communities do not have a moral right to pursue their ends in any way that they please, irrespective of the costs to others. Yet, as we noted in Chapter 5, sovereignty allows communities to make various decisions that can have extremely harmful consequences for third parties. One of the examples given in Chapter 5 was the decision of certain political communities to emit unduly large amounts of carbon dioxide that contribute to dangerous climate change. According to the principle of state sovereignty, this is a decision that communities should be free to make despite its harmful consequences for outsiders. This gives us reason to doubt whether an international system built around the principle of state sovereignty is something that we should want to maintain.[42]

---

41 Michael Walzer, *Just and Unjust Wars: A Moral Argument with Historical Illustrations* (New York: Basic Books, 1977), p. 61.

42 McMahan, "Ethics of international Intervention", p. 93; Fernando R. Tesón, "The Liberal Case for Humanitarian Intervention", in J. L. Holzgrefe and Robert O. Keohane (eds.), *Humanitarian Intervention: Ethical, Legal and Political Dilemmas* (Cambridge: Cambridge University Press, 2003), p. 114; Simon Caney, *Justice Beyond Borders: A Global Political Theory* (Oxford: Oxford University Press, 2005), p. 240; Pattison, *Humanitarian Intervention*, p. 22.

McMahan has argued that if the system of sovereign states were to be replaced by a world government, this would be a welcome development.[43] However, given that many of us will be less sanguine about the prospects of justice in a world governed by a single authority, it is important to stress that world government is not the only alternative to the status quo. We can imagine institutional arrangements that preserve a plurality of independent states (thereby deviating from the model specified by the idea of world government) while dispensing with some of the problematical features of the current system. For example, we can imagine a system that constrains the *scope* of state authority. Under such a system, states would remain the ultimate authority in some domains but not in others. To put the point differently, the range of issues over which states would exercise ultimate authority would be less extensive than it is at present.[44] For example, given the importance of a state's environmental practices for the wellbeing of humans (and non-humans) in other states, responsibility for environmental policy might be transferred to a supranational organization. This organization would not be a world government, for its remit would be narrowly defined, but its existence would nevertheless represent a departure from the system of state sovereignty.

In short, the system of state sovereignty has significant defects, and there appear to be viable institutional alternatives that lack these flaws while also exhibiting certain virtues that characterize the status quo. Given that this is the case, we should perhaps not be unduly worried by the thought that intervention could undermine the system of state sovereignty. The sinking of the current system could be seen as one of the *good* things that humanitarian intervention can contribute toward achieving, rather than as a harm to be weighed against those achievements.

I said that there are two distinct concerns relating to the potentially subversive effects of humanitarian intervention on the international order. So far, we have addressed only one of these. The second concern is that intervention undermines international peace and stability.[45] To the degree that they exist, peace and stability in the international domain are fragile accomplishments, and maintaining a norm of non-intervention is said to be important for their preservation. Acts that disregard that norm set a dangerous precedent. Even benign interventions undertaken by well-intentioned agents can do serious harm by furnishing less scrupulous states with a pretext for predatory attacks. In a world that accepts intervention under certain conditions, it will be easier for states to initiate interventions that are, in fact, unjust. State

---

43 McMahan, "Ethics of International Intervention", p. 93.

44 Caney, *Justice Beyond Borders*, p. 151.

45 Thomas M. Franck and Nigel S. Rodley, "After Bangladesh: The Law of Humanitarian Intervention by Military Force", *The American Journal of International Law*, vol. 67, no. 2, 1973, pp. 275–305, at p. 290; Robert Jackson, *The Global Covenant: Human Conduct in a World of States* (Oxford: Oxford University Press, 2000), p. 291.

leaders will abuse humanitarian rhetoric, and exploit any exceptions made by international law, in order to justify self-interested military incursions that prey on the vulnerable.

Two points should be made in reply to this argument. First, if it could be established that humanitarian intervention makes unjust incursions more likely, it would not follow that humanitarian intervention ought to be prohibited. The appropriate response would instead be to ask, on each occasion that intervention is proposed, whether, by virtue of making unjust incursions more likely, the proposed intervention would be disproportionate. Answering this question will involve paying attention to several different considerations: how much more likely will unjust incursions become? How much harm can those incursions be expected to cause? Will that harm outweigh the good that could be achieved by humanitarian intervention? Our answers to these questions will be speculative, but even if we were to err on the side of caution and adopt a generally pessimistic outlook, it is unlikely that intervention would *always* be ruled out. At least in cases of extreme oppression – genocide, enslavement, expulsion – it is likely that there will be occasions on which intervention can be expected to be proportionate.

An important point to bear in mind here is that although intervention might have a negative influence on the behaviour of others, inaction might also have a negative influence. More specifically, failing to respond to acts of severe oppression might make it more likely that such acts will be repeated in the future.[46] If the oppressors of the world see that they can act with impunity, what is there to prevent them from continuing to brutalize their victims? This consideration bolsters the claim that intervention could sometimes be proportionate *even if* it makes unjust incursions more likely.

The second point to note is that it seems doubtful that humanitarian intervention actually makes unjust incursions more likely. The argument that intervention threatens international peace by undermining a norm of non-intervention assumes that such a norm is actually well established. But this is a dubious assumption. This point is made by Beitz, who writes:

> In international law, non-intervention is the rule; in international politics, it has been the exception. Therefore, it cannot plausibly be argued that interventionary policies should be avoided because they would undermine a convention of respect for national boundaries whose widespread acceptance helps keep the peace.[47]

When powerful states have wanted to intervene in the affairs of others, they have generally found ways to do so. At the outset of the Iraq War, George

---

46 Caney, *Justice Beyond Borders*, p. 256.
47 Charles Beitz, "The Reagan Doctrine in Nicaragua", in Steven Luper-Foy (ed.), *Problems of International Justice* (Boulder, CO: Westview, 1988), p. 187.

W. Bush declared: "Our mission is clear: to disarm Iraq of weapons of mass destruction, to end Saddam Hussein's support for terrorism, and to free the Iraqi people". I doubt anyone believes that the Bush administration would have decided against war had it been unable to appeal to the third of these stated aims (freeing the Iraqi people). If this rationale had been unavailable, Bush and his associates presumably would have simply fallen back on the first two proposed justifications (both of which were subsequently discredited). It is, of course, vitally important that international society find ways to curb the predatory behaviour of powerful states, but opposing humanitarian intervention does not look like a promising approach.

10.2.3 Right intention and the selectivity of intervention

We have acknowledged that humanitarian rationales can be employed disingenuously. States might claim to have humanitarian intentions when, in fact, their ends are considerably less benevolent. A common objection to humanitarian intervention builds upon this observation. According to one line of argument, ostensibly humanitarian interventions are rarely well intentioned and this fact is revealed by the *selectivity* of the practice. Critics point out that states choose to intervene in some humanitarian crises but not in others.[48] During the Arab Spring, for example, Britain chose to intervene in Libya but not in Bahrain. This selectivity, say the critics, reveals that intervening states do not really have humanitarian intentions; if they did, they would intervene more consistently. We can call this the *selectivity argument*.

This argument can be framed in terms of the *jus ad bellum* principle of "right intention". As we saw in the previous chapter, a war requires a just cause in order to be morally permissible, and, according to the right intention principle, war may be waged only if it is intended to achieve that cause: if it is fought in order to achieve some other aim, it will be classed as unjust. The selectivity argument maintains that the right intention principle is rarely satisfied by allegedly humanitarian interventions. The selectiveness of intervention reveals that, when interventions are undertaken, their architects intend to achieve something other than humanitarian ends. For example, their aim might be to economically exploit the country that they invade.

We might suspect that this argument is not always made in good faith. How many of those who criticize the selectivity of intervention would actually be happier if interventions were undertaken more frequently? (Tony Blair was a fairly consistent interventionist – he proposed humanitarian justifications for deploying the military to Kosovo, Sierra Leone, Afghanistan, and Iraq – yet he is generally reviled by anti-war protesters for precisely that reason.) But let us set this suspicion aside in order to assess the argument on its own merits.

---

48 Franck and Rodley, "After Bangladesh", p. 290.

The argument begins with the thought that if a state (Britain, say) intervenes in one country (Eritrea, for example) but not in another (Equatorial Guinea, for example) and the two countries are suffering humanitarian crises of comparable magnitudes, there must be some non-humanitarian consideration that explains Britain's discrepant behaviour (i.e., the fact that it intervenes in Eritrea but not in Equatorial Guinea). Call this the *alternative explanation claim*. The argument goes on to assert that the alternative explanation must be that Britain can attain an important benefit for itself by intervening in Eritrea but not by intervening in Equatorial Guinea. Call this the *benefit explanation*.

As we shall now see, both of these claims are false. Let us start by considering the *alternative explanation claim*. It is simply not true that there must be a non-humanitarian consideration that explains why Britain intervenes in Eritrea but not Equatorial Guinea. Suppose Britain has good reason to believe that intervention in Equatorial Guinea stands a poor chance of achieving its humanitarian goal and will therefore be disproportionate. Intervention will inevitably cause some degree of collateral harm, and, given that it will probably fail to achieve its ends, intervention is unlikely to accomplish any good significant enough to outweigh those harms. If Britain refrains from intervening in Equatorial Guinea for this reason, then it refrains from intervening *for humanitarian reasons*. It declines to intervene because it does not want to inflict further, unnecessary, suffering on Equatorial Guinea's people.

These reflections are also sufficient to defeat the *benefit explanation*, for they reveal that Britain's discrepant behaviour can be explained by something other than the expectation that intervention in Eritrea will yield an important benefit. But notice that in order to defeat the *benefit explanation*, it is not necessary to identify a *humanitarian* reason for Britain's discrepant behaviour. Suppose Britain refused to intervene in Equatorial Guinea not because it worried that intervention would impose disproportionate harms on the country's people but rather because intervention was opposed by British corporations, whose executives regard the country's dictator as good for business. Or suppose Britain's government declined to intervene because a general election was approaching, and intervention was known to be unpopular among voters. If Britain refrained from intervention for either of these reasons, then it refrained for reasons that are non-humanitarian in character, but its discrepant behaviour is nevertheless explained by something other than the expectation that intervention in Eritrea will enable Britain to capture important benefits for itself. Britain intervenes selectively because it has a non-humanitarian reason for non-intervention in Equatorial Guinea (appeasing big business or deferring to the electorate), not because it has a non-humanitarian reason for intervention in Eritrea (such as exploiting the country's inhabitants). This is important because it suggests that what we should criticize and oppose is not the intervention in Eritrea but rather the *non*-intervention in Equatorial Guinea.

One thought underlying the preceding remarks is as follows. States will sometimes recognize both humanitarian reasons for intervention and non-humanitarian reasons for non-intervention. Sometimes, they will decide (to their discredit) that the non-humanitarian reasons outweigh the humanitarian ones. But this clearly gives us no reason to oppose intervention on those occasions when states reach the opposite conclusion.

I have criticized the selectivity argument on the grounds that it cannot establish that an intervening state has non-humanitarian intent. But suppose that a state *does* intervene with non-humanitarian intent. To return to our example, suppose that Britain is largely indifferent to the achievement of humanitarian ends and intervenes in Eritrea for a self-interested reason that does not constitute a just cause. Surprising as it may seem, even this would not necessarily give us a reason to oppose intervention. This is because Britain's pursuit of its self-interested goal may achieve humanitarian ends *as a side effect*. Suppose that Britain intends to depose a dictator on the grounds that his rule undermines Britain's economic interests in the region. If the dictator is a murderous tyrant, his deposition may serve humanitarian ends. If this is the case, then we may have good reason to encourage Britain to go to war and thereby "exploit its wrongdoing in the service of a just cause".[49] (In case you are wondering, this is not intended as a defence of the 2003 Iraq War. The invasion of Iraq precipitated a humanitarian catastrophe that was largely predictable and should have been anticipated by the war's architects.)

Before we move on, it is worth noting the distinction between a humanitarian intention and a humanitarian motive. If I act with a humanitarian *intention*, then I identify a humanitarian state-of-affairs as the outcome that I wish to achieve by acting.[50] In order for my *motive* to be humanitarian, then my underlying reason for wishing to achieve that outcome must also be humanitarian.[51] To illustrate, suppose that Australia intervened in East Timor in order to end the killing of East Timorese civilians but did so because it wanted to reduce refugee flows into its own territory. If this were the case, then Australia would have acted with a humanitarian intention (end the killing of civilians) but a non-humanitarian motive (reduce refugee flows).

Now, it is likely that interveners will sometimes have both humanitarian *and* non-humanitarian motives; their efforts to end oppression will be motivated by a desire both to alleviate the suffering of the victims *and* to further their own ends. This is not to be regretted. In fact, it may actually be *desirable* for an intervener's humanitarian motive to be supplemented by a

---

49 Jeff McMahan, "Just War", in Robert E. Goodin, Philip Pettit, and Thomas Pogge (eds.), *A Companion to Contemporary Political Philosophy: Volume 2*, Second Edition (Malden, MA: Blackwell Publishing, 1993), p. 673.
50 Pattison, *Humanitarian Intervention*, pp. 154–155.
51 Ibid., p. 155.

self-interested motive, for this may ensure that the intervener is more committed to seeing the war through and to providing the resources necessary for a successful resolution.[52]

10.2.4 Reasonable chance of success and the argument of John Stuart Mill

As we saw at the beginning of the previous chapter, one criterion of *jus ad bellum* is that the war must have a reasonable chance of achieving its just cause. If there is not a reasonable chance of success, then the war is unlikely to do enough good to outweigh the harm that it will inevitably inflict. Whether humanitarian intervention has a reasonable chance of succeeding is a question that will generally have to be answered on a case-by-case basis. Some interventions will have greater prospects of success than others. However, it might also be the case that an intervention's likelihood of success is influenced by the nature of its aims. As we have seen, interventions can have different goals. They might aim to eliminate "extreme" oppression, or they might aim to eliminate "ordinary" oppression. Alternatively, they might aim to assist a national community fighting for its independence. According to an influential argument originally developed by the 19th century philosopher John Stuart Mill, interventions whose aim is to assist domestic rebels fighting for a greater degree of liberty and self-governance are almost always bound to fail.[53] Let us examine Mill's reasoning.

Mill's argument is as follows. If liberal institutions are to survive, there must be an adequate number of sufficiently liberal people in the populace who are willing and able to maintain them. Furthermore, if domestic rebels are unable to establish liberal institutions by themselves, without outside assistance, then we can infer from this that the populace lacks the requisite degree of liberal virtue. Mill writes: "The only test possessing any real value, of a people's having become fit for popular institutions, is that they, or a sufficient portion of them to prevail in the contest, are willing to brave labour and danger for their liberation".[54] (This passage is actually somewhat misleading, for it gives the impression that a willingness merely *to fight* for liberty is sufficient evidence of being "fit for popular institutions". As evidenced by the quote provided below, Mill's considered view is that an ability to *secure and maintain* freedom is what is actually required.)

When domestic rebels are unable to achieve victory by themselves, foreign powers might step in to assist them, and liberal institutions could be established as a result. But, in Mill's view, these institutions will not last, for

---

52 Ibid., p. 159-160.

53 John Stuart Mill, "A Few Words on Non-Intervention", in John M. Robson (ed.), *The Collected Works of John Stuart Mill, Volume XXI - Essays on Equality, Law, and Education* (London: Routledge and Kegan Paul, 1984).

54 Ibid., p. 122.

the environment in which they are built will not be capable of sustaining their existence. If the people "have not sufficient love of liberty to be able to wrest it from merely domestic oppressors, the liberty which is bestowed on them by other hands than their own, will have nothing real, nothing permanent".[55] Mill adds:

> If a people – especially one whose freedom has not yet become prescriptive – does not value it sufficiently to fight for it, and maintain it against any force which can be mustered within the country, even by those who have the command of the public revenue, it is only a question in how few years or months that people will be enslaved. Either the government which it has given to itself, or some military leader or knot of conspirators who contrive to subvert the government, will speedily put an end to all popular institutions… [U]nless the spirit of liberty is strong in a people, those who have the executive in their hands easily work institutions to the purposes of despotism.[56]

Presumably, "the government which [the people] has given to itself" will be composed of people with suitably liberal dispositions. (In all likelihood, its members will be drawn from the revolutionaries who disposed of its predecessor.) But Mill argues that this is not enough. There must be a liberal polity, animated by a "spirit of liberty", whose constituents can prevent those in power from becoming corrupted and abusing the state apparatus now at their disposal. And if the people were not capable, on their own, of restraining their previous government, it is unlikely that they will fare any better against its successor.

Now, Mill acknowledges that a people who have been long dominated by a tyrannical government will have been deprived of meaningful opportunities to develop liberal dispositions. He concedes that "the virtues of freemen cannot be learnt in the school of slavery".[57] Moreover, he recognizes "that if a people are not fit for freedom, to have any chance of becoming so they must first be free".[58] His worry is apparently that liberal institutions installed with outside assistance will not endure long enough for a previously subjugated people to acquire liberal virtues. These institutions will collapse (or rather be demolished) before there is sufficient time for them to instil in the people the liberal dispositions necessary for their preservation.

In reply to Mill, we should make two points. The first relates to the suggestion that, because the people were unable, by themselves, to defeat their

---

55 Ibid.
56 Ibid.
57 Ibid.
58 Ibid.

previous government, they will be unable to prevent members of the new government from becoming corrupted and from depriving them of their newly won liberty. It is surely a mistake to regard the people as symmetrically placed vis-à-vis the old and new regimes. One obvious reason why it is so difficult to restrain an autocratic government is that there are no mechanisms in place that enable one to do so. This is what makes it autocratic. Dissidents are required to oppose the government through unofficial channels because there are no official channels available to them. They take to the streets, they take up arms, and they are readily crushed because of the massive advantages afforded to an opponent with unimpeded access to the levers of state power. By contrast, if the new institutions installed after a successful revolutionary struggle (with or without outside support) really are *liberal* institutions, then the relationship between people and government will look very different. The executive will find itself constrained by the legislature, by the need to win approval in popular elections, and by a judiciary charged with ensuring that it does not deviate from the constitution. It hardly seems reasonable to conclude that, because the people were incapable of prevailing in mortal combat with an authoritarian juggernaut (perhaps because they were unable to convince enough people that participation in such a dangerous conflict was prudent), they will therefore be unable to tame a government bound by an elaborate system of checks and balances.

The second point to make is that Mill seems to assume that interveners will abandon their charges as soon as the old guard is deposed. This is presumably why he frets that freshly planted liberal institutions will perish before having had a chance to take root. But there is no reason to think that intervention must necessarily be a brief affair. Instead of departing the second that the conflict has been resolved, interveners may remain to midwife the nascent liberal institutions that they have helped to install. By sharing their resources and expertise, intervening parties can help to nurture these institutions through a possibly difficult infancy. In this way, they can ensure that liberal institutions last long enough to create the liberal citizens required for their long-term survival.

There is a well-known aspect of Mill's argument that I have not yet addressed. According to Mill, revolutionary struggle provides a valuable arena in which liberal virtues can be learned. He writes:

> When a people has had the misfortune to be ruled by a government under which the feelings and the virtues needful for maintaining freedom could not develop themselves, it is during an arduous struggle to become free by their own efforts that these feelings and virtues have the best chance of springing up.[59]

---

59 Ibid., pp. 122–123.

Mill lambasts intervention on the grounds that it truncates such "arduous struggle" or substitutes its local participants with foreign surrogates.

Two points should be noted here. First, Mill clearly does not think that participating in revolutionary struggle is the *only* way in which liberal virtues can be acquired. (If he did, an implication of his view would be that the citizens of all long-established contemporary democracies are unfit for popular institutions.) Rather, Mill's view is that revolutionary struggle is an important arena in which liberal virtues can be acquired by those who have been deprived, by oppressive governments, of a more conventional liberal education. This arena assumes special importance for Mill because, as we have seen, he doubts that liberal institutions installed with outside help will survive long enough to serve their educative purpose. However, as was argued above, Mill's pessimism regarding the prospects of institutions set up with foreign assistance is not well grounded. Therefore, we should ascribe less importance than Mill did to the educational role of revolutionary struggles and not regret the fact that such struggles are often arrested by intervention.

Second, contrary to what Mill's argument seems to assume, protracted revolutionary struggle is often harmful to a community's prospects of achieving freedom. As Allen Buchanan has explained, revolutions are often characterized by a "spiral of coercion".[60] The regime attempts to discourage participation in the revolution by punishing those who take part, while the rebels attempt to encourage participation by punishing those who do not take part. This leads to a situation in which the regime and the rebels attempt to offset each other's efforts by ratcheting up the severity of the punishments that they impose. One concern here is that the rebel leadership may become "accustomed to wrongdoing toward its fellow victims of oppression during the revolutionary struggle, [and] this may increase the probability that [it] will mistreat citizens once it comes to power".[61] One lesson to take from this is that we should reject the rosy image of revolutionary struggle as a domain in which liberal virtues flourish. The unchecked power enjoyed by revolutionaries can corrupt just as readily as that enjoyed by state officials. Given that this is the case, an intervention that accelerates the revolutionary process can actually *increase* the likelihood that a revolution will accomplish its liberal aims.

In short, Mill's arguments fail to establish that humanitarian intervention necessarily lacks a reasonable chance of success on those occasions when its aim is to assist in the fight for liberty.

---

60 Allen Buchanan, "The Ethics of Revolution and its Implications for the Ethics of Intervention", *Philosophy & Public Affairs*, vol. 41, no. 4, 2013, pp. 291–323, at pp. 319–320.
61 Ibid., p. 319.

10.3 Massacres and poverty

I want to finish this chapter, and the book as a whole, by returning to an issue that we first encountered at the outset of our enquiry, namely, world poverty. Our discussion of humanitarian intervention enables us to view this issue in a new light. As noted in Chapter 3, six million children below the age of five die each year, and a large proportion of the deaths have poverty-related causes. For example, almost half of the deaths are attributable to poor nutrition. Now, it will be instructive to compare these statistics with those relating to deaths caused by the kinds of injustices that typically provoke calls for humanitarian intervention. If we go with a liberal estimate of how many Tutsis were killed during the Rwandan genocide and suppose that there were one million victims, the number of infants killed by poor nutrition each year (2,700,000) is over two and a half times higher than the number of people murdered in Rwanda. However, notwithstanding the fact that intervention in Rwanda came shamefully late, there is a tendency to grant less attention to poverty deaths than to massacres. Many public figures who rally to the cause of humanitarian war have little to say about the deaths of numerous children caused each year by famine, measles, and other poverty-related ills.

There are a variety of possible explanations for this. First, poverty is an ongoing and seemingly unchanging phenomenon, "a constant background condition to which most people who are not among the victims have become inured", whereas massacres provide journalists with dramatic new events to report and discuss.[62] Second, deaths attributable to diseases like diarrhoea and measles might seem less newsworthy than deaths inflicted with machetes or rifles.[63] And, third, rescues executed with fighter jets can seem more heroic than those involving the provision of food parcels and medicine.[64]

These are each plausible explanations for the differential reactions elicited by massacres and by poverty, but they do not demonstrate that the extra attention garnered by the former is merited. In other words, they do not provide us with good reasons to ascribe to the prevention of massacres greater moral significance than to the prevention of poverty deaths. Can we identify a plausible argument for holding that the prevention of massacres is more important?

One argument begins with the premise that the victims of massacres suffer as a result of human agency whereas the victims of poverty are disadvantaged by impersonal forces such as famine and disease. In McMahan's words, the thought is that "humanitarian intervention is intended not only to prevent serious *harms* but also to prevent serious *wrongdoing*, or seriously immoral *action*... [H]umanitarian intervention is a response not just to misfortune, but to *evil*".[65] To this observation, we might add a second premise, according

---

62 McMahan, "Humanitarian Intervention, Consent, and Proportionality", p. 58.
63 Ibid.
64 Ibid.
65 Ibid., p. 60.

to which our reasons to prevent harms produced by wrongdoing are weightier than our reasons to prevent harms attributable to impersonal forces.[66] From these two premises, it can then be inferred that preventing massacres is more important than preventing poverty. Call this the *wrongdoing argument*.

There are two problems with this argument. To begin with, the first premise is highly dubious. As we saw in Chapter 3, there are good reasons to think that much world poverty is not a natural phenomenon but a product of the rules that govern the global economy, rules that could (and should) be re-written. This means that it is inappropriate to think of the poor as people who are merely unfortunate rather than as people who have been wrongfully harmed. But even if we were to set this point aside and accept that poverty is not a product of wrongdoing, there is a second problem with the wrongdoing argument. This problem relates to the argument's second premise. Although preventing harms produced by wrongdoing might be more important than preventing harms attributable to impersonal forces, the difference in importance is unlikely to be very great. To illustrate this point, consider the following two thought experiments, which I have adapted from McMahan.[67] (Assume that all of the people involved are strangers to you.)

<u>Scenario A</u>: You can either (1) prevent Anita from being wrongfully pushed off a cliff or (2) prevent Billy from being blown off the cliff by a strong gust of wind.

> If we think that preventing harms caused by wrongdoing is more important than preventing harms caused by impersonal forces, then our choice of whom to save should not be made randomly. Rather, we should choose to save Anita from being murdered. This seems like a reasonable decision. But now consider a second case.

<u>Scenario B</u>: You can either (1) prevent Claire from being wrongfully pushed off a cliff or (2) prevent David from being blown off the cliff by a strong gust of wind *and* prevent Edie from tripping and breaking her leg.

In this case, it seems reasonably clear that we should take the second option. The fact that we can prevent slightly more harm by taking this option (because, in addition to saving a life, we can prevent a non-fatal injury) seems decisive. But this means that preventing harms caused by wrongdoing cannot be *significantly* more important than preventing harms that are not caused by wrongdoing. The fact that a harm is attributable to wrongdoing gives us *some* reason to prioritize its prevention but that reason is easily outweighed by countervailing considerations.

---

66 Ibid.
67 Ibid., pp. 60–61.

Let us continue to suppose, for the sake of argument, that poverty is not caused by wrongdoing. Given that massacres *are* a product of wrongdoing, it follows from what has been said above that we have *some* reason to prioritize their prevention over the prevention of poverty. Moreover, there may be an additional reason to prioritize the prevention of massacres. Intervening militarily against tyrants who are attempting to slaughter innocent people may prevent them from committing further crimes in the future. Moreover, it may deter other dictators from acting in similar ways.[68] These considerations are not insignificant. However, they might be outweighed by considerations that tell in favour of prioritizing the prevention of poverty.

As we saw in Chapter 3, preventing poverty-related deaths is reasonably cheap. Recall that it costs roughly $250 to provide rehydration therapy to impoverished children whose lives are threatened by diarrhoea and roughly $820 to provide life-saving anti-malarial bed nets. By contrast, intervention is staggeringly expensive. For example, in the case of Bosnia, one commentator remarks: "if one assumes that without military action a quarter of the two million Muslims living there would have been killed (a highly unrealistic figure), the intervention cost $120,000 per life saved".[69] If saving lives by intervening militarily to prevent massacres is much less cost-effective than saving lives by addressing poverty, then it will be difficult to defend the claim that, all-things-considered, we ought to attribute greater importance to preventing massacres.

This is not to say that we ought to address poverty *instead of* preventing massacres. A genuine commitment to global justice surely requires us to do both. But the foregoing reflections do force us to question the wisdom of prioritizing the latter task. Earlier in the chapter, we addressed the claim that supposedly humanitarian interveners are suspiciously selective. Although we saw that this objection does not discredit intervention, there is surely something to it. After all, some massacres (those in Rwanda and Darfur, for example) were disgracefully allowed to continue while the international community sat idly by. But the point to be stressed here is that, as the preceding discussion has made clear, a more wide-ranging complaint can also be levelled. This complaint focuses on our peculiarly selective attitude to humanitarian crises more generally and prompts us to confront our tendency to downplay the significance of tackling global poverty. It forces us to ask why, instead of addressing this catastrophe with the urgency that it demands, we have instead allowed it to fester and to become a permanent and disfiguring feature of our world.

---

68 Ibid., p. 60.
69 Benjamin A. Valentino, "The True Costs of Humanitarian Intervention: The Hard Truth About a Noble Notion", *Foreign Affairs*, vol. 90, no. 6, 2011, pp. 60–73, at p. 67.

BIBLIOGRAPHY

Abbott, K. W., "Defensive Unfairness: The Normative Structure of Section 301", in J. Bhagwati and R. E. Hudec (eds.), *Fair Trade and Harmonization: Volume 2 – Legal Analysis* (Cambridge, Mass: MIT Press, 1996).

Abizadeh, A., "Cooperation, Pervasive Impact, and Coercion: On the Scope (not Site) of Distributive Justice", *Philosophy & Public Affairs*, Vol. 35, No. 4, 2007, pp. 318–358.

Abizadeh, A., Pandey, M., and Abizadeh, S., "Wage competition and the special-obligations challenge to more open borders", *Politics, Philosophy & Economics*, Vol. 14, No. 3, 2015, pp. 255–269.

Allen, M. (et al.), "Warming Caused by Cumulative Carbon Emissions Towards the Trillionth Tonne", *Nature*, Vol. 458, 2009, pp. 1163–1166.

Anscombe, E., "Mr. Truman's Degree," in Anscombe, E. (ed.), *Ethics, Religion, and Politics: Collected Philosophical Papers*, Vol. 3 (Minneapolis: University of Minnesota Press, 1981).

Appiah, K. A., *Cosmopolitanism* (New York: Norton, 2006).

Armstrong, C., "Coercion, Reciprocity, and Equality Beyond the State", *Journal of Social Philosophy*, Vol. 40, No. 3, 2009, pp. 297–316.

Armstrong, C., "National Self-Determination, Global Equality and Moral Arbitrariness", *Journal of Political Philosophy*, Vol. 18, No. 3, 2010, pp. 313–334.

Arneson, R. J., "Moral Limits on the Demands of Beneficence?", in Deen K. Chatterjee (ed.), *The Ethics of Assistance: Morality and the Distant Needy* (Cambridge: Cambridge University Press, 2004).

Ashford, E., "The Demandingness of Scanlon's Contractualism", *Ethics*, Vol. 113, No. 2, 2003, pp. 273–302.

Ashford, E., "Obligations of Justice and Beneficence to Aid the Severely Poor", in Patricia Illingworth, Thomas Pogge, and Leif Wenar (eds.), *Giving Well: The Ethics of Philanthropy* (New York: Oxford University Press, 2011).

Barry, B., "Statism and Nationalism: A Cosmopolitan Critique", *Nomos*, Vol. 41, 1999, pp. 12–66.

Beitz, C. R., *Political Theory and International Relations* (Princeton, NJ: Princeton University Press, 1979).

Beitz, C. R., "The Reagan Doctrine in Nicaragua", in Steven Luper-Foy (ed.), *Problems of International Justice* (Boulder: Westview, 1988).

Beitz, C. R., "Cosmopolitan Liberalism and the States System", in Chris Brown (ed.), *Political Restructuring in Europe: Ethical Perspectives* (London: Routledge, 1994).

Beitz, C. R., "Social and Cosmopolitan Liberalism", *International Affairs*, Vol. 75, No. 3, 1999, pp. 515–529.

Beitz, C. R., "Rawls's Law of Peoples", *Ethics*, Vol. 110, No. 4, 2000, pp. 669–696.

Beitz, C. R., "Human Rights as a Common Concern", *The American Political Science Review*, Vol. 95, No. 2, 2001, pp. 269–282.

Beitz, C. R., *The Idea of Human Rights* (Oxford: Oxford University Press, 2009a).

Beitz, C. R., "The Moral Standing of States Revisited", *Ethics and International Affairs*, Vol. 23, No. 4, 2009b, pp. 325–347.

Black, I., "Syrian Regime Document Trove Shows Evidence of 'Industrial Scale' Killing of Detainees", *The Guardian*, 21st January 2014, available at https://www.theguardian.com/world/2014/jan/20/evidence-industrial-scale-killing-syria-war-crimes

Black, S., "Individualism at an Impasse", *Canadian Journal of Philosophy*, Vol. 21, No. 3, 1991, pp. 347–377.

Blake, M., "Distributive Justice, State Coercion, and Autonomy", *Philosophy & Public Affairs*, Vol. 30, No. 3, 2002a, pp. 257–296.

Blake, M., "Discretionary Immigration", *Philosophical Topics*, Vol. 30, No. 2, 2002b, pp. 273–289.

Blake, M., "Immigration", in R. G. Frey and Christopher Heath Wellman (eds.), *A Companion to Applied Ethics* (Malden, MA: Blackwell Publishing, 2005).

Blake, M., "Coercion and Egalitarian Justice", *The Monist*, Vol. 94, No. 4, 2011, pp. 555–570.

Blake, M., "Immigration, Jurisdiction, and Exclusion", *Philosophy & Public Affairs*, Vol. 41, No. 2, 2013, pp. 103–130.

Borjas, G. J., *Heaven's Door: Immigration Policy and the American Economy* (Princeton, NJ: Princeton University Press, 1999).

Boudet, A. M. M., (et al.), *Gender Differences in Poverty and Household Composition Through the Life-Cycle: A Global Perspective* (Washington, DC: World Bank Group, 2018).

Brock, G., *Global Justice: A Cosmopolitan Account* (Oxford: Oxford University Press, 2009).

Brown, A. G. and Stern, R. M., "Concepts of Fairness in the Global Trading System", *Pacific Economic Review*, Vol. 12, No. 3, 2007, pp. 293–318.

Buchanan, A., "The Internal Legitimacy of Humanitarian Intervention", *Journal of Political Philosophy*, Vol. 7, No. 1, 1999, pp. 71–87.

Buchanan, A., *The Heart of Human Rights* (New York: Oxford University Press, 2013a).

Buchanan, A., "The Ethics of Revolution and its Implications for the Ethics of Intervention", *Philosophy & Public Affairs*, Vol. 41, No. 4, 2013b, pp. 291–323.

Caney, S., "Global Equality of Opportunity and the Sovereignty of States", in Tony Coates (ed.), *International Justice* (Aldershot: Ashgate, 2000).

Caney, S., "Cosmopolitanism and the Law of Peoples", *Journal of Political Philosophy*, Vol. 10, No. 1, 2002.

Caney, S., *Justice Beyond Borders* (Oxford: Oxford University Press, 2005).

Caney, S., "Climate Change, Human Rights, and Moral Thresholds", in Stephen Humphreys (ed.), *Human Rights and Climate Change* (Cambridge: Cambridge University Press, 2009a).

Caney, S., "Cosmopolitanism and Justice", in Thomas Christiano and John Christman (eds.), *Contemporary Debates in Political Philosophy* (Malden, MA: Blackwell, 2009b).

Caney, S., "Climate Change and the Duties of the Advantaged", *Critical Review of International Social and Political Philosophy*, Vol. 13, No. 1, 2010, pp. 203–228.

Caney, S., "Humanity, Associations and Global Justice: A Defence of Humanity-Centred Cosmopolitan Egalitarianism", *The Monist*, Vol. 94, No. 4, 2011, pp. 506–534.

Caney, S., "Climate Change, Intergenerational Equity and The Social Discount Rate", *Politics, Philosophy & Economics*, Vol. 13, No. 4, 2014, pp. 320–342.

Carens, J., "Migration and Morality: A Liberal Egalitarian Perspective", in Brian Barry and Robert E. Goodin (eds.), *Free Movement: Ethical Issues in the Transnational Migration of People and Money* (Hemel Hempstead: Harvester Wheatsheaf, 1992).

Carens, J., *The Ethics of Immigration* (New York: Oxford University Press, 2013).

Casal, P., "Global Taxes on Natural Resources", *Journal of Moral Philosophy*, Vol. 8, No. 3, 2011, pp. 307–328.

Christensen, J., *Trade Justice* (Oxford: Oxford University Press, 2017).

Clausing, K., *Open: The Progressive Case for Free Trade, Immigration, and Global Capital* (Cambridge, MA: Harvard University Press, 2019).

Cohen, J., "Philosophy, Social Science, Global Poverty", in Alison M. Jaggar (ed.), *Thomas Pogge and his Critics* (Cambridge: Polity Press, 2010).

Cohen, M., "Moral Skepticism and International Relations", *Philosophy & Public Affairs*, Vol. 13, No. 4, 1984, pp. 299–346.

Coughlin, C. C., "The Controversy over Free Trade: The Gap Between Economists and the General Public", *The Federal Reserve Bank of St. Louis*, January/February, 2002, pp. 1–22.

Cumming-Bruce, N. and Barnard, A., "U.N. Investigators Say Syria Bombed Convoy and Did So Deliberately", *New York Times*, 1st March 2017, available at https://www.nytimes.com/2017/03/01/world/middleeast/united-nations-war-crimes-syria.html

Dukas, H. and Hoffmann, B. (eds.), *Albert Einstein: The Human Side* (Princeton, NJ: Princeton University Press, 1979).

Elster, J., *Sour Grapes: Studies in the Subversion of Rationality* (Cambridge: Cambridge University Press, 1983).

Executive Board, American Anthropological Association, "Statement on Human Rights", *American Anthropologist*, Vol. 49, No. 4, 1947, pp. 539–543.

Fabre, C., "Global Egalitarianism: An Indefensible Theory of Justice?", in Daniel A. Bell and Avner de-Shalit (eds.), *Forms of Justice: Critical Perspectives on David Miller's Political Philosophy* (Lanham, MD: Rowman & Littlefield, 2002).

Fabre, C., "Global Distributive Justice: An Egalitarian Perspective", *Canadian Journal of Philosophy*, Vol. 35, Supp. 1, 2005, pp. 139–164.

Fabre, C., *Cosmopolitan War* (Oxford: Oxford University Press, 2012).

Fankhauser, S., "The Social Costs of Greenhouse Gas Emissions: An Expected Value Approach", *The Energy Journal*, Vol. 15, No. 2, 1994, pp. 157–184.

Franck, T. M. and Rodley, N. S., "After Bangladesh: The Law of Humanitarian Intervention by Military Force", *The American Journal of International Law*, Vol. 67, No. 2, 1973, pp. 275–305.

Frowe, H., *The Ethics of War and Peace: An Introduction*, Second Edition (New York: Routledge, 2016).

Gardiner, S. M., "Ethics and Global Climate Change", *Ethics*, Vol. 114, No. 3, 2004, pp. 555–600.

Griffin, J., *On Human Rights* (New York: Oxford University Press, 2008).

Halper, S., *The Beijing Consensus: Legitimizing Authoritarianism in our Time* (New York: Basic Books, 2012).

Hobbes, T., *De Cive* [1642] (New York: Appleton-Century-Crofts, 1949).

Hobbes, T., *Leviathan* [1651], in William Molesworth (ed.), The English Works of Thomas Hobbes: Volume 3 (London: John Bohn, 1841).

Hohfeld, W., *Fundamental Legal Conceptions as Applied in Judicial Reasoning* (New Haven: Yale University Press, 1919).

Hudec, R. E., "Broadening the Scope of Remedies in WTO Dispute Settlement", in Friedl Weiss and Jochem Wiers (eds.), *Improving WTO Dispute Settlement Procedures* (Folkestone: Cameron May Publishers, 2000).

Hug, L., Sharrow, D., and You, D., *Levels and Trends in Child Mortality (2017)* (New York: United Nations Children's Fund, 2017).

http://trillionthtonne.org/

Hurka, T., "Proportionality in the Morality of War", *Philosophy and Public Affairs*, Vol. 33, No. 1, 2005, pp. 34–66.

International Committee of the Red Cross, "Preamble," Protocol Additional to the Geneva Conventions of 12 August 1949, and Relating to the Protection of Victims of International Armed Conflicts (Protocol I), 8 June 1977, hosted at the International Committee of the Red Cross, available at https://ihl-databases.icrc.org/applic/ihl/ihl.nsf/7c4d08d9b287a42141256739003e636b/f6c8b9fee14a77fdc125641e0052b079?.

International Labour Organization, *Global Estimates of Modern Slavery: Forced Labour and Forced Marriage* (Geneva: International Labour Office, 2017).

International Panel on Climate Change, "IPCC Fact Sheet: What Literature does the IPCC Assess?", 30 August 2013, available at https://archive.ipcc.ch/news_and_events/docs/factsheets/FS_ipcc_assess.pdf

Irwin, D. A., *Against the Tide: An Intellectual History of Free Trade* (Princeton, NJ: Princeton University Press, 1996).

Irwin, D. A., *Free Trade Under Fire*, Third Edition (Princeton, NJ: Princeton University Press, 2009).

Jackson, R., *The Global Covenant: Human Conduct in a World of States* (Oxford: Oxford University Press, 2000).

Jahan, S., (et al.), *The Human Development Report 2016: Human Development for Everyone* (New York: United Nations Development Programme: 2016).

James, A., *Fairness in Practice: A Social Contract for a Global Economy* (New York: Oxford University Press, 2012).

Jones, C., "The Human Right to Subsistence", *Journal of Applied Philosophy*, Vol. 30, No. 1, 2013, pp. 57–72.

Joseph, S., *Blame it on the WTO? A Human Rights Critique* (New York: Oxford University Press, 2011).

Julius, A. J., "Nagel's Atlas", *Philosophy and Public Affairs*, Vol. 34, No. 2, 2006, pp. 176–192.

Keohane, R. O., "The Demand for International Regimes", in Keohane (ed.), *International Institutions andz State Power: Essays in International Relations Theory* (Boulder, CO: Westview Press, 1989).

Kukathas, C., "The Case for Open Immigration", in Andrew I. Cohen and Christopher Heath Wellman (eds.), *Contemporary Debates in Applied Ethics*, Second Edition (Malden, MA: Blackwell Publishing, 2005).

Kuper, A., "Rawlsian Global Justice: Beyond The Law of Peoples to a Cosmopolitan Law of Persons", *Political Theory*, Vol. 28, No. 5, 2000, pp. 640–674.

Kuper, A., "Facts, Theories, and Hard Choices: Reply to Peter Singer", *Ethics and International Affairs*, Vol. 16, No. 1, 2002, pp. 125–126.

Kymlicka, W., *Contemporary Political Philosophy: An Introduction* (New York: Oxford University Press, 2002).

Lazar, S., "Evaluating the Revisionist Critique of Just War Theory", *Daedalus*, Vol. 146, No. 1, 2017, pp. 113–124.

Lippert-Rasmussen, K., "Global Justice and Redistributive Wars", *Law, Ethics, and Philosophy*, Vol. 1, 2013, pp. 65–86.

Luban, D., "The Romance of the Nation State", *Philosophy & Public Affairs*, Vol. 9, No. 4, 1980, pp. 392–397.

Macedo, S., "The Moral Dilemma of U.S. Immigration Policy: Open Borders Versus Social Justice?", in Carol M. Swain (ed.), *Debating Immigration* (New York: Cambridge University Press, 2007).

Mahlman, J. D., "The Long Timescales of Human-Caused Climate Warming: Further Challenges for the Global Policy Process", in W. Sinnott-Armstrong and R. B. Howarth (eds.), *Perspectives on Climate Change: Science, Economics, Politics, Ethics* (Oxford: Elsevier, 2005).

McDonald, P. J., "Peace through Trade or Free Trade?", *Journal of Conflict Resolution*, Vol. 48, No. 4, 2004, pp. 547–572.

McLuhan, M., *The Gutenberg Galaxy: The Making of Typographic Man* (London: Routledge and Kegan Paul, 1962).

McMahan, J., "The Ethics of International Intervention", in K. Kipnis and D. T. Meyers (eds.), *Political Realism and International Morality: Ethics in the Nuclear Age* (Boulder: Westview Press, 1988).

McMahan, J., "Innocence, Self-Defense and Killing in War", *Journal of Political Philosophy*, Vol. 2, No. 3, 1994, pp. 193–221.

McMahan, J., "Realism, Morality, and War", in Terry Nardin (ed.), *The Ethics of War and Peace: Religious and Secular Perspectives* (Princeton, NJ: Princeton University Press, 1996).

McMahan, J., "The Ethics of Killing in War", *Ethics*, Vol. 114, No. 4, 2004, pp. 693–733.

McMahan, J., "Just Cause for War", *Ethics and International Affairs*, Vol. 19, No. 3, 2005, pp. 1–21.

McMahan, J., *Killing in War* (New York: Oxford University Press, 2009).

McMahan, J., "Pacifism and Moral Theory", *Diametros*, Vol. 23, 2010a, pp. 44–68.

McMahan, J., "Humanitarian Intervention, Consent, and Proportionality", in N. Ann Davis, Richard Keshen, and Jeff McMahan (eds.), *Ethics and Humanity: Themes from the Philosophy of Jonathan Glover* (New York: Oxford University Press, 2010b).

McMahan, J., "Just War", in Robert E. Goodin, Philip Pettit, and Thomas Pogge (eds.), *A Companion to Contemporary Political Philosophy, Volume 2*, Second Edition (Malden, MA: Blackwell Publishing, 2012).

McMahan, J., "Proportionality and Time", *Ethics*, Vol. 125, No. 3, 2015a, pp. 696–719.

McMahan, J., "Syria is a Modern-Day Holocaust. We Must Act", *The Washington Post*, 30th November 2015b, available at https://www.washingtonpost.com/news/in-theory/wp/2015/11/30/syria-is-a-modern-day-holocaust-we-must-act/?utm_term=.1e2ff34a56a7

McMahan, J. and McKim, R., "The Just War and the Gulf War", *Canadian Journal of Philosophy*, Vol. 23, No. 4, 1993, pp. 501–541.

Mill, J. S., "A Few Words on Non-Intervention", in John M. Robson (ed.), *The Collected Works of John Stuart Mill, Volume XXI – Essays on Equality, Law, and Education* (London: Routledge and Kegan Paul, 1984).

Miller, D., *On Nationality* (Oxford: Oxford University Press, 1995).

Miller, D., "Immigration: The Case for Limits", in Andrew I. Cohen and Christopher Heath Wellman (eds.), *Contemporary Debates in Applied Ethics*, Second Edition (Malden, MA: Blackwell Publishing, 2005).

Miller, D., *National Responsibility and Global Justice* (Oxford: Oxford University Press, 2007).

Miller, R. W., *Globalizing Justice: The Ethics of Poverty and Power* (Oxford: Oxford University Press, 2010).

Moellendorf, D., *The Moral Challenge of Dangerous Climate Change: Values, Poverty, and Policy* (Cambridge: Cambridge University Press, 2014).

Moyn, S., *Not Enough: Human Rights in an Unequal World* (Cambridge, MA: Harvard University Press, 2018).

Murphy, L. B., "The Demands of Beneficence", *Philosophy & Public Affairs*, Vol. 22, No. 4, 1993, pp. 267–292.

Nagel, T., "War and Massacre", *Philosophy & Public Affairs*, Vol. 1, No. 2, 1972, pp. 123–144.

Nagel, T., "The Problem of Global Justice", *Philosophy & Public Affairs*, Vol. 33, No. 2, 2005, pp. 113–147.

Nickel, J., *Making Sense of Human Rights*, Second Edition (Malden, MA: Blackwell Publishing, 2007).

Nordhaus, W. D., "Discounting in Economics and Climate Change: an Editorial Comment", *Climatic Change*, Vol. 37, No. 2, 1997, pp. 315–328.

Nussbaum, M., *Women and Human Development* (New York: Cambridge University Press, 2000).

Nussbaum, M., "Beyond 'Compassion and Humanity': Justice for Nonhuman Animals", in C. Sunstein and M. Nussbaum (eds.), *Animal Rights: Current Debates and New Directions* (New York: Oxford University Press, 2004).

Nussbaum, M., *Frontiers of Justice: Disability, Nationality, Species Membership* (Cambridge, MA: Harvard University Press, 2006).

Nussbaum, M., *Creating Capabilities: The Human Development Approach* (Cambridge, MA: Harvard University Press, 2011).

Oberman, K., "Poverty and Immigration Policy", *American Political Science Review*, Vol. 109, No. 2, 2015, pp. 239–251.

Pachauri, R. K. and Meyer, L. A., (eds.), *Climate Change 2014: Synthesis Report. Contribution of Working Groups I, II and III to the Fifth Assessment Report of the Intergovernmental Panel on Climate Change* (Geneva: IPCC, 2014).

Page, E., "Climatic Justice and the Fair Distribution of Atmospheric Burdens: A Conjunctive Account", *The Monist*, Vol. 94, No. 3, pp. 412–432.

Pattison, J., *Humanitarian Intervention & the Responsibility to Protect: Who Should Intervene?* (Oxford: Oxford University Press, 2010).

Pevnick, R., "Political Coercion and the Scope of Distributive Justice", *Political Studies*, Vol. 56, 2008, pp. 399–413.

Pevnick, R., "Social Trust and the Ethics of Immigration Policy", *Journal of Political Philosophy*, Vol. 17, No. 2, 2009, pp. 146–167.

Pogge, P., "An Egalitarian Law of Peoples", *Philosophy & Public Affairs*, Vol. 23, No. 3, 1994, pp. 195–224.

Pogge, T., "Migration and Poverty", in Veit Bader (ed.), *Citizenship and Exclusion* (Basingstoke: Macmillan, 1997).

Pogge, T., "'Assisting' the Global Poor", in Deen K. Chatterjee (ed.), *The Ethics of Assistance: Morality and the Distant Needy* (Cambridge: Cambridge University Press, 2004).

Pogge, T., "Do Rawls's Two Theories of Justice Fit Together?", in Rex Martin and David A. Reidy (eds.), *Rawls's Law of Peoples: A Realistic Utopia?* (Oxford: Blackwell, 2006).

Pogge, T., "Severe Poverty as a Human Rights Violation", in Thomas Pogge (ed.), *Freedom from Poverty as a Human Right: Who Owes What to the Very Poor?* (New York: Oxford University Press, 2007).

Pogge, T., *World Poverty and Human Rights*, Second Edition (Cambridge: Polity Press, 2008).

Pogge, T., "Response to the Critics", in Alison M. Jaggar (ed.), *Thomas Pogge and his Critics* (Cambridge: Polity Press, 2010).

Poon, J. and Rigby, D. L., *International Trade* (New York: Routledge, 2017).

Rawls, J., *Political Liberalism* (New York: Columbia University Press, 1993a).

Rawls, J., "The Law of Peoples", in Stephen Shute and Susan Hurley (eds.), *On Human Rights* (New York: Basic Books, 1993b).

Rawls, J., *A Theory of Justice*, Revised Edition (Cambridge, MA: Harvard University Press, 1999a).

Rawls, J., *The Law of Peoples* (Cambridge, MA: Harvard University Press, 1999b)

Raz, J., "Human Rights without Foundations", in Samantha Besson and John Tasioulas (eds.), *The Philosophy of International Law* (Oxford: Oxford University Press, 2010).

Reidy, D., "Philosophy and Human Rights: Contemporary Perspectives", in Claudio Corradetti (ed.), *Philosophical Dimensions of Human Rights: Some Contemporary Views* (New York: Springer, 2012).

Ricardo, D., *On the Principles of Political Economy and Taxation* (London: John Murray, 1817).

Risse, M., "Fairness in Trade I: Obligations from Trading and the Pauper-Labor Argument", *Politics, Philosophy & Economics*, Vol. 6, No. 3, 2007, pp. 355–77.

Risse, M., *On Global Justice* (Princeton, NJ: Princeton University Press, 2012).

Risse, M. and Wollner, G., "Critical notice of Aaron James, Fairness in Practice: A Social Contract for a Global Economy", *Canadian Journal of Philosophy*, Vol. 43, No. 3, 2013, pp. 382–401.

Rodrik, D., *The Globalization Paradox: Why Global Markets, States, and Democracy Can't Coexist* (Oxford: Oxford University Press, 2011).

Roth, P., *American Pastoral* (London: Vintage, 1997).

Sangiovanni, A., "Global Justice, Reciprocity, and the State", *Philosophy & Public Affairs*, Vol. 35, No. 1, 2007, pp. 3–39.

Sangiovanni, A., "The Irrelevance of Coercion, Imposition, and Framing to Distributive Justice", *Philosophy & Public Affairs*, Vol. 40, No. 2, 2012, pp. 79–110.

Scheffler, S., "Immigration and the significance of culture", *Philosophy and Public Affairs*, Vol. 35, No. 2, 2007, pp. 93–125.

Schelling, T. C., "Intergenerational Discounting", *Energy Policy*, Vol. 23, No. 4/5, 1995, pp. 395–401.

Sen, A., *Human Rights and Asian Values* (New York: Carnegie Council on Ethics and International Affairs, 1997).

Shaheen, K., "Dozens Killed in Suspected Chemical Attack on Syrian Rebel Enclave", *The Guardian*, 8th April 2018, available at https://www.theguardian.com/world/2018/apr/08/syrian-government-accused-of-chemical-attacks-on-civilians-in-eastern-ghouta

Shue, H., *Basic Rights: Subsistence, Affluence, and U.S. Foreign Policy* (Princeton, NJ: Princeton University Press, 1980).

Shue, H., *Climate Justice: Vulnerability and Protection* (Oxford: Oxford University Press, 2014).

Singer, P., "Famine, Affluence, and Morality", *Philosophy and Public Affairs*, Vol. 1, No. 3, 1972, pp. 229–243.

Singer, P., *Animal Liberation* (London: Pimlico, 1995).

Singer, P., *One World: The Ethics of Globalization* (New Haven, CT: Yale University Press, 2002a).

Singer, P., "Achieving the Best Outcome: Final Rejoinder", *Ethics and International Affairs*, Vol. 16, No. 1, 2002b, pp. 127–128.

Singer, P., *The Life You Can Save: Acting Now to End World Poverty* (London: Picador, 2009).

Smith, A., *An Inquiry into the Nature and Causes of the Wealth of Nations* (London: Strahan and Cadell, 1776).

Soroka, S. N., Johnston, R., and Banting, K., "Ethnicity, Trust, and the Welfare State", in Philippe Van Parijs (ed.), *Cultural Diversity versus Economic Solidarity* (Brussels: De Boeck, 2004).

Stevens, C., "Special and Differential Treatment", in Ivan Mbirimi, Bridget Chilala, and Roman Grynberg (eds.) *From Doha to Cancun: Delivering a Development Round* (London: Commonwealth Secretariat, 2003).

Stiglitz, J. E. and Charlton, A., *Fair Trade for All: How Trade can Promote Development* (Oxford: Oxford University Press, 2005).

Tan, K-C., "Liberal Toleration in Rawls's Law of Peoples", *Ethics*, Vol. 108, No. 2, 1998, pp. 276–295.

Tan, K-C., *Justice Without Borders: Cosmopolitanism, Nationalism, and Patriotism* (Cambridge: Cambridge University Press, 2004).

Tasioulas, J., "From Utopia to Kazanstan: John Rawls and the Law of Peoples", *Oxford Journal of Legal Studies*, Vol. 22, No. 2, 2002, pp. 367–396.

Tesón, F. R., "The Liberal Case for Humanitarian Intervention", in J. L. Holzgrefe and Robert O. Keohane (eds.), *Humanitarian Intervention: Ethical, Legal and Political Dilemmas* (Cambridge: Cambridge University Press, 2003).

Tesón, F. R., "Why Free Trade is Required by Justice", *Social Philosophy and Policy*, Vol. 29, No. 1, 2012, pp. 126–153.

Unger, P., *Living High and Letting Die* (New York: Oxford University Press, 1996).

Valentino, B. A, "The True Costs of Humanitarian Intervention: The Hard Truth About a Noble Notion", *Foreign Affairs*, Vol. 90, No. 6, 2011, pp. 60–73.

Vanderheiden, S., *Atmospheric Justice: A Political Theory of Climate Change* (New York: Oxford University Press, 2008).

Waldron, J., *Liberal Rights: Collected Papers 1981–1991* (New York: Cambridge University Press, 1993).

Walzer, M., *Just and Unjust Wars: A Moral Argument with Historical Illustrations* (New York: Basic Books, 1977).

Walzer, M., "The Moral Standing of States: A Response to Four Critics", *Philosophy & Public Affairs*, Vol. 9, No. 3, 1980, pp. 209–229.

Walzer, M., *Arguing about War* (New Haven, CT: Yale University Press, 2004).

Weber, M., "Politics as a Vocation", in H. H. Gerth and C. W. Mills (eds.), *From Max Weber* (London: Routledge and Kegan Paul, 1970).

Weinstock, D. M., "Miller on Distributive Justice", in Daniel A. Bell and Avner de-Shalit (eds.), *Forms of Justice*.

Wellman, C., *The Moral Dimensions of Human Rights* (New York: Oxford University Press, 2011).
Wellman, C. H., "Immigration and Freedom of Association", *Ethics*, Vol. 119, No. 1, 2008, pp. 109–141.
Wenar, L., "The Nature of Rights", *Philosophy & Public Affairs*, Vol. 33, No. 3, 2005, pp. 223–252.
Wenar, L., "Property Rights and the Resource Curse", *Philosophy & Public Affairs*, 2008, Vol. 36, No. 1, pp. 2–32.
Wheeler, N. J., *Saving Strangers: Humanitarian Intervention in International Society* (New York: Oxford University Press, 2000).
Widdows, H., *Global Ethics: An Introduction* (Durham: Acumen, 2011).
Wolff, C., *Jus gentium methodo scientifica pertractatum* (1749), trans. Joseph H. Drake (Oxford: Clarendon Press, 1934).
Wolff, M., *Why Globalization Works* (New Haven, CT: Yale University Press, 2005).
Wollner, G., "Equality and the Significance of Coercion", *Journal of Social Philosophy*, Vol. 42, No. 4, 2011, pp. 363–381.
Worldwide Fistula Fund, "What is Fistula: Defining Obstetric Fistula", available at http://worldwidefistulafund.org/fistula-faqs.aspx.
World Health Organization, "Drinking Water", 7 February 2018, available at https://www.who.int/news-room/fact-sheets/detail/drinking-water
Yong, C., "Justice in Labor Immigration Policy", *Social Theory and Practice*, Vol. 42, No. 4, 2016, pp. 817–844.
Ypi, L., "Justice in Migration: A Closed Borders Utopia?", *Journal of Political Philosophy*, Vol. 16, No. 4, 2008, pp. 391–418.
Ypi, L., Goodin, R. E., and Barry, C., "Associative Duties, Global Justice, and the Colonies", *Philosophy & Public Affairs*, Vol. 37, No. 2, 2009, pp. 103–135.

INDEX

A

Ability to pay principle (APP), 157, 158, 162–164
Abizadeh, Arash, 80, 112
Allende, Salvador, 59
American Pastoral (Roth), 1
Amnesty International, 11, 35
Appiah, Kwame Anthony, 53
Arrhenius, Svante, 147
Ashford, Elizabeth, 52
al-Assad, Bashar, 191–192

B

Beitz, Charles, 11, 19, 198, 199, 204
Blake, Michael, 72–78, 80, 92, 123, 124
Blameworthiness of unjust combatants, 187–190
"Borrowing privilege," 60
Brain drain, 111, 132
Brock, Gillian, 102
Brown, Gordon, 101
Buchanan, Allen, 21, 211
Bush, George W., 204–205

C

Caney, Simon, 153, 159, 166, 168
Carens, Joseph, 105, 107, 108, 110, 117–121, 125, 126
Central human capabilities, 27
Charlton, Andrew, 139
"China Model," 30
Climate change, 147–148
    burden, sharing, 156–164
    problem, nature of, 148–151
    rights of future generations, 164–169
    uncertainty, problem of, 169–170
    violation of human rights, 151–155
Cohen, Marshall, 13
Cold War, 45
Communal self-determination, 193–199
Concept vs Conception of justice, 6
Conventional vs Critical morality, 17
Cosmopolitanism, 65–68
Culpable vs Innocent polluters, 159
Cultural critique of human rights, 30
Cultural preservation, immigration and, 121–125
Cultural relativism, 29–33

D

Daesh, 191–192
Developing countries, special and differential treatment for, 137–140
Doctrine of double effect, 181
Domestic labour argument, for trade restrictions, 133–136
Domestic poor, immigration and, 114–117
Dynamic conception of comparative advantage, 139

E

Egalitarianism, 65
Einstein, Albert, 86
Elster, Jon, 37
Equatorial Guinea, 206
Ethnicity vs Nationality, 86
European Court of Human Rights, 34
Executive Board of the American Anthropological Association, 30
Export-oriented firms, 134

F

Fabre, Cecile, 69
Factory farming, 67

INDEX

Fair trade
    as equality, 142–145
    as reciprocity, 140–142
First order vs Second order rights, 171
First World, 46, 65
Formal vs Substantive egalitarianism, 142
Freedom of movement, 117–120
Free trade, world poverty argument for, 127–129
Frowe, Helen, 174, 201

G

Gandhi, Mahatma, 35
Gardiner, Stephen, 147
Generalized System of Preferences, 138
Geneva Conventions, 183
Global egalitarianism, 66, 71, 72, 77, 82–83, 144–145
    and national responsibility, 96–98
    national self-determination and, 92–94
    and special duties, 95–96
Global equality
    case against, 71–80
    case for, 68–71
"Good Samaritanism," 152
Greenhouse gases (GHGs), 148–161
Griffin, James, 31
Growth discounting, 165

H

Hobbes, Thomas, 12–13
Hohfeldian incidents, 21–22, 24
Hohfeld, Wesley, 20
Humanitarian intervention, 6, 191, 192–193, 199–211
Human motivation, limits of, 98–102
Human rights, 19, 24
    and global justice, 3–6
    violation of, 151–155

I

Identarian value of self-determination, 199
Immigration, 105–106
    and cultural preservation, 121–125
    and domestic poor, 114–117
    freedom of movement, 117–120
    and radical global inequality, 106–113
Import-sensitive industries, 134
Inequality, 4, 65
    case against global equality
        coercion argument I, 71–77
        coercion argument II, 77–80
        cooperation, 80–83
    case for global equality, 68–71
    cosmopolitanism, 65–68
International Covenant on Civil and Political Rights (1966), 22, 118, 153
International Covenant on Economic, Social and Cultural Rights (1966), 22, 154, 155
International customary law, 23
International Labour Organization, 132
International Panel on Climate Change (IPCC), 148, 159
International redistribution, national self-determination and, 90–92
Irwin, Douglas, 56

J

James, Aaron, 142–143
Jones, Charles, 3
Jus ad bellum, 205
    vs. *Jus in bello*, 173–180, 180–186
Justice
    arguing about, 8–11
    nature of, 6–8
Justifying human rights, 26–29
"Just war" tradition, 172

K

Kauṭilya, 34
Keohane, Robert, 14
Kissinger, Henry, 182
Kukathas, Chandran, 107
Kuper, Andrew, 54–55

L

Lazar, Seth, 185
Lee Kuan Yew, 30, 32
Liability, 175
Luban, David, 196

INDEX

M

Macedo, Stephen, 114
Mahlman, Jerry, 149
Massacres, 212–214
McKim, Robert, 183
McMahan, Jeff, 173–176, 183, 184, 186–189, 194, 197, 203, 212, 213
Miller, David, 66, 86–90, 95–97, 99–103, 118, 119, 121, 136, 137
Mill, John Stuart, 208–211
Moral vs Distributive equality, 68
Moral equality of combatants, 183
Moral vs Artificial human rights, 22–23
Morally arbitrary inequalities, 72, 144, 168
Most Favoured Nation (MFN) rule, 138
Murphy, Liam, 51–52

N

Nagel, Thomas, 77–80, 180–181, 184
National culture, 89
Nationalism, 85
National responsibility, global egalitarianism and, 96–98
National self-determination, 88–90
    and global egalitarianism, 92–94
    and international redistribution, 90–92
Nations and nationality, 85–88
Natural lottery, 68
Nehru, Jawaharlal, 35
Neo-colonialism, 74
Nickel, James, 32, 34
Nixon, Richard, 182
Non-combatant deaths, 181
Non-ideal vs Ideal theory, 131
Nordhaus, William, 164–165
Nussbaum, Martha, 20, 26–29, 33, 36–38

O

Open-borders policy, 111
Orthodox view of human rights, 23

P

Part IV of the General Agreement on Tariffs and Trade, 138
Pattison, James, 200, 201

Pevnick, Ryan, 116
Pogge, Thomas, 58–64, 69, 97, 108
Political Theory and International Relations (Beitz), 11
Polluter-beneficiary argument, 159–160
Polluter pays principle (PPP), 157–162
Poverty, 4, 45–46, 212–214
    local/global factors, 55–61
    Singer, Peter, 46–54
Principle of non-combatant immunity, 180
Protectionist measures, 141
"Purely Domestic Poverty Thesis" (Pogge), 63
Pure time discounting, 167

R

Radical global inequality, immigration and, 106–113
Rawls, John, 27, 48, 56, 68, 131
    domestic inequality, 69
    on toleration, 38–42
Realism, 11, 16–17
Reciprocity, fair trade as, 140–142
Reflective equilibrium, 48
Refugee Convention (1951), 108
Resource curse, 58, 59
Resource privilege, 59
Ricardo, David, 128
Rights, 19
    cultural relativism, 29–33
    diversity, 42–43
    justifying human rights, 26–29
    Rawls on toleration, 38–42
    toleration and respect, 35–38
    understanding human rights, 22–25
    understanding rights, 20–22
    Western ideas, 33–35
Risse, Mathias, 67, 68, 131, 143, 144
Roth, Philip, 1

S

Saddam Hussein, 179
Sangiovanni, Andrea, 75, 76, 80–83
Scheffler, Samuel, 122, 123
Schindler, Oskar, 55
Sen, Amartya, 34, 41

INDEX

'Sense of justice,' 19
Shue, Henry, 150, 152–154, 156, 166, 169, 170
Singer, Peter, 46–55, 61, 64, 67, 99, 152
Smith, Adam, 128
Sovereignty, 88
Soviet invasion of Czechoslovakia, 176
Stiglitz, Joseph, 139
Subsistence rights, 3
Sweatshop argument, for trade restrictions, 129–133

T

Tan, Kok-Chor, 91, 100
Tarkovsky, Andrei, 86
A Theory of Justice (Rawls), 68, 82, 131
Third Reich, 86
Third World, 56, 71, 109, 110, 112, 115, 127, 155
Trade, 127
    domestic labour and, 133–136
    equality, fair trade as, 142–145
    nationalist perspective, 136–137
    reciprocity, fair trade as, 140–142
    special and differential treatment for developing countries, 137–140
    sweatshops and, 129–133
    world poverty argument for, 127–129
Troubles in Northern Ireland, 34
Trump, Donald, 105, 106

U

Unger, Peter, 49
United Nations Charter, 24
United Nations Environment Programme, 148
Universal Declaration of Human Rights (1948), 22, 24, 25, 30
Unjust combatants, blameworthiness of, 187–190
UN Refugee Agency (UNHCR), 108
US Department of Energy, 182

V

Vietnam War, 188
Violation of human rights, 151–155

W

Waldron, Jeremy, 24
Walzer, Michael, 184, 194–197, 200
War, 6, 171–173
    blameworthiness of unjust combatants, 187–190
    jus ad bellum, 173–180, 183–186
    jus in bello, 180–186
Weinstock, Daniel, 103
Wellman, Carl, 24, 33
Wellman, Christopher Health, 109
Wenar, Leif, 21, 59, 60
Western conception of human rights, 31
Wheeler, Nicholas, 200
"White Australia" policy, 124
Wolff, Christian, 193
Wolf, Martin, 57
Wollner, Gabriel, 143, 144
World Health Organization, 4
World Meteorological Organization, 148
World poverty argument, for trade, 127–129
World Trade Organization (WTO), 5, 56, 91–92
Worldwide Fistula Fund, 46

Y

Yong, Caleb, 112, 115

Made in the USA
Monee, IL
28 April 2026

49136483R00133